PRENTICE HALL

SCIENCE EXPLORER

Environmental Science

PRENTICE HALL
Needham, Massachusetts
Upper Saddle River, New Jersey

PRENTICE HALL
SCIENCE EXPLORER

Environmental Science

Program Resources
Student Edition
Annotated Teacher's Edition
Teaching Resources Book with Color Transparencies
Environmental Science Materials Kits

Program Components
Integrated Science Laboratory Manual
Integrated Science Laboratory Manual, Teacher's Edition
Inquiry Skills Activity Book
Student-Centered Science Activity Books
Program Planning Guide
Guided Reading English Audiotapes
Guided Reading Spanish Audiotapes and Summaries
Product Testing Activities by Consumer Reports™
Event-Based Science Series (NSF funded)
Prentice Hall Interdisciplinary Explorations
Cobblestone, Odyssey, Calliope, and *Faces* Magazines

Media/Technology
Science Explorer Interactive Student Tutorial CD-ROMs
Odyssey of Discovery CD-ROMs
Resource Pro® (Teaching Resources on CD-ROM)
Assessment Resources CD-ROM with Dial-A-Test®
Internet site at www.science-explorer.phschool.com
Life, Earth, and Physical Science Videodiscs
Life, Earth, and Physical Science Videotapes

Science Explorer Student Editions

From Bacteria to Plants

Animals

Cells and Heredity

Human Biology and Health

Environmental Science

Inside Earth

Earth's Changing Surface

Earth's Waters

Weather and Climate

Astronomy

Chemical Building Blocks

Chemical Interactions

Motion, Forces, and Energy

Electricity and Magnetism

Sound and Light

Staff Credits

The people who made up the *Science Explorer* team—representing editorial, editorial services, design services, field marketing, market research, marketing services, on-line services/multimedia development, product marketing, production services, and publishing processes—are listed below. Bold type denotes core team members.

Kristen E. Ball, **Barbara A. Bertell,** Peter W. Brooks, **Christopher R. Brown, Greg Cantone,** Jonathan Cheney, **Patrick Finbarr Connolly,** Loree Franz, Donald P. Gagnon, Jr., **Paul J. Gagnon, Joel Gendler,** Elizabeth Good, Kerri Hoar, **Linda D. Johnson,** Katherine M. Kotik, Russ Lappa, Marilyn Leitao, David Lippman, **Eve Melnechuk, Natania Mlawer,** Paul W. Murphy, **Cindy A. Noftle,** Julia F. Osborne, Caroline M. Power, Suzanne J. Schineller, **Susan W. Tafler,** Kira Thaler-Marbit, Robin L. Santel, Ronald Schachter, **Mark Tricca,** Diane Walsh, Pearl B. Weinstein, Beth Norman Winickoff

Acknowledgment for page 198: Excerpt from *The Amateur Naturalist* by Gerald Durrell. Copyright ©1982 by Dorling Kindersley Ltd., London. Reprinted by permission of Alfred A. Knopf, Inc.

ISBN 0-13-434486-3
6 7 8 9 10   03 02 01 00

Cover: A snail and a flower are just
two examples of Earth's biodiversity.

Program Authors

Michael J. Padilla, Ph.D.
Professor
Department of Science Education
University of Georgia
Athens, Georgia

Michael Padilla is a leader in middle school science education. He has served as an editor and elected officer for the National Science Teachers Association. He has been principal investigator of several National Science Foundation and Eisenhower grants and served as a writer of the National Science Education Standards.

As lead author of *Science Explorer,* Mike has inspired the team in developing a program that meets the needs of middle grades students, promotes science inquiry, and is aligned with the National Science Education Standards.

Ioannis Miaoulis, Ph.D.
Dean of Engineering
College of Engineering
Tufts University
Medford, Massachusetts

Martha Cyr, Ph.D.
Director, Engineering
   Educational Outreach
College of Engineering
Tufts University
Medford, Massachusetts

Science Explorer was created in collaboration with the College of Engineering at Tufts University. Tufts has an extensive engineering outreach program that uses engineering design and construction to excite and motivate students and teachers in science and technology education.

Faculty from Tufts University participated in the development of *Science Explorer* chapter projects, reviewed the student books for content accuracy, and helped coordinate field testing.

CHAPTER PROJECT

Book Authors

Fred Holtzclaw
Science Instructor
Oak Ridge High School
Oak Ridge, Tennessee

Linda Cronin Jones, Ph.D.
College of Education
University of Florida
Gainesville, Florida

Steve Miller
Science Writer
State College, Pennsylvania

Contributing Writers

Thomas R. Wellnitz
Science Instructor
The Paideia School
Atlanta, Georgia

Theresa K. Holtzclaw
Former Science Instructor
Clinton, Tennessee

Reading Consultant

Bonnie B. Armbruster, Ph.D.
Department of Curriculum
   and Instruction
University of Illinois
Champaign, Illinois

Interdisciplinary Consultant

Heidi Hayes Jacobs, Ed.D.
Teacher's College
Columbia University
New York City, New York

Safety Consultants

W. H. Breazeale, Ph.D.
Department of Chemistry
College of Charleston
Charleston, South Carolina

Ruth Hathaway, Ph.D.
Hathaway Consulting
Cape Girardeau, Missouri

Tufts University Program Reviewers

Behrouz Abedian, Ph.D.
Department of Mechanical
    Engineering

Wayne Chudyk, Ph.D.
Department of Civil and
    Environmental Engineering

Eliana De Bernardez-Clark, Ph.D.
Department of Chemical Engineering

Anne Marie Desmarais, Ph.D.
Department of Civil and
    Environmental Engineering

David L. Kaplan, Ph.D.
Department of Chemical Engineering

Paul Kelley, Ph.D.
Department of Electro-Optics

George S. Mumford, Ph.D.
Professor of Astronomy, Emeritus

Jan A. Pechenik, Ph.D.
Department of Biology

Livia Racz, Ph.D.
Department of Mechanical Engineering

Robert Rifkin, M.D.
School of Medicine

Jack Ridge, Ph.D.
Department of Geology

Chris Swan, Ph.D.
Department of Civil and
    Environmental Engineering

Peter Y. Wong, Ph.D.
Department of Mechanical Engineering

Content Reviewers

Jack W. Beal, Ph.D.
Department of Physics
Fairfield University
Fairfield, Connecticut

W. Russell Blake, Ph.D.
Planetarium Director
Plymouth Community
    Intermediate School
Plymouth, Massachusetts

Howard E. Buhse, Jr., Ph.D.
Department of Biological Sciences
University of Illinois
Chicago, Illinois

Dawn Smith Burgess, Ph.D.
Department of Geophysics
Stanford University
Stanford, California

A. Malcolm Campbell, Ph.D.
Assistant Professor
Davidson College
Davidson, North Carolina

Elizabeth A. De Stasio, Ph.D.
Associate Professor of Biology
Lawrence University
Appleton, Wisconsin

John M. Fowler, Ph.D.
Former Director of Special Projects
National Science Teacher's Association
Arlington, Virginia

Jonathan Gitlin, M.D.
School of Medicine
Washington University
St. Louis, Missouri

Dawn Graff-Haight, Ph.D., CHES
Department of Health, Human
    Performance, and Athletics
Linfield College
McMinnville, Oregon

Deborah L. Gumucio, Ph.D.
Associate Professor
Department of Anatomy and Cell Biology
University of Michigan
Ann Arbor, Michigan

William S. Harwood, Ph.D.
Dean of University Division and Associate
    Professor of Education
Indiana University
Bloomington, Indiana

Cyndy Henzel, Ph.D.
Department of Geography
    and Regional Development
University of Arizona
Tucson, Arizona

Greg Hutton
Science and Health
    Curriculum Coordinator
School Board of Sarasota County
Sarasota, Florida

Susan K. Jacobson, Ph.D.
Department of Wildlife Ecology
    and Conservation
University of Florida
Gainesville, Florida

Judy Jernstedt, Ph.D.
Department of Agronomy and Range Science
University of California, Davis
Davis, California

John L. Kermond, Ph.D.
Office of Global Programs
National Oceanographic and
    Atmospheric Administration
Silver Spring, Maryland

David E. LaHart, Ph.D.
Institute of Science and Public Affairs
Florida State University
Tallahassee, Florida

Joe Leverich, Ph.D.
Department of Biology
St. Louis University
St. Louis, Missouri

Dennis K. Lieu, Ph.D.
Department of Mechanical Engineering
University of California
Berkeley, California

Cynthia J. Moore, Ph.D.
Science Outreach Coordinator
Washington University
St. Louis, Missouri

Joseph M. Moran, Ph.D.
Department of Earth Science
University of Wisconsin–Green Bay
Green Bay, Wisconsin

Joseph Stukey, Ph.D.
Department of Biology
Hope College
Holland, Michigan

Seetha Subramanian
Lexington Community College
University of Kentucky
Lexington, Kentucky

Carl L. Thurman, Ph.D.
Department of Biology
University of Northern Iowa
Cedar Falls, Iowa

Edward D. Walton, Ph.D.
Department of Chemistry
California State Polytechnic University
Pomona, California

Robert S. Young, Ph.D.
Department of Geosciences and
    Natural Resource Management
Western Carolina University
Cullowhee, North Carolina

Edward J. Zalisko, Ph.D.
Department of Biology
Blackburn College
Carlinville, Illinois

Teacher Reviewers

Stephanie Anderson
Sierra Vista Junior
    High School
Canyon Country, California

John W. Anson
Mesa Intermediate School
Palmdale, California

Pamela Arline
Lake Taylor Middle School
Norfolk, Virginia

Lynn Beason
College Station Jr. High School
College Station, Texas

Richard Bothmer
Hollis School District
Hollis, New Hampshire

Jeffrey C. Callister
Newburgh Free Academy
Newburgh, New York

Judy D'Albert
Harvard Day School
Corona Del Mar, California

Betty Scott Dean
Guilford County Schools
McLeansville, North Carolina

Sarah C. Duff
Baltimore City Public Schools
Baltimore, Maryland

Melody Law Ewey
Holmes Junior High School
Davis, California

Sherry L. Fisher
Lake Zurich Middle
    School North
Lake Zurich, Illinois

Melissa Gibbons
Fort Worth ISD
Fort Worth, Texas

Debra J. Goodding
Kraemer Middle School
Placentia, California

Jack Grande
Weber Middle School
Port Washington, New York

Steve Hills
Riverside Middle School
Grand Rapids, Michigan

Carol Ann Lionello
Kraemer Middle School
Placentia, California

Jaime A. Morales
Henry T. Gage Middle School
Huntington Park, California

Patsy Partin
Cameron Middle School
Nashville, Tennessee

Deedra H. Robinson
Newport News Public Schools
Newport News, Virginia

Bonnie Scott
Clack Middle School
Abilene, Texas

Charles M. Sears
Belzer Middle School
Indianapolis, Indiana

Barbara M. Strange
Ferndale Middle School
High Point, North Carolina

Jackie Louise Ulfig
Ford Middle School
Allen, Texas

Kathy Usina
Belzer Middle School
Indianapolis, Indiana

Heidi M. von Oetinger
L'Anse Creuse Public School
Harrison Township, Michigan

Pam Watson
Hill Country Middle School
Austin, Texas

Activity Field Testers

Nicki Bibbo
Russell Street School
Littleton, Massachusetts

Connie Boone
Fletcher Middle School
Jacksonville Beach, Florida

Rose-Marie Botting
Broward County
    School District
Fort Lauderdale, Florida

Colleen Campos
Laredo Middle School
Aurora, Colorado

Elizabeth Chait
W. L. Chenery Middle School
Belmont, Massachusetts

Holly Estes
Hale Middle School
Stow, Massachusetts

Laura Hapgood
Plymouth Community
    Intermediate School
Plymouth, Massachusetts

Sandra M. Harris
Winman Junior High School
Warwick, Rhode Island

Jason Ho
Walter Reed Middle School
Los Angeles, California

Joanne Jackson
Winman Junior High School
Warwick, Rhode Island

Mary F. Lavin
Plymouth Community
    Intermediate School
Plymouth, Massachusetts

James MacNeil, Ph.D.
Concord Public Schools
Concord, Massachusetts

Lauren Magruder
St. Michael's Country
    Day School
Newport, Rhode Island

Jeanne Maurand
Glen Urquhart School
Beverly Farms, Massachusetts

Warren Phillips
Plymouth Community
    Intermediate School
Plymouth, Massachusetts

Carol Pirtle
Hale Middle School
Stow, Massachusetts

Kathleen M. Poe
Kirby-Smith Middle School
Jacksonville, Florida

Cynthia B. Pope
Ruffner Middle School
Norfolk, Virginia

Anne Scammell
Geneva Middle School
Geneva, New York

Karen Riley Sievers
Callanan Middle School
Des Moines, Iowa

David M. Smith
Howard A. Eyer Middle School
Macungie, Pennsylvania

Derek Strohschneider
Plymouth Community
    Intermediate School
Plymouth, Massachusetts

Sallie Teames
Rosemont Middle School
Fort Worth, Texas

Gene Vitale
Parkland Middle School
McHenry, Illinois

Zenovia Young
Meyer Levin Junior
    High School (IS 285)
Brooklyn, New York

Contents

Environmental Science

Activities

Real-World Lab

Everyday application of science concepts

EXPLORING

Visual exploration of concepts

Interdisciplinary Activities

Math Toolbox

Science and History

Science and Society

Connection

PROTECTING DESERT WILDLIFE

Elroy Masters likes working outdoors. One day he hikes a mountain trail, looking for desert tortoises. The next morning he may be in a boat on the Colorado River, counting birds along the riverbank. Another day he may be in the Arizona hills, building a water container for thirsty bighorn sheep. Elroy is a biologist working for the federal government's Bureau of Land Management (BLM). His job is to protect wildlife habitat in the desert along the Colorado River between California and Arizona.

"People may come in wanting to run a pipeline across public land or needing to build a road," he explains. "Part of my job is to check out the biological effect of that action on different species of animals and plants. If people are going to build a road where there are a lot of tortoises, we might try to have them work from November to March. Since tortoises hibernate during those months, we reduce the chance of a tortoise getting run over."

Growing up in Arizona, Elroy lived in a farming community. "I was always outdoors. I was able to have animals that a lot of people don't have—chickens, pigeons, ducks, and a horse. I always loved animals. I always hoped for some type of career with them."

Elroy Masters studied biology at Phoenix College and Northern Arizona University. He started working for the Bureau of Land Management when he was still a college student. He now works as a Wildlife Management Biologist. In this photograph, Elroy is about to release a razorback sucker, an endangered species of fish, into the Colorado River.

Today, Elroy and his co-workers make surveys of desert animals. They count the animals in different areas and make maps of their habitats. They locate where the animals live, what they eat, and where they build their nests and raise their young. Elroy uses that information to protect the animals when natural events or human activities threaten them.

Elroy Masters works in the area around Lake Havasu in western Arizona.

TALKING WITH ELROY MASTERS

Q *What wildlife do you protect?*

A One of the neatest animals we deal with is the desert bighorn sheep. In an average summer, it can get as hot as 120 degrees here. Sometimes the heat lasts for weeks. But with the number of people living around the river, the animals are no longer able to travel to water. So we go up into the mountains to construct catchments (containers) to collect water and store it. That way the sheep can stay in the mountains without trying to cross freeways to get to water.

We fly in big storage tanks that hold about 10,000 gallons of water. We bury them in the ground or put them on a platform. We use paint to mask them into the color of the scenery. We sometimes build a dam or put out a metal sheet to catch drizzle rain.

A catchment can hold 10,000 gallons of water (right). It is buried in the ground. The drinking container provides water for desert bighorn sheep (below), mule deer, and other wildlife.

Q *What else are you doing to protect the bighorn sheep?*

A We're going to work with the Fish and Wildlife Department to capture and transplant bighorn sheep to a mountain range in my area. There are already sheep and some mountain lions here. But the sheep aren't doing as well as we expected. We want to bring in some bighorn sheep that are used to lions. We hope these lion-savvy sheep will teach the sheep in our area how to avoid lions. To catch the sheep, we'll use a helicopter. We'll shoot a net over the sheep and a couple of guys will jump out to secure the animals and then bring them to our herd.

The Colorado River valley is home to the Southwestern willow flycatcher and the desert tortoise.

Q *What other animals are you responsible for protecting?*

A I work a lot with desert tortoises. I'm responsible for two different populations, one on either side of the river. The tortoises live in the drier, hilly areas away from the river. Any time we go out into the field, we try to collect data. We keep track of where they've been and where they feed.

Q *How do you find the tortoises?*

A We have maps that indicate their habitat. Based on the habitat, we'll go out, walk around, and look under rocks and boulders to see if we can find a burrow. The tortoises are good diggers. They find a good boulder and go underground 10 or 12 feet. That's where they'll spend the winter.

Southwestern willow flycatcher

Desert tortoise

Q *Do you also work with birds?*

A Right now we're working with the Southwestern willow flycatcher. It's a small bird that depends on thick riparian (riverbank) vegetation to build nests and breed. The flycatcher is a migratory bird. Each spring, the birds fly to Arizona from Central America and Mexico. In the early summer months, we go out to find how many are breeding. We're trying to learn what's needed to prevent flycatchers from becoming extinct. We need to survey and protect the remaining stands of habitat. The flycatchers like to nest in thick stands of willow. But they will also build nests in another tree, salt cedar. The birds don't prefer it, but sometimes salt cedar is the only vegetation remaining, so they use it.

Q *What's threatening the riverbank plants?*

A The low water level in the river—due to human use—is a big threat. So is fire. During summer months, there are large numbers of recreational boats. Careless boaters can cause fires. Some fires get pretty big along the river and destroy a lot of the habitat where the birds nest and raise their young.

Q *Can you see the benefits of your work?*

A Yes, I see it especially in riverbank zones where areas are protected so that vegetation and trees can grow back. This year we did a new bird count in one area. Species that hadn't been seen in a while, like tanagers, showed up. Some of the migratory birds are already stopping in young cottonwood trees. That's the best gauge I've had—seeing birds returning to these new trees.

There are also quick results with the water catchments in the hills. We put the water in a year ago. They're aimed at bighorn sheep and mule deer. But now we've also got a lot of different birds—doves and quails— that come into the area.

Elroy Masters also works with populations of the California leaf-nosed bat. This bat has large ears and a leaf-shaped, turned-up nose. The bats are threatened by the loss of their habitat.

In Your Journal

Elroy Masters and his co-workers "survey" the wildlife in their area in order to learn how to protect them. Think of a wild animal that lives in a park or open area near you—squirrels, frogs, birds, even insects. Work out a step-by-step plan to draw a simple map marking the places where the animal is found.

CHAPTER

1

Populations and Communities

WHAT'S AHEAD

SECTION 1
Living Things and the Environment

Discover What's in the Scene?
Try This With or Without Salt?
Skills Lab A World in a Jar

Integrating Mathematics
SECTION 2
Studying Populations

Discover What's the Population of Beans in a Jar?
Sharpen Your Skills Calculating
Try This Elbow Room
Real-World Lab Counting Turtles

SECTION 3
Interactions Among Living Things

Discover How Well Can You Hide a Butterfly?
Sharpen Your Skills Classifying

What's a Crowd?

How many sunflowers are there in this photograph? Certainly too many to count! But there is a limit to how many more sunflowers can grow in this fertile field. The limit is determined by what the sunflowers need to survive.

In this chapter, you will explore how living things obtain the things they need from their surroundings. You will also learn how organisms interact with the living and nonliving things around them. As you study this chapter, you will observe plants as sample organisms.

Your Goal To design and conduct an experiment to determine the effect of crowding on plant growth.

To complete your project successfully, you must
◆ develop a plan for planting different numbers of seeds in identical containers
◆ observe and collect data on the growing plants
◆ present your results in a written report and a graph
◆ follow the safety guidelines in Appendix A

Get Started With your group, brainstorm ideas for your plan. What conditions do plants need to grow? How will you arrange your seeds in their containers? What types of measurements will you make when the plants begin to grow? Submit your draft plan to your teacher for review.

Check Your Progress You'll be working on this project as you study this chapter. To keep your project on track, look for Check Your Progress boxes at the following points.

Section 1 Review, page 21: Plant the seeds. Measure the plants' growth and record your observations.

Section 3 Review, page 38: Analyze your data and prepare your report.

Wrap Up At the end of the chapter (page 41), your group will present your results and conclusions to the class.

Row after row of bright sunflowers blanket a field in Provence, France.

SECTION 1
Living Things and the Environment

DISCOVER · · · · · · · · · ·

What's in the Scene?

1. Choose a magazine picture of a nature scene. Paste the picture onto a sheet of paper, leaving space all around the picture.

2. Identify all the things in the picture that are alive. Use a colored pencil to draw a line from each living thing, or organism. Label the organism if you know its name.

· · · · · · · · · · · · ·ACTIVITY· · · · ·

3. Use a different colored pencil to draw a line from each nonliving thing and label it.

Think It Over

Inferring How do the organisms in the picture depend on the nonliving things? Using a third color, draw lines connecting organisms to the nonliving things they need.

GUIDE FOR READING

◆ **What needs are met by an organism's surroundings?**

◆ **What are the levels of organization within an ecosystem?**

Reading Tip Write the section headings in your notebook. As you read, make a list of main ideas and supporting details under each heading.

Black-tailed prairie dogs ▼

As the sun rises on a warm summer morning, the Nebraska town is already bustling with activity. Some residents are hard at work building homes for their families. They are building underground, where it is dark and cool. Other inhabitants are collecting seeds for breakfast. Some of the town's younger residents are at play, chasing each other through the grass.

Suddenly, an adult spots a threatening shadow approaching—an enemy has appeared in the sky! The adult cries out several times, warning the others. Within moments, the town's residents disappear into their underground homes. The town is silent and still, except for a single hawk circling overhead.

Have you guessed what kind of town this is? It is a prairie dog town on the Nebraska plains. As these prairie dogs dug their burrows, searched for food, and hid from the hawk, they interacted with their environment, or surroundings. The prairie dogs interacted with living things, such as the grass and the hawk, and with nonliving things, such as the soil. All the living and nonliving things that interact in a particular area make up an **ecosystem.**

A prairie is just one of the many different ecosystems found on Earth. Other ecosystems in which living things make their homes include mountain streams, deep oceans, and dense forests.

Habitats

A prairie dog is one type of organism, or living thing. Organisms live in a specific place within an ecosystem. **An organism obtains food, water, shelter, and other things it needs to live, grow, and reproduce from its surroundings.** The place where an organism lives and that provides the things the organism needs is called its **habitat.**

A single ecosystem may contain many habitats. For example, in a forest ecosystem, mushrooms grow in the damp soil, rabbits live on the forest floor, termites live under the bark of tree trunks, and flickers build nests in the trunks.

Organisms live in different habitats because they have different requirements for survival. A prairie dog obtains the food and shelter it needs from its habitat. It could not survive in a tropical rain forest or on the rocky ocean shore. Likewise, the prairie would not meet the needs of a gorilla, a penguin, or a hermit crab.

Figure 1 A stream tumbles over mossy rocks in a lush Tennessee forest. This ecosystem contains many different habitats. *Comparing and Contrasting How is the mushrooms' habitat in the forest different from the flicker's habitat?*

Biotic Factors

An organism interacts with both the living and nonliving things in its environment. The living parts of an ecosystem are called **biotic factors** (by AHT ik factors). Biotic factors in the prairie dogs' ecosystem include the grass and plants that provide seeds and berries. The hawks, ferrets, badgers, and eagles that hunt the prairie dogs are also biotic factors. In addition, worms, fungi, and bacteria are biotic factors that live in the soil underneath the prairie grass. These organisms keep the soil rich in nutrients as they break down the remains of other living things.

✓ *Checkpoint Name a biotic factor in your environment.*

Figure 2 This eastern banjo frog is burrowing in the sand to stay cool in the hot Australian desert. *Interpreting Photographs With which abiotic factors is the frog interacting in this scene?*

With or Without Salt?

In this activity you will explore salt as an abiotic factor.

1. Label four 600-mL beakers A, B, C, and D. Fill each with 500 mL of room-temperature spring water.

2. Set beaker A aside. It will contain fresh water. To beaker B, add 2.5 grams of noniodized salt. Add 7.5 grams of salt to beaker C and 15 grams of salt to beaker D. Stir beakers B, C, and D.

3. Add $\frac{1}{8}$ teaspoon of brine shrimp eggs to each beaker.

4. Cover each beaker with a square of paper. Keep them away from direct light or heat. Wash your hands.

5. Observe the beakers daily for three days.

Drawing Conclusions In which beakers did the eggs hatch? What can you conclude about the amount of salt in the shrimps' natural habitat?

Abiotic Factors

The nonliving parts of an ecosystem are called **abiotic factors** (ay by AHT ik factors). Abiotic factors that affect living things in the prairie are similar to those found in most ecosystems. They include water, sunlight, oxygen, temperature, and soil.

Water All living things require water to carry out their life processes. Water also makes up a large part of the bodies of most organisms. Your body, for example, is about 65 percent water. A watermelon consists of more than 95 percent water! Water is particularly important to plants and algae. These organisms use water, along with sunlight and carbon dioxide, to make food in a process called **photosynthesis** (foh toh SIN thuh sis). Other living things eat the plants and algae to obtain energy.

Sunlight Because sunlight is necessary for photosynthesis, it is an important abiotic factor for plants, algae, and other living things. In places that do not receive sunlight, such as dark caves, plants cannot grow. Without plants or algae to provide a source of food, few other organisms can live.

Oxygen Most living things require oxygen to carry out their life processes. Oxygen is so important to the functioning of the human body that you can live only a few minutes without it. Organisms that live on land obtain oxygen from the air, which is about 20 percent oxygen. Fish and other water organisms obtain dissolved oxygen from the water around them.

Temperature The temperatures that are typical of an area determine the types of organisms that can live there. For example, if you took a trip to a warm tropical island, you would see palm trees, bright hibiscus flowers, and tiny lizards. These organisms could not survive on the frozen plains of Siberia. But the thick, warm fur of wolves and short, strong branches of dwarf willows are suited to the blustery winters there.

Some animals alter their environments to overcome very hot or very cold temperatures. For example, prairie dogs dig underground dens to find shelter from the blazing summer sun. They line the dens with grass. The grass keeps the prairie dogs warm during the cold and windy winters.

Soil Soil is a mixture of rock fragments, nutrients, air, water, and the decaying remains of living things. Soil in different areas consists of varying amounts of these materials. The type of soil in an area influences the kinds of plants that can grow there. Many animals, such as the prairie dogs, use the soil itself as a home. Billions of microscopic organisms such as bacteria also live in the soil. These tiny organisms play an important role in the ecosystem by breaking down the remains of other living things.

☑ *Checkpoint* **How do biotic factors differ from abiotic factors?**

Populations

In 1900, travelers saw a prairie dog town in Texas covering an area twice the size of the city of Dallas. The sprawling town contained more than 400 million prairie dogs! These prairie dogs were all members of one species, or single kind, of organism. A **species** (SPEE sheez) is a group of organisms that are physically similar and can reproduce with each other to produce fertile offspring.

All the members of one species in a particular area are referred to as a **population.** The 400 million prairie dogs in the Texas town are one example of a population. All the pigeons in New York City make up a population, as do all the daisies in a field. In contrast, all the trees in a forest do not make up a population, because they do not all belong to the same species. There may be pines, maples, birches, and many other tree species in the forest.

Figure 3 This milkweed plant is home to a small population of ladybug beetles.

The area in which a population lives can be as small as a single blade of grass or as large as the whole planet. Scientists studying a type of organism usually limit their study to a population in a defined area. For example, they might study the population of bluegill fish in a pond, or the population of alligators in the Florida Everglades.

Some populations, however, do not stay in a contained area. For example, to study the population of finback whales, a scientist might need to use the entire ocean.

Organism

Population

Communities

Of course, most ecosystems contain more than one type of organism. The prairie, for instance, includes prairie dogs, hawks, grasses, badgers, and snakes, along with many other organisms. All the different populations that live together in an area make up a **community.**

Figure 4 shows the levels of organization in the prairie ecosystem. **The smallest unit of organization is a single organism, which belongs to a population of other members of its species. The population belongs to a community of different species. The community and abiotic factors together form an ecosystem.**

To be considered a community, the different populations must live close enough together to interact. One way the populations in a community may interact is by using the same resources, such as food and shelter. For example, the tunnels dug by the prairie dogs also serve as homes for burrowing owls and black-footed ferrets. The prairie dogs share the grass with other animals. Meanwhile, prairie dogs themselves serve as food for many species.

What Is Ecology?

Because the populations in the prairie ecosystem interact with one another, any changes in a community affect all the different populations that live there. The study of how living things interact with each other and with their environment is called **ecology.** Ecologists, scientists who study ecology, look at how all the biotic and abiotic factors in an ecosystem are related.

Community

Ecosystem

Figure 4 The smallest level of ecological organization is an individual organism. The largest is the entire ecosystem.

As part of their work, ecologists study how organisms react to changes in their environment. Living things constantly interact with their surroundings, responding to changes in the conditions around them. Some responses are very quick. When a prairie dog sees a hawk overhead, it gives a warning bark. The other prairie dogs hear the bark and respond by returning to their burrows to hide. Other responses to change in the environment occur more slowly. For example, after a fire on the prairie, it takes some time for the grass to reach its former height and for all the animals to return to the area.

Section 1 Review

1. What basic needs are provided by an organism's habitat?
2. List these terms in order from the smallest unit to the largest: population, organism, ecosystem, community.
3. Explain how water and sunlight are two abiotic factors that are important to all organisms.
4. Why do ecologists study both biotic and abiotic factors in an ecosystem?
5. **Thinking Critically** Applying Concepts Would all the insects in a forest be considered a population? Why or why not?

Check Your Progress

CHAPTER PROJECT 1

After your teacher has reviewed your plan, prepare the containers and plant the seeds. Design a data table to record the information you will use to compare the growth in the different containers. When the plants begin to grow, examine them daily and record your observations. Be sure to continue caring for your plants according to your plan. *(Hint:* Use a metric ruler to measure your growing plants. Besides size, look for differences in leaf color and the number of buds among the plants.)

A World in a Jar

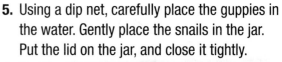

In this lab, you will study the interactions that take place between biotic and abiotic factors in a model ecosystem.

Problem

How can organisms live in a closed ecosystem?

Materials

aquarium gravel
plastic stirring rod
2-day-old tap water
2 guppies
metric ruler
dip net
4 aquatic plants
4 small pond snails
large jar with cover (about 2 liters)
UL-listed lamp with a 60-watt bulb

Procedure

1. In this lab, you will put guppies, snails, and plants together in a sealed jar of water. Record your prediction about whether this habitat will meet the needs of these organisms.
2. Find a safe location for the jar away from windows and other areas where light and temperature are likely to change often. There should be an electrical outlet nearby for the lamp.
3. Add aquarium gravel to the jar to a depth of 3 cm. Add water to about 6 cm from the top.
4. Place the plants in the jar one at a time. Use a stirring rod to gently brush aside a little gravel. Position the roots of each plant against the bottom of the jar. Move gravel back over the roots to hold the plant in place.

5. Using a dip net, carefully place the guppies in the water. Gently place the snails in the jar. Put the lid on the jar, and close it tightly.
6. Position the lamp so that the light shines into the jar. The light bulb should be 15 to 20 cm from the jar. **CAUTION:** *Lighted bulbs get very hot. Do not allow the bulb to touch any objects.*
7. Observe the jar every day. Record your observations in your notebook.
8. Within 5 days, the water in the jar should turn slightly green. The green color indicates the presence of algae. If the water is bright green, move the light away from the jar. If the water is not green after 5 days, move the light closer to the jar. Record in your notebook any changes to the setup.
9. Observe the jar for at least one more week.

Analyze and Conclude

1. What biotic and abiotic factors are part of the ecosystem in the jar?
2. Are any biotic or abiotic factors able to enter the sealed jar? If so, which one(s)?
3. Where did the green algae come from?
4. Draw a diagram of the interactions between the biotic and abiotic factors in the jar.
5. Would the guppies, snails, and plants be able to live alone in separate jars? Why or why not?
6. **Think About It** Explain how your jar and its contents model an ecosystem. How is your model different from an ecosystem on Earth?

More to Explore

Make a plan to model a saltwater or land ecosystem. How would this model be different from the freshwater ecosystem? Obtain your teacher's approval before carrying out your plan.

SECTION 2 Studying Populations

DISCOVER ·· ACTIVITY

What's the Population of Beans in a Jar?

1. Fill a plastic jar with dried beans. This is your model population.

2. Your goal is to determine the number of beans in the jar, but you will not have time to count every bean. You may use any of the following to help you determine the size of the bean population: a ruler, a small beaker, another large jar. Set a timer for two minutes when you are ready to begin.

3. After two minutes, record your answer. Then count the actual number of beans. How close was your answer?

Think It Over
Forming Operational Definitions
In this activity, you came up with an estimate of the size of the bean population. Write a definition of the term *estimate* based on what you did.

How would you like to change jobs for the day? Instead of being a student, today you are an ecologist. You are working on a project to study the bald eagle population in your area. One question you might ask is how the population has changed over time. Is the number of bald eagles more, less, or the same as it was 50 years ago? To answer these questions, you must first determine the present size of the bald eagle population.

Population Density

One way to state the size of a population is in terms of **population density** — the number of individuals in a specific area. Population density can be written as an equation:

$$Population\ density = \frac{Number\ of\ individuals}{Unit\ area}$$

For instance, suppose you counted 50 monarch butterflies in a garden measuring 10 square meters. The population density would be 50 butterflies per 10 square meters, or 5 butterflies per square meter.

GUIDE FOR READING

◆ How do ecologists determine the size of a population?

◆ What causes populations to change in size?

◆ What factors limit population growth?

Reading Tip Before you read, predict some factors that might cause a population to increase or decrease.

Bald eagles in Alaska ▶

Figure 5 These cone-shaped structures are nests built by cliff swallows in Dinosaur National Monument, Utah. Counting the nests is one way to estimate the cliff swallow population.

Determining Population Size

In your work as an ecologist, how can you determine the size of the population you are studying? **Some methods of determining the size of a population are direct and indirect observations, sampling, and mark-and-recapture studies.**

Direct Observation The most obvious way to determine the size of a population is to count, one by one, all of its members. You could count all the bald eagles that live along a river, all the red maple trees in a forest, or all the elephants in a valley in Kenya.

Indirect Observation The members of a population may be small or hard to find. It may then be easier to observe their tracks or other signs rather than the organisms themselves. Look at the mud nests built by cliff swallows in Figure 5. Each nest has one entrance hole. By counting the entrance holes, you can determine the number of swallow families nesting in this area. Suppose that the average number of swallows per nest is four: two parents and two offspring. If there are 120 nests in an area, you can find the number of swallows by multiplying 120 by 4, or 480 swallows.

Sampling In most cases, it is not possible to count every member of a population. The population may be very large, or it may be spread over a wide area. It may be hard to find every individual or to remember which ones have already been counted. Instead, ecologists usually make an estimate. An **estimate** is an approximation of a number, based on reasonable assumptions.

One type of estimating involves counting the number of organisms in a small area (a sample), and then multiplying to find the number in a larger area. To get an accurate estimate, the sample should have the same population density as the larger area. For example, suppose you count 8 red maples in a 10 meter-by-10 meter area of the forest. If the entire forest were 100 times that size, you would multiply your count by 100 to estimate the total population, or 800 red maples.

Mark-and-Recapture Studies Another estimating method is a technique called "mark and recapture." This technique gets its name because some animals are first captured, marked, and released into the environment. Then another group of animals is captured. The

Sharpen your Skills

Calculating
ACTIVITY

A bed of oysters measures 100 meters long and 50 meters wide. In a one-square-meter area you count 20 oysters. Estimate the population of oysters in the bed. (*Hint:* Drawing a diagram may help you set up your calculation.)

number of marked animals in this second group indicates the population size. For example, if half the animals in the second group are marked, it means that the first sample represented about half the total population.

Here's an example showing how mark and recapture works. First, deer mice in a field are caught in a trap that does not harm the mice. Ecologists count the mice and mark each mouse's belly with a dot of hair dye before releasing it again. Two weeks later, the researchers return and capture mice again. They count how many mice have marks, showing that they were captured the first time, and how many are unmarked. Using a mathematical formula, the scientists can estimate the total population of mice in the field. You can try this technique for yourself in the Real-World Lab at the end of this section.

Figure 6 This young hawk is part of a mark-and-recapture study in a Virginia marsh. *Inferring What is the purpose of the silver band on the hawk's leg?*

✓ *Checkpoint* When is sampling used to estimate a population?

Changes in Population Size

By returning to a location often and using one of the methods described above, ecologists can monitor the size of a population over time. **Populations can change in size when new members enter the population or when members leave the population.**

Births and Deaths The major way in which new individuals are added to a population is through the birth of offspring. The **birth rate** of a population is the number of births in a population in a certain amount of time. For example, suppose a population of 1,000 snow geese produces 1,400 goslings in a year. The birth rate in this population would be 1,400 goslings per year.

Similarly, the major way that individuals leave a population is by dying. The **death rate** is the number of deaths in a population in a certain amount of time. Suppose that in the same population, 100 geese die in a year. The death rate would be 100 geese per year.

Figure 7 The birth of new individuals can increase the size of a population. This cheetah mother added five offspring to the population in her area.

The Population Equation When the birth rate in a population is greater than the death rate, the population will generally increase in size. This statement can be written as a mathematical statement using the "is greater than" sign:

If birth rate > death rate, population size increases.

For example, in the snow goose population, the birth rate of 1,400 goslings per year was greater than the death rate of 100 geese per year, and the population would increase in size.

However, if the death rate in a population is greater than the birth rate, the population size will generally decrease. This can also be written as a mathematical statement:

If death rate > birth rate, population size decreases.

Immigration and Emigration The size of a population also can change when individuals move into or out of the population, just as the population of your town changes when families move into town or move away. **Immigration** (im ih GRAY shun) means moving into a population. **Emigration** (em ih GRAY shun) means leaving a population. Emigration can occur when part of a population gets cut off from the rest of the population. For instance, if food is scarce, some members of an antelope herd may wander off in search of better grassland. If they become permanently separated from the original herd, they will no longer be part of that population.

Graphing Changes in Population You can see an example of changes in a population of rabbits in Figure 8. The vertical axis shows the numbers of rabbits in the population, while the horizontal axis shows time. The graph shows the size of the population over a 10-year period.

☑ *Checkpoint* *Name two ways individuals can join a population.*

Figure 8 From Year 0 to Year 4, more rabbits joined the population than left it, so the population increased. From Year 4 to Year 8, more rabbits left the population than joined it, so the population decreased. From Year 8 to Year 10, the rates of rabbits leaving and joining the population were about equal, so the population remained steady. *Interpreting Graphs In what year did the rabbit population reach its highest point? What was the size of the population in that year?*

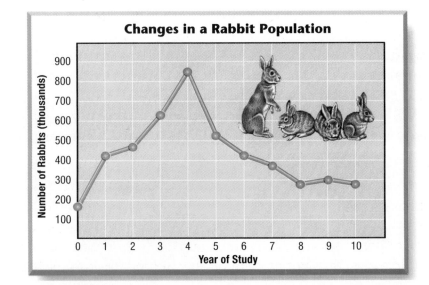

Changes in a Rabbit Population

Number of Rabbits (thousands) vs. Year of Study

Figure 9 These gannets seem to have heard the saying "Birds of a feather flock together." When there are more birds than the space can support, the population will have exceeded the carrying capacity of the shore.

Limiting Factors

When conditions are good, a population will generally increase. But a population does not keep growing forever. Eventually, some factor in its environment causes the population to stop growing. A **limiting factor** is an environmental factor that prevents a population from increasing. **Some limiting factors for populations are food, space, and weather conditions.**

Food Organisms require food to survive. In an area where food is scarce, this becomes a limiting factor. Suppose a giraffe needs to eat 10 kilograms of leaves each day to survive. The trees in an area can provide 100 kilograms of leaves a day while remaining healthy. Five giraffes could live easily in this area, since they would only require a total of 50 kilograms of food. But 15 giraffes could not all survive—there would not be enough food for all of them. No matter how much shelter, water, and other resources there might be, the population will not grow much higher than 10 giraffes. The largest population that an environment can support is called its **carrying capacity.** The carrying capacity of this environment is 10 giraffes.

Space The birds in Figure 9 are rarely seen on land. These birds, called gannets, spend most of their lives flying over the ocean. They only land on this rocky shore to nest. But as you can see, the shore is very crowded. If a pair of gannets does not have room to build a nest, that pair will not be able to produce any offspring.

Elbow Room

Using masking tape, mark off several one-meter squares on the floor of your classroom. Your teacher will form groups of 2, 4, and 6 students. Each group's task is to put together a small jigsaw puzzle in one of the squares. All the group members must keep their feet within the square. Time how long it takes your group to finish the puzzle.

Making Models How long did it take each group to complete the task? How does this activity show that space can be a limiting factor? What is the carrying capacity of puzzle-solvers in a square meter?

Those gannets will not contribute to an increase in the gannet population. This means that space for nesting is a limiting factor for these gannets. If the shore were bigger, more gannets would be able to nest there, and the population would increase.

Space is often a limiting factor for plants. The amount of space in which a plant grows can determine how much sunlight, water, and other necessities the plant can obtain. For example, many pine seedlings sprout each year in a forest. But as the trees get bigger, those that are too close together do not have room to spread their roots underground. Other tree branches block out the sunlight they need to live. Some of the seedlings die, limiting the size of the pine population.

Weather Weather conditions such as temperature and amount of rainfall can also limit population growth. Many insect species breed in the warm spring weather. As winter begins, the first frost kills many of the insects. This sudden rise in the death rate causes the insect population to decrease.

A single severe weather event can dramatically change the size of a population by killing many organisms. For instance, a flood or hurricane can wash away nests and burrows just as it damages the homes of humans. If you live in a northern state, you may have seen an early frost limit the population of tomatoes in a vegetable garden.

Figure 10 A snowstorm can limit the size of the orange crop.

 Section 2 Review

Science at Home

1. List four ways of determining population size.
2. How is birth rate related to population size?
3. List three limiting factors for populations. Choose one and explain how this factor can limit population growth.
4. Explain why it is often necessary for ecologists to estimate the size of a population.
5. **Thinking Critically** Problem Solving A field measures 50 meters by 90 meters. In one square meter, you count 3 mice. Estimate the total population of mice in the field. What method did you use to make your estimate?

Choose a page of a dictionary or other book that has a lot of type on it. Challenge your family members to estimate the number of words on the page. After everyone has come up with an estimate, have each person explain the method he or she used. Now count the actual number of words on the page. Whose estimate was closest?

Counting Turtles

For three years, ecologists have been using the mark-and-recapture method to monitor the population of turtles in a pond. In this lab, you will model recapturing the turtles to complete the study. Then you will analyze the results.

Problem

How can the mark-and-recapture method help ecologists monitor the size of a population?

Skills Focus

calculating, graphing, predicting

Materials

model paper turtle population
calculator   graph paper

Procedure

1. The data table shows the results from the first three years of the study. Copy it into your notebook, leaving spaces for your data as shown.
2. Your teacher will give you a box representing the pond. Fifteen of the paper turtles have been marked, as shown in the data table.
3. Capture a member of the population by randomly selecting one turtle. Set it aside.
4. Repeat Step 3 nine times. Record the total number of turtles you captured.
5. Examine each turtle to see whether it has a mark. Count the number of recaptured (marked) turtles. Record this number in your data table.

Analyze and Conclude

1. Use the equation below to estimate the turtle population for each year. The first year is done for you as a sample. If your answer is a decimal, round it to the nearest whole number so that your estimate is in "whole turtles." Record the population for each year in the last column of the data table.

$$\text{Total population} = \frac{\text{Number marked} \times \text{Total number captured}}{\text{Number recaptured (with marks)}}$$

Sample (Year 1):
$$\frac{32 \times 28}{15} = 59.7 \text{ or } 60 \text{ turtles}$$

2. Graph the estimated total populations for the four years. Mark years on the horizontal axis. Mark population size on the vertical axis.
3. Describe how the turtle population has changed over the four years of the study. Suggest three possible causes for the changes.
4. **Apply** Use your graph to predict the turtle population in Year 5. Explain your prediction.

Getting Involved

Find out whether any wildlife populations in your area are being monitored by national, state, or local agencies. Make a poster or write an article for the school paper about the population and the method being used to study it.

DATA TABLE

Year	Number Marked	Total Number Captured	Number Recaptured (with Marks)	Estimated Total Population
1	32	28	15	
2	25	21	11	
3	23	19	11	
4	15			

Animal Overpopulation: How Can People Help?

Populations of white-tailed deer are growing rapidly in many parts of the United States. As populations soar, food becomes a limiting factor. Many deer die of starvation. Others grow up small and unhealthy. In search of food, hungry deer move closer to where humans live. There they eat farm crops, garden vegetables, shrubs, and even trees. This affects birds and small animals that depend on the plants for shelter or food. In addition, increased numbers of deer near roads can cause more automobile accidents.

People admire the grace, beauty, and swiftness of deer. Most people don't want these animals to suffer from starvation or illness. Should people take action to limit growing deer populations?

The Issues

Should People Take Direct Action?

Many people argue that hunting is the simplest way to reduce animal populations. Wildlife managers look at the supply of resources in an area and determine its carrying capacity. Then hunters are issued licenses to help reduce the number of deer to the level that can be supported.

Other people favor nonhunting approaches to control deer populations. One plan is to trap the deer and relocate them. But this method is expensive and requires finding another location that can accept the deer without unbalancing its own system. Few such locations are available.

Scientists are also working to develop chemicals to reduce the birth rate in deer populations. This plan will help control overpopulation, but it is effective for only one year at a time.

Should People Take Indirect Action?

Some suggest bringing in natural enemies of deer, such as wolves, mountain lions, and bears, to areas with too many deer. But these animals could also attack cattle, dogs, cats, and even humans. Other communities have built tall fences around areas they don't want deer to invade. Although this solution can work for people with small yards, it is impractical for farmers or ranchers.

Should People Do Nothing?
Some people oppose any kind of action. They support leaving the deer alone and allowing nature to take its course. Animal populations in an area naturally cycle up and down over time. Doing nothing means that some deer will die of starvation or disease. But eventually, the population will be reduced to a size within the carrying capacity of the environment.

You Decide

1. Identify the Problem
In your own words, explain the problem created by the over-population of white-tailed deer.

2. Analyze the Options
List the ways that people can deal with overpopulation of white-tailed deer. State the negative and positive points of each method.

3. Find a Solution
Suppose you are an ecologist in an area that has twice as many deer as it can support. Propose a way for the community to deal with the problem.

3 Interactions Among Living Things

DISCOVER · ACTIVITY · · ·

How Well Can You Hide a Butterfly?

1. Using the outline at the right, trace a butterfly on a piece of paper.

2. Look around the classroom and pick a spot where you will place your butterfly. The butterfly must be placed completely in the open. Color your butterfly so it will blend in with the spot you choose.

3. Tape your butterfly to its spot. Someone will now enter the room to look for the butterflies. This person will have one minute to find all the butterflies he or she can. Will your butterfly be found?

Think It Over

Predicting Over time, how do you think the population size would change for butterflies that blend in with their surroundings?

Imagine giving a big hug to the plant in the photo. Ouch! The sharp spines on its trunk would make you think twice before hugging—or even touching—the saguaro (suh GWAHR oh) cactus. But if you could spend a day hidden inside a saguaro, you would see that many species do interact with this spiky plant.

As the day breaks, you hear a twittering noise coming from a nest tucked in one of the sagauro's arms. Two young red-tailed hawks are preparing to fly for the first time. Farther down the trunk, a tiny elf owl peeks out of its nest in a small hole. The elf owl is so small it could fit in your palm! A rattlesnake slithers around the base of the saguaro, looking for lunch. Spying a nearby shrew, the snake moves in for the kill. With a sudden movement, it strikes the shrew with its sharp fangs.

The activity around the saguaro doesn't stop after the sun goes down. At night, long-nosed bats feed on the nectar from the saguaro's blossoms. They stick their faces into the flowers to feed, covering their long snouts with a dusting of white pollen in the process. As the bats move from plant to plant, they carry the pollen along. This enables the cactuses to reproduce.

GUIDE FOR READING

◆ How do an organism's adaptations help it to survive?

◆ What are the major types of interactions among organisms?

◆ What are the three forms of symbiotic relationships?

Reading Tip As you read, use the section headings to make an outline. Fill in details under each heading.

◀ Saguaro cactus in the Arizona desert

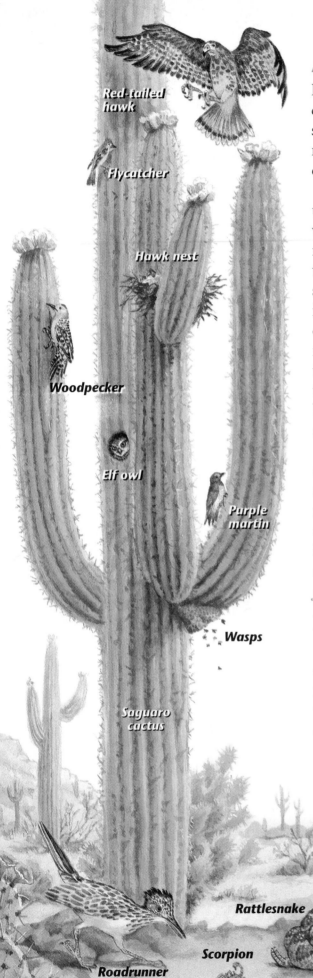

Red-tailed hawk

Flycatcher

Hawk nest

Woodpecker

Elf owl

Purple martin

Wasps

Saguaro cactus

Roadrunner

Scorpion

Rattlesnake

Gila monster

Adapting to the Environment

Each organism in this desert ecosystem has some unique characteristics. In response to their environments, species evolve, or change over time. The changes that make organisms better suited to their environments develop through a process called **natural selection.**

Natural selection works like this: Individuals in a population have different characteristics. Those individuals whose characteristics are best suited for their environment tend to survive and produce offspring. Offspring that inherit the characteristics that made their parents successful also live to reproduce. Over many generations individuals with those characteristics continue to reproduce. Individuals that are poorly suited to the environment are less likely to survive and reproduce. Over time, these poorly suited characteristics may disappear from the population. This process results in **adaptations,** the behaviors and physical characteristics of species that allow them to live successfully in their environment.

Every organism has a variety of adaptations that are suited to its specific living conditions. The adaptations of the organisms in the desert ecosystem create unique roles for each organism. An organism's particular role, or how it makes its living, is called its **niche.** A niche includes the type of food the organism eats, how it obtains this food, and which other species use the organism as food. The niche also includes when and how the organism reproduces and the physical conditions it requires to survive.

An organism's niche may include how it interacts with other organisms. During your day in the saguaro community, you observed a range of such interactions. **There are three major types of interactions among organisms: competition, predation, and symbiosis.**

Figure 11 The organisms in the saguaro community are well adapted to their desert environment.
Observing Identify two interactions between organisms that are taking place in this scene.

The bay-breasted warbler *feeds in the middle part of the tree.*

The Cape May warbler *feeds at the tips of branches near the top of the tree.*

The yellow-rumped warbler *feeds in the lower part of the tree and at the bases of the middle branches.*

Figure 12 Each of these warblers occupies a different niche in its spruce tree habitat. By feeding in different areas of the tree, the birds avoid competing with each other for food.

Competition

Different species can share the same habitat, such as the many animals that live in and around the saguaro. Different species can also share similar food requirements. For example, the red-tailed hawk and the elf owl both live on the saguaro and eat similar food. However, these two species do not occupy exactly the same niche. The hawk is active during the day, while the owl is active mostly at night. If two species occupy the same niche, one of the species will eventually die off. The reason for this is **competition,** the struggle between organisms to survive in a habitat with limited resources.

An ecosystem cannot satisfy the needs of all the living things in a particular habitat. There is a limited amount of food, water, and shelter. Organisms that survive have adaptations that enable them to reduce competition. For example, the three species of warblers in Figure 12 live in the same spruce forest habitat. They all eat insects that live in the spruce trees. How do these birds avoid competing for the limited insect supply? Each warbler "specializes" in feeding in a certain part of a spruce tree. By finding their own places to feed, the three species can coexist.

INTEGRATING CHEMISTRY Many plants use chemicals to ward off their competition. Plants often compete with one another for growing space and water. Some shrubs release toxic, or poisonous, chemicals into the ground around them. These chemicals keep grass and weeds from growing around the shrubs, sometimes forming a ring of bare ground a meter or two wide.

✓ *Checkpoint* *Why can't two species occupy the same niche?*

Predation

A tiger shark lurks beneath the surface of the clear blue water, looking for shadows of young albatross floating above it. The shark sees a chick and silently swims closer. Suddenly, the shark bursts through the water and seizes the albatross with one snap of its powerful jaw. This interaction between two organisms has an unfortunate ending for the albatross.

An interaction in which one organism kills and eats another is called **predation.** The organism that does the killing, in this case the tiger shark, is the **predator.** The organism that is killed, the albatross, is the **prey.**

Predator Adaptations Predators have adaptations that help them catch and kill their prey. For example, a cheetah can run very fast for a short time, enabling it to catch its prey. A jellyfish's tentacles contain a poisonous substance that paralyzes tiny water

EXPLORING *Defense Strategies*

Organisms display a wide array of adaptations that help them avoid becoming prey.

Protective Coverings
This sea urchin sends a clear message to predators: "Don't touch!" Porcupines, hedgehogs, and cactuses all use the same spiny strategy. After a few painful encounters, a predator will look for less prickly prey. ▼

Camouflage ▲
These delicate spiny bugs are a perfect match for their branch habitat. The more an organism resembles its surroundings, the less likely it is that a predator will notice it. Some animals, such as flounder, can even change their colors to match a variety of settings.

animals. You can probably think of many predators that have claws, sharp teeth, or stingers. Some plants, too, have adaptations for catching prey. The sundew is covered with sticky bulbs on stalks—when a fly lands on the plant, it remains snared in the sticky goo while the plant digests it.

Some predators have adaptations that enable them to hunt at night. For example, the big eyes of an owl let in as much light as possible to help it see in the dark. Bats can hunt without seeing at all. Instead, they locate their prey by producing pulses of sound and listening for the echoes. This precise method enables a bat to catch a flying moth in complete darkness.

Prey Adaptations How do prey organisms manage to avoid being killed by such effective predators? In *Exploring Defense Strategies,* below, you can see some examples of how an organism's physical characteristics can help protect it.

Warning Coloring ▲
A frog this bright certainly can't hide. How could such a color be an advantage? The bright red and blue of this poison arrow frog warn predators not to eat it— glands on the frog's back that release toxic chemicals make it a bad choice for a meal.

Mimicry
If you've ever been stung by a bee, you'd probably keep your distance from this insect. But actually this "bee" is a harmless fly. The fly's resemblance to a stinging bee protects it from birds and other predators, who are fooled into staying away. ▼

◀ **False Coloring**
Which way is this butterfly fish swimming? The black dot on its tail is a false eye. A predator may bite this end of the fish, allowing it to escape with only part of its tail missing.

Figure 13 The populations of wolves and moose on Isle Royale are related. The predator wolf population depends on the size of the prey moose population, and vice versa.
Predicting How might a disease in the wolf population one year affect the moose population the next year?

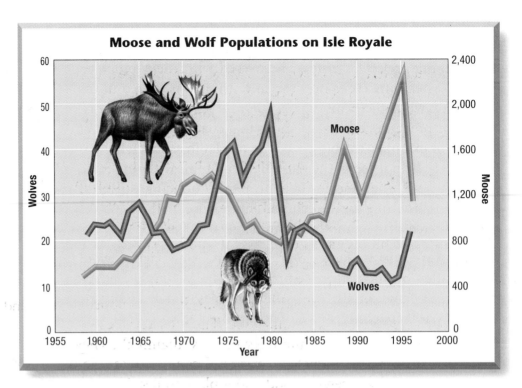

Moose and Wolf Populations on Isle Royale

The Effect of Predation on Population Size

Predation can have a major effect on the size of a population. As you learned in Section 2, when the death rate exceeds the birth rate in a population, the size of the population usually decreases. If predators are very effective at hunting their prey, the result is often a decrease in the size of the prey population. But a decrease in the prey population in turn affects the predator population.

To see how predator and prey populations can affect each other, look at the graph above. The graph shows the number of moose and wolves living on Isle Royale, an island in Lake Superior. From 1965 to 1975, the number of prey moose increased. The wolves now had enough to eat, so more of them survived. Within a few years, the wolf population began to increase. The growing number of wolves killed more and more moose. The moose population decreased. By 1980, the lack of moose had greatly affected the wolves. Some wolves starved, and others could not raise as many young. Soon the moose population began to climb again. This cycle for the two species has continued.

Of course, other factors also affect the populations on Isle Royale. For instance, cold winters and disease can also reduce the size of one or both of the populations.

✓ *Checkpoint* *If predation removes more members of a population than are born, how will the population change?*

Symbiosis

Many of the interactions in the saguaro community you read about earlier are examples of symbiosis. **Symbiosis** (sim bee OH sis) is a close relationship between two species that benefits at least one of the species. **The three types of symbiotic relationships are mutualism, commensalism, and parasitism.**

Mutualism   A relationship in which both species benefit is called **mutualism** (MYOO choo uh liz um). The relationship between the saguaro and the long-eared bats is an example of mutualism. The bat benefits because the cactus flowers provide it with food. The saguaro benefits as its pollen is carried to another plant on the bat's nose.

 INTEGRATING HEALTH   At this very moment, you are participating in a mutualistic relationship with a population of bacteria in your large intestine. These bacteria, called *Escherichia coli*, live in the intestines of most mammals. They break down some foods that the mammal cannot digest. The bacteria benefit by receiving food and a place to live. You also benefit from the relationship because the bacteria help you digest your food. Your *Escherichia coli* also provide you with vitamin K, a nutrient that is needed to make your blood clot.

Commensalism   A relationship in which one species benefits and the other species is neither helped nor harmed is called **commensalism** (kuh MEN suh liz um). The red-tailed hawks' interaction with the saguaro is an example of commensalism. The hawks are helped by having a place to build their nest, while the cactus is not affected by the birds.

Commensalism is not very common in nature because two species are usually either helped or harmed a little by any interaction. For example, by creating a small hole for its nest in the cactus trunk, the elf owl slightly damages the cactus.

Classifying

Classify each interaction as an example of mutualism, commensalism, or parasitism. Explain your answers.

- ◆ a remora fish attaches itself to the underside of a shark without harming the shark, and eats leftover bits of food from the shark's meals
- ◆ a vampire bat drinks the blood of horses
- ◆ bacteria living in cows' stomachs help them break down the cellulose in grass

Figure 14 Three yellow-billed oxpeckers get a cruise and a snack aboard an obliging hippopotamus. The oxpeckers eat ticks living on the hippo's skin. Since both the birds and the hippo benefit from this interaction, it is an example of mutualism.

Figure 15 The white objects on this sphinx moth larva are wasp cocoons. When the wasps emerge, they will feed on the larva.
Applying Concepts Which organism in this interaction is the parasite? Which organism is the host?

Parasitism The third type of symbiosis is called parasitism. **Parasitism** (PA ruh sit iz um) involves one organism living on or inside another organism and harming it. The organism that benefits is called a **parasite,** and the organism it lives on or in is called a **host.** The parasite is usually smaller than the host. In a parasitic relationship, the parasite benefits from the interaction while the host is harmed.

Some common parasites you may be familiar with are fleas, ticks, and leeches. These parasites have adaptations that enable them to attach to their host and feed on its blood. Other parasites live inside the host's body, such as tapeworms that live inside the digestive systems of dogs and wolves.

Unlike a predator, a parasite does not usually kill the organism it feeds on. If the host dies, the parasite loses its source of food. An interesting example of this rule is shown by a species of mite that lives in the ears of moths. The mites almost always live in just one of the moth's ears. If they live in both ears, the moth's hearing is so badly affected that it is likely to be quickly caught and eaten by its predator, a bat.

Section 3 Review

1. How do an organism's adaptations help it to survive?
2. Name and define the three major types of interactions among organisms.
3. List the three types of symbiosis. For each one, explain how the two organisms are affected.
4. A walking stick is an insect that resembles a small twig. How do you think this insect avoids predators?
5. **Thinking Critically** **Comparing and Contrasting** How are parasitism and predation similar? How are they different?

Check Your Progress

CHAPTER PROJECT
1

By now you should be making your final observations of your plants and planning your report. How can you present your data in a graph? Think about what you should put on each axis of your graph. *(Hint: Draft the written portion of your report early enough to look it over and make any necessary changes.)*

SECTION 1 Living Things and the Environment

Key Ideas

◆ An organism's habitat provides food, water, shelter, and other things the organism needs to live, grow, and reproduce.

◆ An ecosystem includes both biotic and abiotic factors. Abiotic factors found in many environments include water, sunlight, oxygen, temperature, and soil.

◆ A population consists of a single species. The different populations living together in one area make up a community. The community plus abiotic factors form an ecosystem.

◆ Ecologists study how the biotic and abiotic factors interact within an ecosystem.

Key Terms

ecosystem	species
habitat	population
biotic factor	community
abiotic factor	ecology
photosynthesis	

SECTION 2 Studying Populations

INTEGRATING MATHEMATICS

Key Ideas

◆ Ecologists can estimate population size by direct and indirect observations, sampling, and mark-and-recapture studies.

◆ A population changes in size as a result of changes in the birth rate or death rate, or when organisms move into or out of the population.

◆ Population size is controlled by limiting factors such as food, space, and weather conditions.

Key Terms

population density	immigration
estimate	emigration
birth rate	limiting factor
death rate	carrying capacity

SECTION 3 Interactions Among Living Things

Key Ideas

◆ Over time, species of organisms develop specialized adaptations and behaviors that help them succeed in their environments.

◆ The major types of interactions among organisms are competition, predation, and symbiosis.

◆ Predators have many adaptations that enable them to catch their prey, while prey organisms have adaptations to protect themselves from predators.

◆ Symbiosis is a close relationship between two species. The three types of symbiotic relationships are mutualism, commensalism, and parasitism.

Key Terms

natural selection	predator	commensalism
adaptation	prey	parasitism
niche	symbiosis	parasite
competition	mutualism	host
predation		

ACTIVITY

USING THE INTERNET

www.science-explorer.phschool.com

Reviewing Content

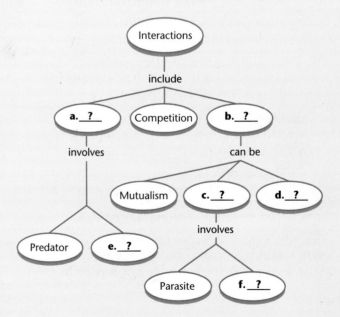

For more review of key concepts, see the Interactive Student Tutorial CD-ROM.

Multiple Choice

Choose the letter of the best answer.

1. A prairie dog, a hawk, and a badger all are members of the same
   a. habitat.
   b. community.
   c. species.
   d. population.

2. Which of the following is *not* an example of a population?
   a. the pets in your neighborhood
   b. the people in a city
   c. the rainbow trout in a stream
   d. the ants in an anthill

3. All of the following are examples of limiting factors for populations *except*
   a. space
   b. food
   c. time
   d. weather

4. Which of these relationships is an example of parasitism?
   a. a bird building a nest on a tree branch
   b. a bat pollinating a saguaro cactus
   c. a flea living on a cat's blood
   d. *Escherichia coli* bacteria making vitamin K in your intestine

5. In which type of interaction do both species benefit?
   a. predation
   b. mutualism
   c. commensalism
   d. parasitism

True or False

If the statement is true, write true. If it is false, change the underlined word or words to make the statement true.

6. Grass is an example of a(n) <u>abiotic</u> factor in a habitat.

7. A rise in birth rate while the death rate remains steady will cause a population to <u>increase</u> in size.

8. The struggle between organisms for limited resources is called <u>mutualism</u>.

9. A parasite lives on or inside its <u>predator</u>.

10. An organism's specific role in its habitat is called its <u>niche</u>.

Checking Concepts

11. Name two biotic and two abiotic factors you might find in a forest ecosystem.

12. Explain how sunlight is used by plants and algae. How is this process important to other living things in an ecosystem?

13. Describe how ecologists use the technique of sampling to estimate population size.

14. Give an example showing how space can be a limiting factor for a population.

15. What are two adaptations that prey organisms have developed to protect themselves? Describe how each adaptation protects the organism.

16. **Writing to Learn** Write a description of your niche in the environment. Include details about your habitat, including both biotic and abiotic factors around you. Be sure to describe your feeding habits as well as any interactions you have with members of other species.

Thinking Visually

17. **Concept Map** Copy the concept map about interactions among organisms onto a separate sheet of paper. Complete the concept map and add a title. (For more on concept maps, see the Skills Handbook.)

Applying Skills

Ecologists monitoring a deer population collected data during a 30-year study. Use the data to answer Questions 18–21.

18. Graphing Make a line graph using the data in the table. Plot years on the horizontal axis and population on the vertical axis.

Year	0	5	10	15	20	25	30
Population (thousands)	15	30	65	100	40	25	10

19. Interpreting Data In which year did the deer population reach its highest point? Its lowest point?

20. Communicating Write a few sentences describing how the deer population changed during the study.

21. Developing Hypotheses In Year 16 of the study, this region experienced a very severe winter. How might this have affected the deer population?

Thinking Critically

22. Making Generalizations Explain why ecologists usually study a specific population of organisms rather than studying the entire species.

23. Problem Solving As a summer job working for an ecologist, you have been assigned to estimate the population of grasshoppers in a field. Propose a method to get an estimate and explain how you would carry it out.

24. Comparing and Contrasting Explain how parasitism and mutualism are similar and how they are different.

25. Relating Cause and Effect Competition for resources in an area is usually more intense within a single species than between two different species. Can you suggest an explanation for this observation? (*Hint:* Consider how niches help organisms avoid competition.)

Performance Assessment

CHAPTER PROJECT 1 Wrap Up

Present Your Project Review your report and graph to be sure that they clearly state your conclusion about the effects of crowding on plant growth. With your group, decide how you will present your results. Do a practice run-through to make sure all group members feel comfortable with their part.

Reflect and Record Compare your group's results with those of your classmates. Suggest possible explanations for any differences. How could you have improved your plan for your experiment? Record these thoughts in your project notebook.

Getting Involved

In Your School Get permission to set up a bird observation center outside your school. Work with other students to make a bird feeder from a plastic jug. Use a birdwatching guide or contact a local wildlife organization to determine what type of feed to put in your container. Hang the feeder in a location that is safe from neighborhood cats. Nearby, place a shallow pan of water for the birds to drink and bathe in. Refill the food and water regularly. Keep a log of the species that visit your center, what type of food they prefer, and how they interact.

Chapter 1 **E ◆ 41**

WHAT'S AHEAD

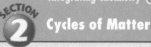

Breaking It Down

Nothing in this toad's ecosystem is wasted. Even when the living things die, they will be recycled by other organisms like the mushrooms. This natural breakdown process is called decomposition. In this chapter, you will study decomposition and other processes in ecosystems.

When fallen leaves and other waste products decompose, a fluffy, brown mixture called compost is formed. You can observe decomposition firsthand by building a compost chamber.

Your Goal To design an experiment to learn more about the process of decomposition.

To complete your project successfully, you must
◆ build two compost chambers
◆ investigate the effect of one of the following variables on decomposition: moisture, oxygen, temperature, or activity of soil organisms
◆ analyze your data and present your results
◆ follow the safety guidelines in Appendix A

Get Started Your teacher will provide you with a sample of compost material. Observe the wastes in the mixture with a hand lens. Write a hypothesis about which kinds of waste will decay and which will not. Begin thinking about which variable you will test.

Check Your Progress You'll be working on this project as you study this chapter. To keep your project on track, look for Check Your Progress boxes at the following points.

Section 1 Review, page 50: Build your compost chambers and design your experimental plan.
Section 2 Review, page 55: Observe your compost chambers and collect data.
Section 4 Review, page 73: Analyze your data.

Wrap Up At the end of the chapter (page 81), you will compare the compost produced in each of your compost chambers. Will your results support your hypothesis?

This toad is right at home in its habitat. It is surrounded by living leaves, grass, and mushrooms, as well as nonliving rocks, soil, and air.

SECTION
4 Earth's Biomes

Discover **How Much Rain Is That?**
Try This **Desert Survival**
Sharpen Your Skills **Inferring**
Sharpen Your Skills **Interpreting Data**
Real-World Lab **Biomes in Miniature**

SECTION
5 Succession

Discover **What Happened Here?**
Skills Lab **Change in a Tiny Community**

Where Did Your Dinner Come From?

1. Across the top of a page, list the different types of foods you ate for dinner last night.

2. Under each item, write the name of the plant, animal, or other organism that is the source of that food. Some foods have more than one source. For example, bread is made from flour (which is made from a plant such as wheat) and yeast (which is a fungus).

Think It Over

Classifying Count the different organisms that contributed to your dinner. How many of your food sources were plants? How many were animals?

GUIDE FOR READING

◆ What energy roles do organisms play in an ecosystem?

◆ How much energy is available at each level of an energy pyramid?

Reading Tip As you read, create a flowchart showing one possible path of energy through an ecosystem.

Pushing off from its perch on an oak tree limb, the kestrel glides over a field dotted with yellow flowers. In the middle of the field, the bird pauses. It hovers above the ground like a giant hummingbird. Despite strong gusts of wind, the bird's head remains steady as it looks for prey. It takes a lot of energy for the kestrel to hover in this way, but from this position it can search the field below for food.

Soon the kestrel spots a mouse munching the ripening seedhead of a blade of grass. Seconds later the kestrel swoops down and grasps the mouse in its talons. The bird carries the mouse back to the tree to feed.

Meanwhile, a lynx spider hides among the petals of a nearby flower. An unsuspecting bee lands on the flower for a sip of nectar. The spider grabs the bee and injects its venom into the bee's body. The venom kills the bee before it can respond with its own deadly sting.

This sunny field is an ecosystem, made up of living and nonliving things that interact with one another. You can see that many interactions in this ecosystem involve eating. The spider eats a bee that eats nectar, while the kestrel eats a mouse that eats grass. Ecologists study such feeding patterns to learn how energy flows within an ecosystem.

Figure 1 Cradled in a gumweed flower, a green lynx spider attacks an unsuspecting bee. These organisms are involved in feeding interactions.

Energy Roles

Do you play an instrument in your school band? If so, you know that each instrument has a role in a piece of music. For instance, the flute may provide the melody, while the drum provides the beat. Although the two instruments are quite different, they both play important roles in creating the band's music. In the same way, each organism has a role in the movement of energy through its ecosystem. This role is part of the organism's niche in the ecosystem. The kestrel's role is different from that of the giant oak tree where it was perched. But all parts of the ecosystem, like all parts of the band, are necessary for the ecosystem to work.

An organism's energy role is determined by how it obtains energy and how it interacts with the other living things in its ecosystem. **An organism's energy role in an ecosystem may be that of a producer, consumer, or decomposer.**

Producers Energy first enters most ecosystems as sunlight. Some organisms, such as plants, algae, and certain microorganisms, are able to capture the energy of sunlight and store it as food energy. As Figure 2 shows, these organisms use the sun's energy to turn water and carbon dioxide into molecules such as sugars and starches. As you recall from Chapter 1, this process is called photosynthesis.

An organism that can make its own food is a **producer.** Producers are the source of all the food in an ecosystem. For example, the grass and oak tree are the producers for the field ecosystem you read about at the beginning of the section.

In a few ecosystems the producers obtain energy from a source other than sunlight. One such ecosystem is found in rocks deep beneath the ground. Since the rocks are never exposed to sunlight, how is energy brought into this ecosystem? Certain bacteria in this ecosystem produce their own food using the energy in a gas, hydrogen sulfide, that is found in their environment.

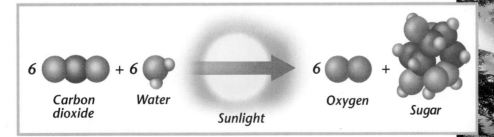

6 Carbon dioxide + 6 Water → Sunlight → 6 Oxygen + Sugar

Figure 2 The sunlight streaming through this redwood forest is the source of energy for the ecosystem. Plants convert the sun's energy to stored food energy through the process of photosynthesis.
Interpreting Diagrams What substances are needed for photosynthesis? What substances are produced?

Figure 3 Consumers are classified by what they eat. **A.** An agile gerenuk stands on its hind legs to reach these leaves. Consumers that eat plants are called herbivores. **B.** Carnivores like this collared lizard eat only animals. **C.** A black vulture is a scavenger, a carnivore that feeds on the remains of dead organisms.

Observing **ACTIVITY**

Sprinkle a few drops of water on a slice of bread. Enclose the bread in a sealable plastic bag. Seal the bag tightly with tape and put it in a warm, dark place. Observe the bread daily for about two weeks. **CAUTION:** *Do not open the bag.* Write a few sentences describing the changes you observe. What is responsible for the change?

Consumers Other members of the ecosystem cannot make their own food. These organisms depend on the producers for food and energy. An organism that obtains energy by feeding on other organisms is a **consumer.**

Consumers are classified by what they eat. Consumers that eat only plants are called **herbivores.** This term comes from the Latin words *herba*, which means grass or herb, and *vorare*, which means to eat. Some familiar herbivores are caterpillars, cattle, and deer. Consumers that eat only animals are called **carnivores.** This term comes from the same root word *vorare*, plus the Latin word for flesh, *carnis*. Lions, spiders, and snakes are some examples of carnivores. A consumer that eats both plants and animals is called an **omnivore.** The Latin word *omni* means all. Crows, goats, and most humans are examples of omnivores.

Some carnivores are scavengers. A **scavenger** is a carnivore that feeds on the bodies of dead organisms. Scavengers include catfish and vultures.

Decomposers What would happen if there were only producers and consumers in an ecosystem? As the organisms in the ecosystem continued to take water, minerals, and other raw materials from their surroundings, these materials would begin to run low. If these materials were not replaced, new organisms would not be able to grow.

All the organisms in an ecosystem produce waste and eventually die. If these wastes and dead organisms were not somehow removed from the ecosystem, they would pile up until they overwhelmed the living things. Organisms that break down wastes and dead organisms and return the raw materials to the environment are called **decomposers.** Two major groups of decomposers are bacteria and fungi, such as molds and mushrooms. While obtaining energy for their own needs, decomposers return simple molecules to the environment. These molecules can be used again by other organisms.

☑ *Checkpoint* *What do herbivores and carnivores have in common?*

Food Chains and Food Webs

As you have read, energy enters most ecosystems as sunlight, and is converted into sugar and starch molecules by producers. This energy is transferred to each organism that eats a producer, and then to other organisms that feed on these consumers. The movement of energy through an ecosystem can be shown in diagrams called food chains and food webs.

A **food chain** is a series of events in which one organism eats another and obtains energy. You can follow one food chain from the field ecosystem below. The first organism in a food chain is always a producer, such as the grass in the field. The second organism is a consumer that eats the producer, and is called a first-level consumer. The mouse is a first-level consumer. Next, a second-level consumer eats the first-level consumer. The second-level consumer in this example is the kestrel.

A food chain shows one possible path along which energy can move through an ecosystem. But just as you do not eat the same thing every day, neither do most other organisms. Most producers and consumers are part of many food chains. A more realistic way to show the flow of energy through an ecosystem is a food web. A **food web** consists of the many overlapping food chains in an ecosystem.

Figure 4 A cluster of honey mushrooms grows among dead leaves. Mushrooms are familiar decomposers.

Kestrel
(Second-level consumer)

Figure 5 These organisms make up one food chain in a field ecosystem.
Classifying Which organism shown is acting as an herbivore? Which is a carnivore?

Grass
(Producer)

Mouse
(First-level consumer)

EXPLORING a Food Web

A food web consists of many inter-connected food chains. Trace the path of energy through the producers, consumers, and decomposers.

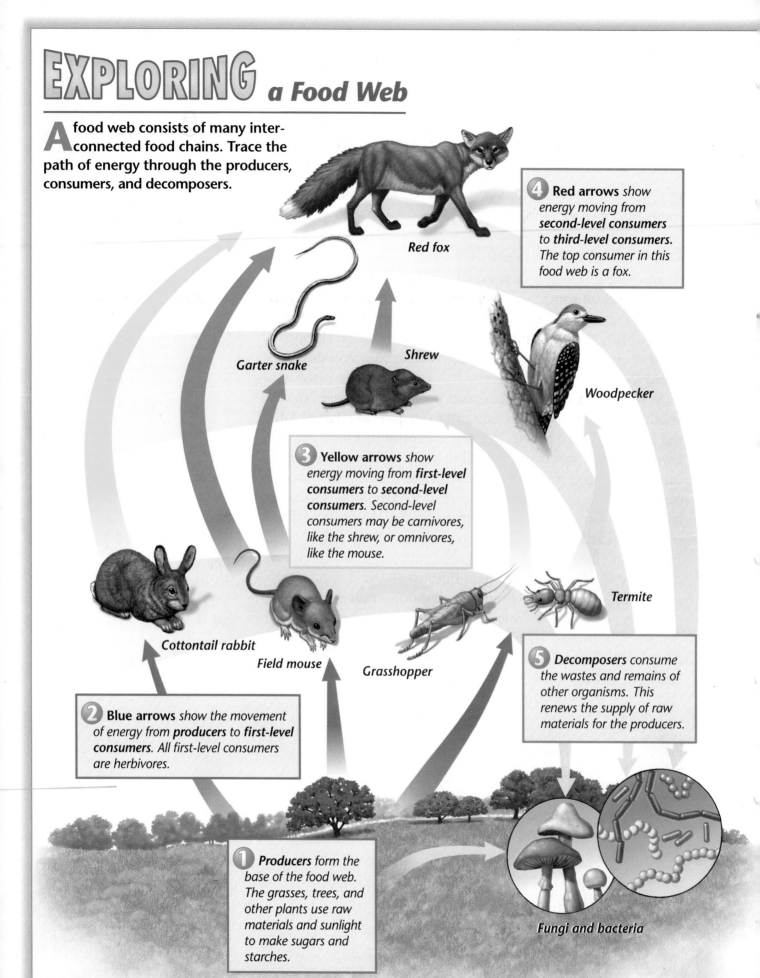

4 **Red arrows** *show energy moving from* ***second-level consumers*** *to* ***third-level consumers.*** *The top consumer in this food web is a fox.*

Red fox

Garter snake

Shrew

Woodpecker

3 **Yellow arrows** *show energy moving from* ***first-level consumers*** *to* ***second-level consumers.*** *Second-level consumers may be carnivores, like the shrew, or omnivores, like the mouse.*

Termite

Cottontail rabbit

Field mouse

Grasshopper

2 **Blue arrows** *show the movement of energy from* ***producers*** *to* ***first-level consumers.*** *All first-level consumers are herbivores.*

5 **Decomposers** *consume the wastes and remains of other organisms. This renews the supply of raw materials for the producers.*

1 **Producers** *form the base of the food web. The grasses, trees, and other plants use raw materials and sunlight to make sugars and starches.*

Fungi and bacteria

In *Exploring a Food Web* on the facing page, you can trace the many food chains in a woodland ecosystem. Note that an organism may play more than one role in an ecosystem. For example, an omnivore such as the mouse is a first-level consumer when it eats grass. But when the mouse eats a grasshopper, it is a second-level consumer.

☑ *Checkpoint* *What are the organisms in one food chain shown in the food web on the facing page?*

Energy Pyramids

When an organism in an ecosystem eats, it obtains energy. The organism uses some of this energy to move, grow, reproduce, and carry out other life activities. This means that only some of the energy will be available to the next organism in the food web.

A diagram called an **energy pyramid** shows the amount of energy that moves from one feeding level to another in a food web. The organisms at each level use some of the energy to carry out their life processes. **The most energy is available at the producer level. At each level in the pyramid, there is less available energy than at the level below.** An energy pyramid gets its name from the shape of the diagram—wider at the base and narrower at the top, resembling a pyramid.

In general, only about 10 percent of the energy at one level of a food web is transferred to the next, higher, level. The other

Weaving a Food Web

This activity shows how the organisms in a food web are interconnected.

ACTIVITY

1. Your teacher will assign you a role in the food web.

2. Hold one end of each of several pieces of yarn in your hand. Give the other ends of your yarn to the other organisms to which your organism is linked.

3. Your teacher will now eliminate one of the organisms. Everyone who is connected to that organism should drop the yarn connecting them to it.

Making Models How many organisms were affected by the removal of one organism? What does this activity show about the importance of each organism in a food web?

Figure 6 Organisms use energy to carry out their life activities. A lioness uses energy to chase her zebra prey. The zebras use energy to flee.

Figure 7 This energy pyramid diagram shows the energy available at each level of a food web. Energy is measured in kilocalories, or kcal. *Calculating* How many times more energy is available at the producer level than at the second-level consumer level?

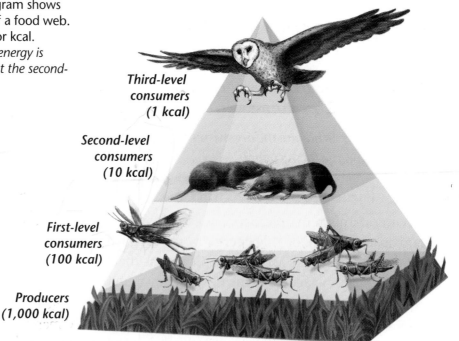

Third-level consumers
(1 kcal)

Second-level consumers
(10 kcal)

First-level consumers
(100 kcal)

Producers
(1,000 kcal)

90 percent of the energy is used for the organism's life processes or is lost as heat to the environment. Because of this, most food webs only have three or four feeding levels. Since 90 percent of the energy is lost at each step, there is not enough energy to support many feeding levels.

But the organisms at higher feeding levels of an energy pyramid do not necessarily require less energy to live than organisms at lower levels. Since so much energy is lost at each level, the amount of energy in the producer level limits the number of consumers the ecosystem can support. As a result, there usually are few organisms at the highest level in a food web.

Section 1 Review

1. Name the three energy roles of organisms in an ecosystem. How does each type of organism obtain energy?
2. How does the amount of available energy change from one level of an energy pyramid to the next level up?
3. Name and define the four types of consumers.
4. What is the source of energy for most ecosystems?
5. **Thinking Critically Making Generalizations** Why are food webs a more realistic way of portraying ecosystems than food chains?

Check Your Progress CHAPTER PROJECT 2
By now you should have constructed your compost chambers and chosen a variable to investigate. Design your plan for observing the effect of this variable on the decomposition process. Submit your plan to your teacher for approval. (*Hint:* As part of your plan, include how you will collect data to measure decomposition in your compost chambers.)

SECTION
2 Cycles of Matter

DISCOVER • **ACTIVITY**

Are You Part of a Cycle?

1. Hold a small mirror a few centimeters from your mouth.

2. Exhale onto the mirror.

3. Observe the surface of the mirror.

Think It Over
Inferring What is the substance that forms on the mirror? Where did this substance come from?

A pile of crumpled cars is ready for loading into a giant compactor. Junkyard workers have already removed many of the cars' parts. The aluminum and copper pieces were removed so that they could be recycled, or used again. Now a recycling plant will reclaim the steel in the bodies of the cars. Earth has a limited supply of aluminum, copper, and the iron needed to make steel. Recycling old cars is one way to provide a new supply of these materials.

Recycling Matter

The way matter is recycled in ecosystems is similar to the way the metal in old cars is recycled. Like the supply of metal for building cars, the supply of matter in an ecosystem is limited. If matter could not be recycled, ecosystems would quickly run out of the raw materials necessary for life.

Energy, on the other hand, is not recycled. You must constantly supply a car with energy in the form of gasoline. Ecosystems must also be constantly supplied with energy, usually in the form of sunlight. Gasoline and the sun's energy cannot be recycled—they must be constantly supplied.

As you read in Section 1, energy enters an ecosystem and moves from the producers to the consumers to the decomposers. In contrast, matter cycles through an ecosystem over and over. Matter in an ecosystem includes water, oxygen, carbon, nitrogen, and many other substances. To understand how these substances cycle through an ecosystem, you need to know a few basic terms that describe the structure of matter. Matter is made

GUIDE FOR READING

◆ What three major processes make up the water cycle?

◆ How is carbon dioxide used by producers?

Reading Tip As you read, use the section headings to make an outline of the section.

Cars awaiting recycling at a Utah plant ▼

Figure 8 In the water cycle, water moves continuously from Earth's surface to the atmosphere and back.
Interpreting Diagrams
In which step of the water cycle does water return to Earth's surface?

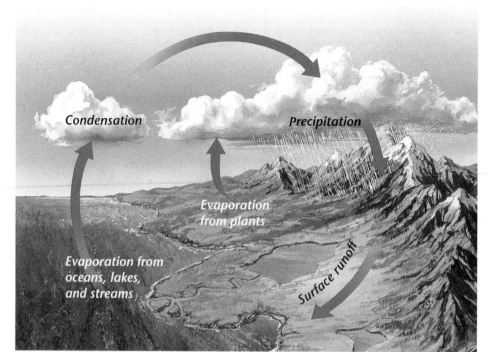

Condensation

Precipitation

Evaporation from plants

Evaporation from oceans, lakes, and streams

Surface runoff

up of tiny particles called atoms. Combinations of two or more atoms chemically bonded together are called molecules. For example, a molecule of water consists of two hydrogen atoms bonded to one oxygen atom. In this section, you will learn about some of the most important cycles of matter: the water cycle, the carbon and oxygen cycles, and the nitrogen cycle.

The Water Cycle

How could you determine whether life has ever existed on another planet in the solar system? One piece of evidence scientists look for is the presence of water. This is because water is the most common compound in all living cells on Earth. Water is necessary for life as we know it.

Water is recycled through the water cycle. The **water cycle** is the continuous process by which water moves from Earth's surface to the atmosphere and back. **The processes of evaporation, condensation, and precipitation make up the water cycle**. As you read about these processes, follow the cycle in Figure 8.

Evaporation   The process by which molecules of liquid water absorb energy and change to the gas state is called **evaporation.** In the water cycle liquid water evaporates from Earth's surface and forms water vapor, a gas, in the atmosphere. Most water evaporates from the surfaces of oceans and lakes. The energy for evaporation comes from the sun.

Sharpen your Skills

Developing Hypotheses

ACTIVITY

You're having cocoa at a friend's house on a cold, rainy day. As your friend boils some water, you notice that a window next to the stove is covered with water droplets. Your friend thinks the window is leaking. Using what you know about the water cycle, can you propose another explanation for the water droplets on the window?

Some water is also given off by living things. For example, plants take in water through their roots and release water vapor from their leaves. You take in water when you drink and eat. You release liquid water in your wastes and water vapor when you exhale.

Condensation What happens next to the water vapor in the atmosphere? As the water vapor rises higher in the atmosphere, it cools down. When it cools to a certain temperature the vapor turns back into tiny drops of liquid water. The process by which a gas changes to a liquid is called **condensation.** The water droplets collect around particles of dust in the air, eventually forming clouds like those in Figure 8.

Precipitation As more water vapor condenses, the drops of water in the cloud grow larger and heavier. Eventually the heavy drops fall back to Earth as a form of **precipitation**—rain, snow, sleet, or hail. Most precipitation falls back into oceans or lakes. The precipitation that falls on land may soak into the soil and become groundwater. Or the precipitation may run off the land, ultimately flowing into a river or ocean once again.

☑ *Checkpoint* *What change of state occurs when water from the surface of the ocean enters the atmosphere as water vapor?*

The Carbon and Oxygen Cycles

Two other chemicals necessary for life are carbon and oxygen. The processes by which they are recycled are linked together, as shown in Figure 9. Carbon is the building block for the matter that makes up the bodies of living things. It is present in the atmosphere in the gas carbon dioxide. Producers take in carbon dioxide from

Figure 9 This scene shows how the carbon and oxygen cycles are linked together. Producers use carbon dioxide to carry out photosynthesis. In this process, carbon is used to create sugar molecules such as those found in apples. The producers release oxygen, which is then used by other organisms. These organisms take in carbon in food and release it in the form of carbon dioxide again.

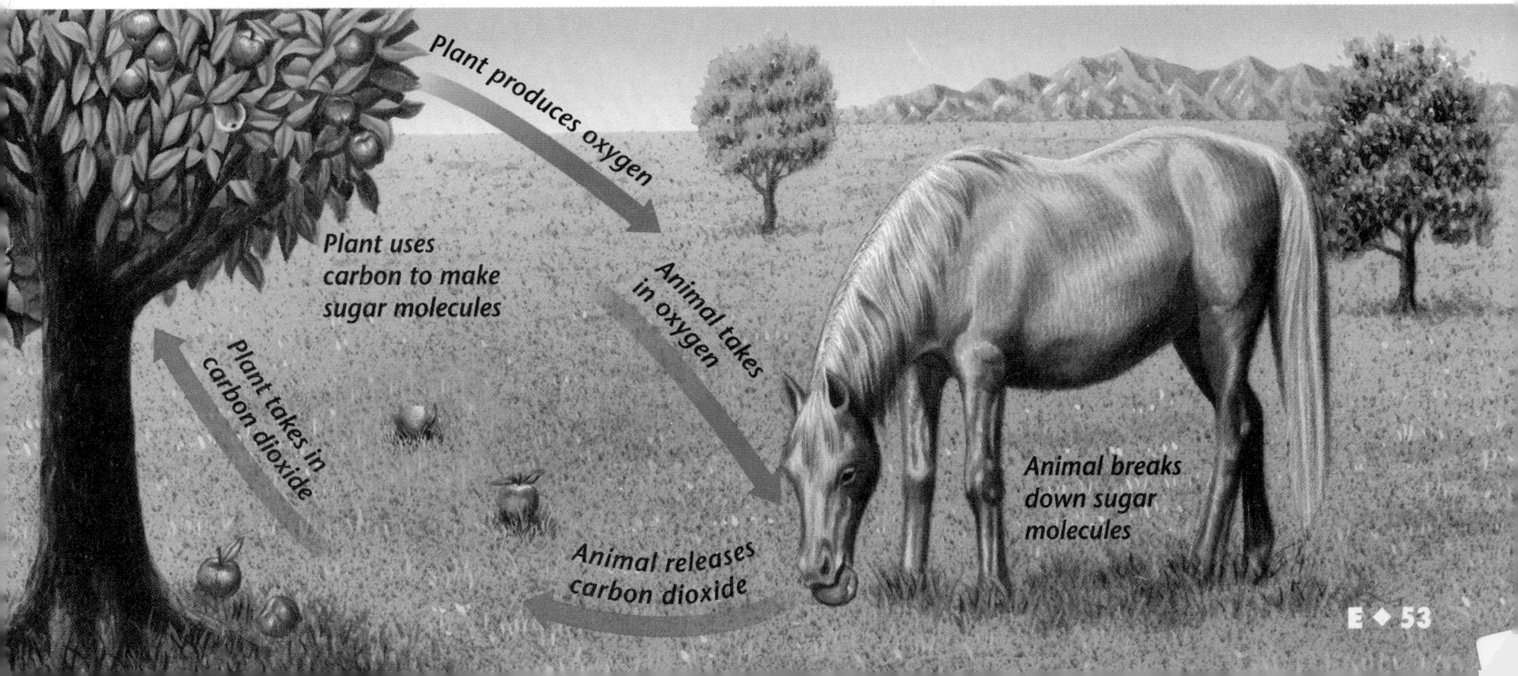

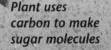

Plant produces oxygen

Plant uses carbon to make sugar molecules

Animal takes in oxygen

Plant takes in carbon dioxide

Animal breaks down sugar molecules

Animal releases carbon dioxide

the atmosphere during photosynthesis. **In this process, the producers use carbon from the carbon dioxide to produce other carbon-containing molecules.** These molecules include sugars and starches. To obtain energy from these molecules, consumers break them down into simpler molecules. Consumers release water and carbon dioxide as waste products.

At the same time, oxygen is also cycling through the ecosystem. Producers release oxygen as a result of photosynthesis. Other organisms take in oxygen from the atmosphere and use it in their life processes.

☑ *Checkpoint* How is oxygen returned to the environment?

The Nitrogen Cycle

Like carbon, nitrogen is a necessary building block in the matter that makes up living things. Since the air around you is about 78 percent nitrogen gas, you might think that it would be easy for living things to obtain nitrogen. However, most organisms cannot use the nitrogen gas in the air. Nitrogen gas is called "free" nitrogen, meaning it is not combined with other kinds of atoms. Most organisms can use nitrogen only once it has been "fixed," or combined with other elements to form nitrogen-containing compounds. You can follow this process in Figure 10 below.

Figure 10 In the nitrogen cycle, nitrogen moves from the air to the soil, into living things, and back into the air.
Interpreting Diagrams How do consumers obtain nitrogen?

Free nitrogen in air

Consumers eat nitrogen compounds in plants

Bacteria release some free nitrogen back to air

Decomposers break down wastes and plant remains and return nitrogen compounds to soil

Bacteria in root nodules fix free nitrogen into compounds

Nitrogen Fixation The process of changing free nitrogen gas into a usable form of nitrogen is called **nitrogen fixation.** Most nitrogen fixation is performed by certain kinds of bacteria. Some of these bacteria live in bumps called **nodules** (NAHJ oolz) on the roots of certain plants. These plants, known as legumes, include clover, beans, peas, alfalfa, and peanuts.

The relationship between the bacteria and the legumes is an example of mutualism. As you recall from Chapter 1, a symbiotic relationship in which both species benefit is called mutualism. Both the bacteria and the plant benefit from this relationship: The bacteria have a place to live, and the plant is supplied with nitrogen in a usable form.

INTEGRATING TECHNOLOGY Many farmers make use of the nitrogen-fixing bacteria in legumes to enrich their fields. Every few years, a farmer may plant a legume such as alfalfa in a field. The bacteria in the alfalfa roots build up a new supply of nitrogen compounds in the soil. The following year, the new crops planted in the field benefit from the improved soil.

Return of Nitrogen to the Environment Once the nitrogen has been fixed into chemical compounds, it can be used by organisms to build proteins and other complex substances. Decomposers break down these complex compounds in animal wastes and in the bodies of dead organisms. This returns simple nitrogen compounds to the soil. Nitrogen can cycle from the soil to producers and consumers many times. At some point, however, bacteria break down the nitrogen compounds completely. These bacteria release free nitrogen back into the air. Then the cycle starts again.

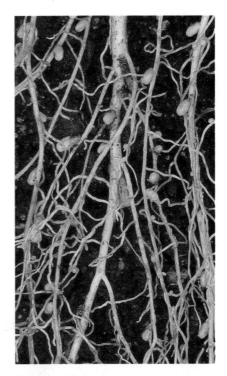

Figure 11 Lumpy nodules are clearly visible on the roots of this clover plant. Bacteria inside the nodules carry out nitrogen fixation.

Section 2 Review

1. Name and define the three major processes that occur during the water cycle.
2. Explain the role of plants in the carbon cycle.
3. How is nitrogen fixation a necessary part of the nitrogen cycle?
4. Where do nitrogen-fixing bacteria live?
5. **Thinking Critically** **Comparing and Contrasting** Explain how the movement of matter through an ecosystem is different than the movement of energy through an ecosystem.

Check Your Progress

CHAPTER PROJECT 2

Once your teacher has approved your plan, place the waste into your compost chambers. Record your hypothesis about the effect of the variable you are investigating. Observe the two containers daily. (*Hint:* If there are no signs of decomposition after several days, you may wish to stir the contents of each chamber. Stirring allows more oxygen to enter the mixture.)

SECTION
3 Biogeography

DISCOVER

How Can You Move a Seed?

1. Place a few corn kernels at one end of a shallow pan.

2. Make a list of ways you could move the kernels to the other side of the pan. You may use any of the simple materials your teacher has provided.

3. Now try each method. Record whether or not each was successful in moving the kernels across the pan.

Think It Over

Predicting How might seeds be moved from place to place on Earth?

GUIDE FOR READING

◆ How does dispersal of organisms occur?

◆ What factors can limit the distribution of a species?

Reading Tip As you read, look for reasons why organisms live in certain places in the world. Make a list of these reasons.

◀ Australian wallaby

Imagine how European explorers must have felt when they saw the continent of Australia for the first time. Instead of familiar grazing animals such as horses and deer, they saw what looked like giant rabbits with long tails. Peering into the branches of eucalyptus trees, these explorers saw bearlike koalas. And who could have dreamed up an egg-laying animal with a beaver's tail, a duck's bill, and a thick coat of fur? You can see why people who heard the first descriptions of the platypus accused the explorers of lying!

Ecologists had many questions about the plants and animals of Australia. Why had no one ever seen a kangaroo, a eucalyptus tree, or a koala in Europe? Why were there no reindeer, camels, or gorillas in Australia?

Different species live in different parts of the world. The study of where organisms live is called **biogeography.** The word *biogeography* is made up of three Greek word roots: *bio,* meaning "life"; *geo,* meaning "Earth"; and *graph,* meaning "description." Together, these root words tell what biogeographers do—they describe where living things are found on Earth.

Continental Drift

INTEGRATING EARTH SCIENCE In addition to studying where species live today, biogeographers also study how these species spread into different parts of the world. One factor that has affected how species are distributed is the motion of Earth's continents. The continents are huge blocks of solid rock floating on a layer of hot, dense liquid. The very slow motion of the continents is called **continental drift.**

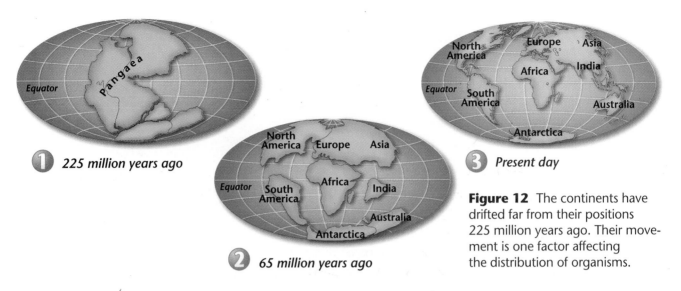

① **225 million years ago**

② **65 million years ago**

③ **Present day**

Figure 12 The continents have drifted far from their positions 225 million years ago. Their movement is one factor affecting the distribution of organisms.

Figure 12 shows how much the continents have moved. About 225 million years ago, all the continents were touching each other. But after millions of years of slow drifting, they have moved apart. Looking at the globe today, it is hard to believe that at one time India was next to Antarctica, or that Europe and North America once were connected.

The movement of the continents has had a great impact on the distribution of species. Consider Australia, for example. Millions of years ago Australia drifted apart from the other land masses. Organisms from other parts of the world could not reach the isolated island. Kangaroos, koalas, and other unique species developed in this isolation.

Means of Dispersal

The movement of organisms from one place to another is called **dispersal.** Organisms may be dispersed in several different ways. **Dispersal can be caused by wind, water, or living things, including humans.**

Wind and Water Many animals move into new areas by simply walking, swimming, or flying. But plants and small organisms need assistance to move from place to place. Wind provides a means of dispersal for seeds, the spores of fungi, tiny spiders, and many other small, light organisms. Similarly, water transports objects that float, such as coconuts and leaves. Insects and small animals may get a free ride to a new home on top of these floating rafts.

Other Living Things Organisms may also be dispersed by other living things. For example, a goldfinch may eat seeds in one area and deposit them elsewhere in its wastes. A duck may carry algae or fish eggs on its feet from pond to pond. And if your dog or cat has ever come home covered with sticky plant burs, you know another way seeds can get around.

Figure 13 The stiff brown pods of the milkweed plant contain seeds fringed with silky threads.
Inferring By what means of dispersal are milkweed seeds spread?

Figure 14 Clumps of purple loosestrife line the banks of a Massachusetts river. Loosestrife is an exotic species that has thrived in its new home, often crowding out native species.

Humans are important to the dispersal of other species. As people move around the globe, they take plants, animals, and other organisms with them. Sometimes this is intentional, such as when people bring horses to a new settlement. Sometimes it is unintentional, such as when someone carries a parasite into a country.

Species that have naturally evolved in an area are referred to as **native species.** When an organism is carried into a new location by people, it is referred to as an **exotic species.** Some exotic species are so common in their new environment that people think of them as native. For example, you probably know the dandelion, one of the most common flowering plants in North America. But the dandelion is not a native species. It was brought by colonists who valued its leaves for eating and for tea for the sick.

☑ *Checkpoint* How can humans disperse a species?

Limits to Dispersal

With all these means of dispersal, you might expect to find the same organisms everywhere in the world. Of course, that's not so. Why not? What determines the limits of a species' distribution? **Three factors that limit dispersal of a species are physical barriers, competition, and climate.**

Physical Barriers Barriers such as water, mountains, and deserts are hard to cross. These features can limit the movement of organisms. For example, once Australia became separated from the other continents, the ocean acted as a barrier to dispersal. Organisms could not easily move to or from Australia.

Competition When an organism enters a new area, it must compete for resources with the species already there. To survive, the organism must find a unique niche. If the existing species are thriving, they may outcompete the new species. In this case competition is a barrier to dispersal. Sometimes, however, the new species is more successful than the existing species. The native species may be displaced.

Social Studies CONNECTION

Many important crops are actually exotic species. When settlers in new lands brought crops with them from their old homes, they caused the dispersal of these species. Some examples of crops dispersed by people are peanuts, potatoes, cotton, corn, and rice.

In Your Journal

Choose a crop to investigate. Research your crop to learn where it is a native species and how it spread to different parts of the world. In what conditions does it grow well? (*Hint:* Almanacs and encyclopedias are good sources of this information.)

Climate The typical weather pattern in an area over a long period of time is the area's **climate.** Climate is different from weather, which is the day-to-day conditions in an area. Climate is largely determined by temperature and precipitation.

Differences in climate can be a barrier to dispersal. For example, conditions at the top of the mountain shown in Figure 15 are very different from those at the base. The base is warm and dry. Low shrubs and cactuses grow there. Just up the mountain, mostly grasses grow. Higher up the mountain, the climate becomes cooler and wetter. Larger trees such as pines, oaks, and firs can grow. The squirrel in the closeup lives in this region. Climate differences act as a barrier that keeps the squirrel species from dispersing down or up the mountain. Near the top of the mountain, it is very cold and windy. Small alpine wildflowers and mosses grow best in this region.

Places with similar climates tend to have similar niches for species to occupy. For example, most continents have a large area of flat, grassy plains. The organisms that occupy the niche of "large, grazing mammal" on each continent have some similarities. In North America, the large, grazing mammals of the grasslands are bison; in Africa, they are wildebeests and antelopes; in Australia, they are kangaroos.

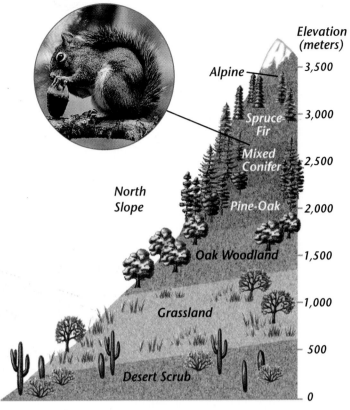

Figure 15 Climate conditions change at different elevations on this mountainside. These conditions determine the distribution of species on the mountain. Each zone begins at a lower elevation on the north slope of the mountain, which is cooler than the south slope.

Section 3 Review

1. List three ways that species can disperse.
2. Explain how mountain ranges and climate can each limit a species' distribution.
3. What is biogeography?
4. Give an example of a physical barrier. How might it affect where species are found?
5. **Thinking Critically** **Predicting** If an exotic insect species were introduced to your area, do you think it would be easy or difficult to eliminate the species? Give reasons to support your answer.

Science at Home

Take an adult family member on a seed hunt. When you spot a new seed, place a plastic bag over your hand. Pick up the seed with the bag and then turn the bag inside out to hold the seed. When you get home, observe the seeds and compare them to one another. Based on your observations, classify the seeds by their methods of dispersal. Staple the bags to a sheet of heavy paper in the groups in which you have classified them.

BIOMES IN MINIATURE

Climate is one factor that affects where organisms live. A group of ecosystems with similar climates and organisms is called a biome. In this lab, you will investigate some key factors that make biomes different from each other.

Problem

What biotic and abiotic factors create different biomes around the world?

Skills Focus

making models, observing, drawing conclusions

Materials

scissors
index card
10 impatiens seeds
5 lima bean seeds
about 30 rye grass seeds
empty, clean cardboard milk carton
sandy soil or potting soil
clear plastic wrap
lamp
tape
stapler

Procedure

1. Your teacher will assign your group a biome. You will also observe the other groups' biomes. Based on the chart below, predict how well you think each of the three kinds of seeds will grow in each set of conditions. Record these predictions in your notebook. Then copy the data table on the facing page four times, once for each biome.
2. Staple the spout of the milk carton closed. Completely cut away one of the four sides of the carton. Poke a few holes in the opposite side for drainage, then place that side down.
3. Fill the carton to 3 centimeters from the top with the type of soil given in the table. Divide the surface of the soil into three sections by making two lines in it with a pencil.
4. In the section near the spout, plant the impatiens seeds. In the middle section, plant the lima bean seeds. In the third section, scatter the rye grass seeds on the surface.

GROWING CONDITIONS			
Biome	**Soil Type**	**Hours of Light Per Day**	**Watering Instructions**
Forest	Potting soil	1–2 hours direct light	Let the surface dry, then add water.
Desert	Sandy soil	5–6 hours direct light	Let the soil dry to a depth of 2.5 cm below the surface.
Grassland	Potting soil	5–6 hours direct light	Let the surface dry, then add water.
Rain forest	Potting soil	No direct light; indirect light for 5–6 hours	Keep the surface of the soil moist.

DATA TABLE

Name of biome: _____

Day	Impatiens	Lima Beans	Rye Grass
1			
2			
3			

5. Water all the seeds well. Then cover the open part of the carton with plastic wrap.

6. On an index card, write the name of your biome, the names of the three types of seeds in the order you planted them, and the names of your group members. Tape the card to the carton. Put it in a warm place where it will not be disturbed.

7. Once the seeds sprout, provide your biome with light and water as specified in the chart. Keep the carton covered with plastic wrap except when you add water.

8. Observe all the biomes daily for at least one week. Record your observations.

Analyze and Conclude

1. In which biome did each type of seed grow best? In which biome did each type of seed grow least well?

2. How was each type of seed affected by the soil type, amount of light, and availability of water? How do your results relate to biomes in nature?

3. Ecologists studying land biomes often begin a description of the biome by describing key abiotic factors and the typical plants. Why do you think they do this?

4. **Apply** Describe the rainfall pattern and other abiotic factors that make up the climate where you live. How do those factors affect the kinds of plants and animals that live there?

Design an Experiment

After reading Section 4, write a plan for setting up a model rain forest or desert terrarium. Include typical plants found in that biome. Obtain your teacher's approval before trying this activity.

DISCOVER •• ACTIVITY ••••

How Much Rain Is That?

The table shows the average amount of precipitation that falls each year in four different regions. With your classmates, you will create a full-size bar graph on a wall to help you visualize these amounts of rain.

Biome	Rainfall (cm)
Mojave Desert	15
Illinois prairie	70
Smoky Mountains	180
Costa Rican rain forest	350

1. Using a meter stick, measure a strip of adding-machine paper 15 centimeters long. Label this piece of paper "Mojave Desert."

2. Repeat Step 1 for the other three locations. If necessary, tape strips of paper together to make the correct length. Label each strip.

3. Now find a place where you can display the four strips vertically. If the wall of your classroom is not tall enough, you may need to use another wall in your school building. Follow your teacher's instructions to hang your precipitation strips.

Think It Over

Developing Hypotheses Which ecosystem receives the most precipitation? Which receives the least? What effect do you think the amount of rainfall might have on the types of species that live in these ecosystems?

GUIDE FOR READING

◆ What determines the type of biome found in an area?

◆ Where can photosynthesis occur in water biomes?

Reading Tip As you read, make a list of the biomes described in this section. Under each biome name, take notes on the characteristics of that biome.

Congratulations! You and your classmates have been selected as the student members of an around-the-world scientific expedition. Your mission is to study the major types of ecosystems on Earth. You will be collecting data on the climate conditions and typical organisms found in each of these ecosystems. The result of this expedition will be a database of information on the biomes you visit. A **biome** is a group of ecosystems with similar climates and organisms.

Classifying ecosystems into biomes helps ecologists describe the world. As you might expect, not all ecologists agree on the exact number and kinds of biomes. The scientists guiding your expedition have chosen to focus on six major land biomes and two major water biomes.

Be sure to pack a variety of clothing for your journey. During your trip, you will visit places ranging from frozen, windy Arctic plains to steamy tropical jungles. **In fact, it is mostly the climate conditions—temperature and rainfall—in an area that determine its biome.** This is because climate limits the distribution of plants in the area. In turn, the types of plants determine the kinds of animals that live there.

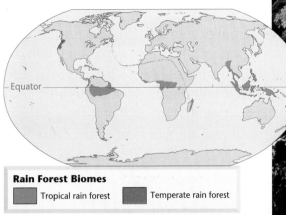

Rain Forest Biomes
- ☐ Tropical rain forest
- ☐ Temperate rain forest

Rain Forest Biomes

The first stop on your expedition is a tropical rain forest close to the equator. The rain forest is warm and humid—in fact, it's pouring rain! Fortunately, you remembered to pack a poncho. After just a short shower, the sun reappears. But even though the sun is shining, very little light penetrates the thick vegetation.

Plants are everywhere in the rain forest. Some, such as the ferns, orchids, and vines you observe hanging from tree limbs, even grow on other plants. Among the plants are many species of birds as bright as the numerous flowers all around you.

Tropical Rain Forests Tropical rain forests are found in warm regions close to the equator. Tropical rain forests typically receive a lot of rain. The warm temperatures do not vary much throughout the year, and the sunlight is fairly constant all year.

Tropical rain forests contain an astounding variety of species. For example, scientists studying a 100-square-meter area of one rain forest identified 300 different kinds of trees! These trees form several distinct layers. The tall trees form a leafy roof called the **canopy.** A few giant trees poke out above the canopy. Below the canopy, a second layer of shorter trees and vines form an **understory.** Understory plants grow well in the shade formed by the canopy. Finally, some plants thrive in the near-darkness of the forest floor.

Figure 16 Tropical rain forests contain an amazing variety of plants and other organisms. In the large photo, a river winds through the lush Indonesian rain forest. The top closeup shows a young orangutan swinging from tree limbs. In the bottom closeup, a tarantula climbs over a brightly colored bracket fungus on the forest floor.

The abundant plant life provides many habitats for animals. The number of insect species in tropical rain forests is not known, but has been estimated to be in the millions. These in turn feed many bird species, which feed other animals. Although tropical rain forests cover only a small part of the planet, they probably contain more species of plants and animals than all the other land biomes combined.

Temperate Rain Forests The land along the northwestern coast of the United States resembles a tropical rain forest in some ways. This region receives more than 300 centimeters of rain a year. Huge trees grow there, including cedars, redwoods, and Douglas firs. However, it is difficult to classify this region. It is too far north and too cool to be a tropical rain forest. Instead many ecologists refer to this ecosystem as a temperate rain forest. The term *temperate* means having moderate temperatures.

Desert Biomes

The next stop on your expedition is a desert. It couldn't be more different from the tropical rain forest you just left. You step off the bus into the searing summer heat. At midday, you cannot even walk into the desert—the sand feels as hot as the hot water that comes from your bathroom faucet at home.

A **desert** is an area that receives less than 25 centimeters of rain per year. The amount of evaporation in a desert is greater than the amount of precipitation. Some of the driest deserts may not receive any rain at all in a year! Deserts often also undergo large shifts in temperature during the course of a day. A scorching hot desert like the

Figure 17 Desert organisms have adaptations that enable them to live in the harsh conditions of their biome. For example, this shovel-snouted lizard "dances" to avoid burning its feet on the hot sand dunes of the Namib Desert in Africa. *Making Generalizations Describe the climate conditions of a typical desert.*

Equator

Desert and Grassland Biomes
Desert   Grassland

Namib Desert cools rapidly each night when the sun goes down. Other deserts, such as the Gobi in central Asia, are cooler, even experiencing freezing temperatures in the winter.

The organisms that live in the desert are adapted to the lack of rain and to the extreme temperatures. For example, the trunk of a saguaro cactus has folds that work like the pleats in an accordion. The trunk of the cactus expands to hold more water when it is raining. Many desert animals are most active at night when the temperatures are cooler. A gila monster, for instance, spends much of its time in a cool underground burrow. It may go for weeks without coming up to the surface of the desert.

✓ *Checkpoint* *What are some adaptations that help an organism to live in the desert?*

Grassland Biomes

The next stop on the expedition is a grassland called a prairie. The temperature here is much more comfortable than that in the desert. The breeze carries the scent of soil warmed by the sun. This rich soil supports grass as tall as you and your classmates. Sparrows flit among the grass stems, looking for their next meal. Startled by your approach, a rabbit quickly bounds away.

Like other grasslands located in the middle latitudes, this prairie receives more rain than deserts, but not enough for many trees to grow. A **grassland** receives between 25 and 75 centimeters of rain each year, and is typically populated by grasses and other non-woody plants. Grasslands that are located closer to the equator than prairies, called **savannas,** receive as much as 120 centimeters of

Desert Survival

✂ Use a hand lens **ACTIVITY** to carefully observe a small potted cactus. Be careful of the spines! With a pair of scissors, carefully snip a small piece from the tip of the cactus. Observe the inside of the plant. Note any characteristics that seem different from those of other plants.

Observing How is the inside of the cactus different from the outside? Suggest how the features you observe might be related to its desert habitat.

Figure 18 Migrating wildebeest make their way across a vast Kenyan savanna.

Forest Biomes

◼ Deciduous forest ◼ Boreal forest

Figure 19 This Michigan forest in autumn is a beautiful example of a deciduous forest. The closeup shows a red fox, a common resident of North American deciduous forests. *Comparing and Contrasting How do deciduous forests differ from rain forests?*

rain each year. Scattered shrubs and small trees grow on savannas along with the grass.

Grasslands are home to many of the largest animals on Earth—herbivores such as bison, antelopes, zebras, rhinoceros, giraffes, and kangaroos. Grazing by these large herbivores helps to maintain the grasslands. They keep young trees and bushes from sprouting and competing with the grass for water and sunlight.

Deciduous Forest Biomes

Your trip to the next biome takes you to another forest. It is now late summer. Cool mornings here give way to warm days. Several members of the expedition are busy recording the numerous plant species. Others are looking through their binoculars, trying to identify the songbirds in the trees. You step carefully to avoid a small salamander on the forest floor. Chipmunks chatter at all the disturbance.

You are now visiting the deciduous forest biome. The trees found in this forest, called **deciduous trees** (dee SIJ oo us), shed their leaves and grow new ones each year. Oaks and maples are examples of deciduous trees. Deciduous forests receive enough rain to support the growth of trees and other plants, at least 50 centimeters per year. Temperatures vary during the year. The growing season usually lasts five to six months. As in the rain forest, different plants grow to different heights, ranging from a canopy of tall trees to small ferns and mosses on the forest floor.

The variety of plants in the forest creates many different habitats. You and your classmates note that different species of birds live at each level, eating the insects and fruits that live and grow there. You observe opossums, mice, and a skunk looking for food in the thick layer of damp leaves on the ground. Other common North American deciduous forest species include wood thrushes, white-tailed deer, and black bears.

If you were to return to this biome in the winter, you would not see much of the wildlife you are now observing. One reason is that many of the bird species migrate to warmer areas. Some of the mammals enter a low-energy state similar to sleep called **hibernation.** During hibernation an animal relies on fat it has stored in its body.

☑ *Checkpoint* *What are deciduous trees?*

Boreal Forest Biomes

Now the expedition heads north into a colder climate. The expedition leaders claim they can identify the next biome, a boreal forest, by its smell. When you arrive, you catch a whiff of the spruce and fir trees that blanket the hillsides. Feeling the chilly early fall air, you pull a jacket and hat out of your bag.

This forest contains **coniferous trees** (koh NIF ur us), that produce their seeds in cones and have leaves shaped like needles. The boreal forest is sometimes referred to by its Russian name, the *taiga* (TY guh). Winters in these forests are very cold. The yearly

Inferring

Observe the map on the facing page showing the locations of deciduous and boreal forests. How do they compare? Can you suggest a reason why no boreal forests are shown in the Southern Hemisphere?

Figure 20 Common organisms of the boreal forest include moose like this one in Alaska's Denali National Park, and porcupines.

snowfall can reach heights well over your head—or even two or three times your height! Even so, the summers are rainy and warm enough to melt all the snow.

A limited number of trees have adapted to the cold climate of boreal forests. Fir, spruce, and hemlock are the most common species because their thick, waxy needles keep water from evaporating. Since water is frozen for much of the year in these areas, prevention of water loss is a necessary adaptation for trees in the boreal forest.

Many of the animals of the boreal forest eat the seeds produced by the conifers. These animals include red squirrels, insects, and birds such as finches and chickadees. Some of the larger herbivores, such as porcupines, deer, elk, moose, and beavers, eat tree bark and new shoots. This variety of herbivores in the boreal forest supports a variety of large predators, including wolves, bears, wolverines, and lynxes.

Tundra Biomes

The driving wind brings tears to the eyes of the members of the expedition as you arrive at your next stop. It is now fall. The slicing wind gives everyone an immediate feel for this biome, the tundra. The **tundra** is an extremely cold, dry, land biome. Expecting deep snow, many are surprised that the tundra may receive no more precipitation than a desert. Most of the soil in the tundra is frozen all year. This frozen soil is called **permafrost**.

Figure 21 Far from being a barren terrain, the tundra explodes with color in summer. Mosses, wildflowers, and shrubs flourish despite the short growing season. *Relating Cause and Effect* Why are there no tall trees on the tundra?

Tundra Biomes, Mountains, and Ice

Equator

Tundra   Mountains   Ice

During the short summer the top layer of soil on the tundra thaws, but the underlying soil remains frozen.

Plants on the tundra include mosses, grasses, shrubs, and dwarf forms of a few trees, such as willows. Looking across the tundra, you observe that the landscape is already brown and gold. The short growing season is over. Most of the plant growth takes place during the long summer days when many hours of sunshine combine with the warmest temperatures of the year. North of the Arctic Circle the sun does not set during midsummer.

If you had visited the tundra during the summer, the animals you might remember most are insects. Swarms of black flies and mosquitos provide food for many birds. The birds take advantage of the plentiful food and long days by eating as much as they can. Then, when winter approaches again, many birds migrate south to warmer climates.

Mammals of the tundra include caribou, foxes, wolves, and hares. The animals that remain in the tundra during the winter grow thick fur coats. What can these animals find to eat on the tundra in winter? The caribou scrape snow away to find lichens, which are fungi and algae that grow together on rocks. Wolves follow the caribou and look for weak members of the herd to prey upon.

✓ *Checkpoint* **What is the climate of the tundra?**

Mountains and Ice

Some areas of land on Earth do not fall into one of the major land biomes. These areas include mountain ranges and land that is covered with thick sheets of ice.

You read in Section 3 that the climate conditions of a mountain change from its base to its summit. As a result, different species of plants and other organisms inhabit different parts of the mountain. If you hiked to the top of a tall mountain, you would pass through a series of biomes. At the base of the mountain, you might find a grassland. As you climbed, you might pass through a deciduous forest, and then a boreal forest. Finally, as you neared the top, the trees would disappear. Your surroundings would resemble the rugged tundra.

Some land on Earth is covered year-round with thick ice sheets. Most of the island of Greenland and the continent of Antarctica fall into this category. Some organisms are adapted to life on the ice, including penguins, polar bears, and seals.

Figure 22 Many waterfowl spend summers on the tundra. This black brant is tending her nest.

Interpreting Data

An ecologist has collected **ACTIVITY** climate data from two locations. The total yearly precipitation is 250 cm in Location A and 14 cm in Location B. The graph below shows the average monthly temperature in the two locations. Based on this information, of which biome is each location a part? Explain.

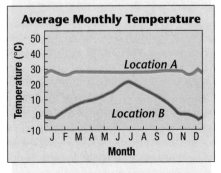

Average Monthly Temperature

Figure 23 Ponds and rivers are two types of freshwater habitats. **A.** At the edge of a pond, two western pond turtles sun themselves on a log. **B.** A brown bear fishes for salmon in the rushing waters of a river.
Comparing and Contrasting How are these habitats similar? How are they different?

Freshwater Biomes

The next stops for the expedition are located in water biomes. Since almost three quarters of Earth's surface is covered with water, it is not surprising that many living things make their homes in the water. Water biomes include both freshwater and saltwater (also called marine) biomes. All of these are affected by the same abiotic factors: temperature, sunlight, oxygen, and salt content.

An especially important factor in water biomes is sunlight. Sunlight is necessary for photosynthesis in the water just as it is on land. **However, because water absorbs sunlight, there is only enough light for photosynthesis near the surface or in shallow water.** The most common producers in most water biomes are algae rather than plants.

Ponds and Lakes First stop among the freshwater biomes is a calm pond. Ponds and lakes are bodies of standing, or still, fresh water. Lakes are generally larger and deeper than ponds. Ponds are often shallow enough that sunlight can reach the bottom even in the center of the pond, allowing plants to grow there. Plants that grow along the shore have their roots in the soil, while their leaves stretch to the sunlit water at the surface. In the center of a lake, algae floating at the surface are the major producers.

Many animals are adapted for life in the still water. Along the shore of the pond you observe insects, snails, frogs, and salamanders. Sunfish live in the open water, feeding on insects and algae from the surface. Scavengers such as catfish live near the pond bottom. Bacteria and other decomposers also feed on the remains of other organisms.

Streams and Rivers When you arrive at a mountain stream, you immediately notice how different it is from the still waters of a lake. Where the stream begins, called the headwaters, the cold, clear water flows rapidly. Animals that live in this part must be adapted to the strong current. Trout, for instance, have stream-lined bodies that allow them to swim despite the pull of the rushing water. Insects and other small animals may have hooks or suckers to help them cling to rocks. Few plants or algae can grow in this fast-moving water. Instead, first-level consumers rely on leaves and seeds that fall into the stream.

As the river flows along, it is joined by other streams. The current slows. The water becomes cloudy with soil. With fewer rapids, the slower-moving, warmer water contains less oxygen. Different organisms are adapted to live in this lower part of the river. More plants take root among the pebbles on the river bottom, providing homes for insects and frogs. As is true in every biome, organisms are adapted to live in this specific habitat.

✓ *Checkpoint* *What are two abiotic factors that affect organisms in a river?*

Marine Biomes

Next the members of the expedition head down the coast to explore some marine biomes. The oceans contain many different habitats. These habitats differ in sunlight amount, water temperature, wave action, and water pressure. Different organisms are adapted to life in each type of habitat. The first habitat, called an **estuary** (ES choo ehr ee), is found where the fresh water of a river meets the salt water of the ocean.

Estuaries The shallow, sunlit water, plus a large supply of nutrients carried in by the river, makes an estuary a very rich habitat for living things. The major producers in estuaries are plants, such as marsh grasses, as well as algae.

Figure 24 Fresh river water and salty ocean water meet in an estuary. Estuaries such as this Georgia salt marsh provide a rich habitat for many organisms, including a wading tricolored heron.

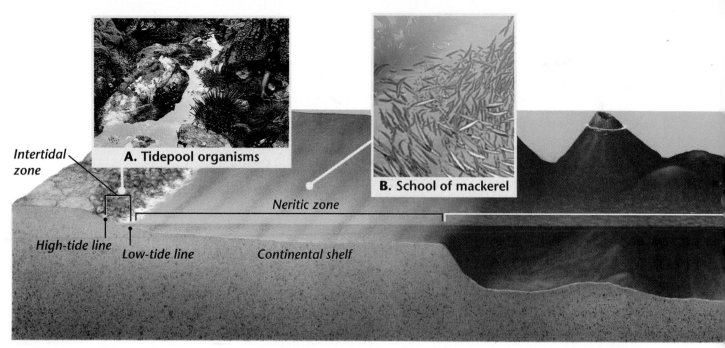

Intertidal zone

A. Tidepool organisms

High-tide line

Low-tide line

Neritic zone

Continental shelf

B. School of mackerel

Figure 25 The marine biome is divided into several zones. **A.** Tidepools are common in the intertidal zone. This zone lies between the highest high-tide line and lowest low-tide line. **B.** Many fish, such as these silvery mackerel, inhabit the shallow waters over the continental shelf, called the neritic zone. **C.** A humpback whale feeds on algae at the surface of the open-ocean zone. **D.** This eerie deep-sea gulper is a predator in the deepest part of the ocean.

These organisms provide food and shelter for a variety of animals, including crabs, worms, clams, oysters, and fish. Many of these organisms use the calm waters of estuaries for breeding grounds.

Intertidal Zone Next, you take a walk along the rocky shoreline. The part of the shore between the highest high-tide line and the lowest low-tide line is called the **intertidal zone.** Organisms here must be able to withstand the pounding action of waves, sudden changes in temperature, and being both covered with water and then exposed to the air. It is a difficult place to live! You observe many animals, such as barnacles and sea stars, clinging to the rocks. Others, such as clams and crabs, burrow in the sand.

Neritic Zone Now it's time to set out to sea to explore the waters near shore. From your research vessel, your group will explore the next type of marine habitat. The edge of a continent extends into the ocean for a short distance, like a shelf. Below the low-tide line is a region of shallow water, called the **neritic zone** (nuh RIT ik), that extends over the continental shelf. Just as in freshwater biomes, the shallow water in this zone allows photosynthesis to occur. As a result, this zone is particularly rich in living things. Many large schools of fish such as sardines and anchovies feed on the algae in the neritic zone. In the warm ocean waters of the tropics, coral reefs may form in the neritic zone. Though a coral reef may look like stone, it is actually a living home to a wide variety of other organisms.

Surface Zone Out in the open ocean, light penetrates through the water only to a depth of a few hundred meters. Algae floating in these surface waters carry out photosynthesis. These algae

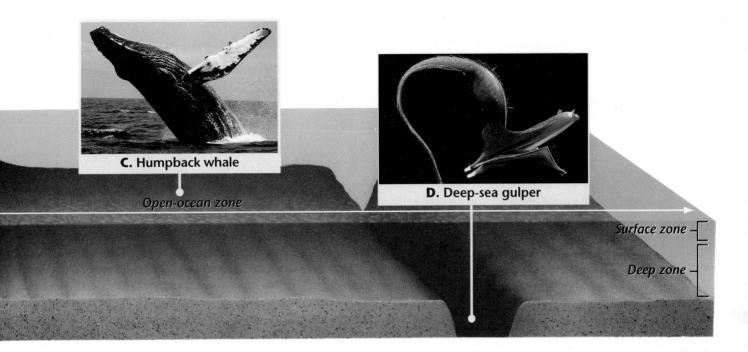

C. Humpback whale

Open-ocean zone

D. Deep-sea gulper

Surface zone

Deep zone

are the producers that form the base of almost all open-ocean food webs. Other marine animals, such as tuna, swordfish, and whales, depend directly or indirectly on the algae for food.

Deep Zone The deep zone is located in the open ocean below the surface zone. Throughout most of the deep ocean, the water is completely dark. Your expedition will need to use a submarine with bright headlights to explore this region. How can anything live in a place with no sunlight? Most animals in this zone feed on remains of organisms that sink down from the surface zone. The deepest parts of the deep zone are home to bizarre-looking animals, such as giant squid that glow in the dark and fish with rows and rows of sharp teeth.

After you have recorded your deep-zone observations, your long expedition is over at last. You can finally return home.

Section 4 Review

1. How does climate determine a biome's characteristics?
2. Where in water biomes can photosynthesis occur?
3. Which land biome receives the most precipitation? Which two receive the least?
4. In which biome would you find large herbivores such as antelope and elephants? Explain your answer.
5. **Thinking Critically Comparing and Contrasting** How are the three forest biomes (rain forests, deciduous forests, and boreal forests) alike? How are they different?

CHAPTER PROJECT 2

Check Your Progress
By now you should be ready to start analyzing the data you have collected about your compost chambers. Do your observations of the two chambers support your hypothesis? Begin to prepare your report.

CHANGE IN A TINY COMMUNITY

The types of organisms in an ecosystem may change gradually over time. You will learn more about this process, called succession, in the next section. In this lab you will observe succession in a pond community.

Problem

How does a pond community change over time?

Materials

hay solution
small baby-food jar
plastic dropper
coverslip

pond water
wax pencil
microscope slide
microscope

Procedure

1. Use a wax pencil to label a small jar with your name.
2. Fill the jar about three-fourths full with hay solution. Add pond water until the jar is nearly full. Examine the mixture, and record your observations in your notebook.
3. Place the jar in a safe location out of direct sunlight where it will remain undisturbed. Always wash your hands thoroughly with soap after handling the jar or its contents.

4. After two days, examine the contents of the jar, and record your observations.
5. Use a plastic dropper to collect a few drops from the surface of the solution in the jar. Make a slide following the procedures in the box at the right. **CAUTION:** *Slides and coverslips are fragile, and their edges are sharp. Handle them carefully.*
6. Examine the slide under a microscope using both low and high power following the procedures in the box at the right. Draw each type of organism you observe. Estimate the number of each type in your sample. The illustration below shows some of the organisms you might see.
7. Repeat Steps 5 and 6 with a drop of solution taken from the side of the jar beneath the surface.
8. Repeat Steps 5 and 6 with a drop of solution taken from the bottom of the jar. When you are finished, follow your teacher's directions about cleaning up.
9. After 3 days, repeat Steps 5 through 8.
10. After 3 more days, repeat Steps 5 through 8 again. Then follow your teacher's directions for returning the solution.

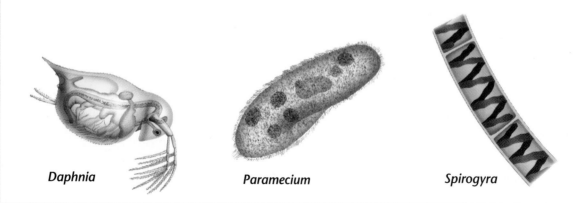

Daphnia   *Paramecium*   *Spirogyra*

Making and Viewing a Slide

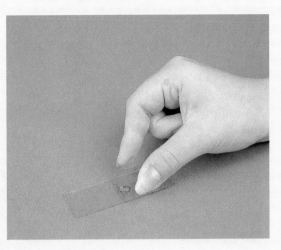

A. Place one drop of the solution to be examined in the middle of a microscope slide. Place one edge of a coverslip at the edge of the drop, as shown above. Gently lower the coverslip over the drop. Try not to trap any air bubbles.

B. Place the slide on the stage of a microscope so the drop is over the opening in the stage. Adjust the stage clips to hold the slide.

C. Look from the side of the microscope, and use the coarse adjustment knob to move the low-power objective close to, but not touching, the coverslip.

D. Look through the eyepiece, and use the coarse adjustment knob to raise the body tube and bring the slide into view. Use the fine adjustment knob to bring the slide into focus.

E. To view the slide under high power, look from the side of the microscope, and revolve the nosepiece until the high-power objective clicks into place just over, but not touching, the slide.

F. While you are looking through the eyepiece, use the fine adjustment knob to bring the slide into focus.

Analyze and Conclude

1. Identify as many of the organisms you observed as possible. Use the diagrams on the facing page and any other resources your teacher provides.

2. How did the community change over the time that you made your observations?

3. What factors may have influenced the changes in this community?

4. Where did the organisms you observed in the jar come from?

5. **Think About It** Do you think your observations gave you a complete picture of the changes in this community? Explain your answer.

Design an Experiment

Write a hypothesis about what would happen if you changed one biotic or abiotic factor in this activity. Design a plan to test your hypothesis. Obtain your teacher's permission before carrying out your experiment.

SECTION 5 Succession

DISCOVER ⋯⋯⋯⋯⋯⋯⋯⋯⋯⋯ ACTIVITY

What Happened Here?

1. The two photographs at the right show the same area in Yellowstone National Park in Wyoming. Photograph A was taken soon after a major fire. Photograph B was taken a few years later. Observe the photographs carefully.

2. Make a list of all the differences you notice between the two scenes.

Think It Over

Posing Questions How would you describe what happened during the time between the two photographs? What questions do you have about this process?

GUIDE FOR READING

◆ How are primary and secondary succession different?

Reading Tip Before you read, write a definition of what you think the term *succession* might mean. As you read, revise your definition.

In 1988, a huge fire raged through Yellowstone National Park. The fire was so hot that it jumped from tree to tree without burning along the ground between them. In an instant, huge trees burst into flame from the intense heat. It took weeks for the fires to burn themselves out. All that remained of that part of the forest were thousands of blackened tree trunks sticking out of the ground like charred toothpicks.

You might think it unlikely that Yellowstone could recover from such a disastrous fire. But within just a few months, signs of life had returned. First tiny green shoots of new grass appeared in the black ground. Then small tree seedlings began to grow again. The forest was coming back!

Fires, floods, volcanoes, hurricanes, and other natural disasters can change communities in a very short period of time. But even without a disaster, communities change. The series of predictable changes that occur in a community over time is called **succession.** This section describes two types of succession: primary succession and secondary succession.

Primary Succession

Primary succession is the series of changes that occur in an area where no ecosystem previously existed. Such an area might be a new island formed by the eruption of an undersea volcano, or an area of rock uncovered by a melting sheet of ice.

You can follow the series of changes an area might undergo in Figure 26 below. These scenes show an area after a violent volcanic eruption. At first there is no soil, just ash and rock. The first species to populate the area are called **pioneer species.** Pioneer species are often lichens and mosses carried to the area by wind or water. These species can grow on bare rocks with little or no soil. As these organisms grow, they help break up the rocks. When they die, they provide nutrients that enrich the thin layer of soil that is forming on the rocks.

Over time, plant seeds land in the new soil and begin to grow. The specific plants that grow depend on the biome of the area. For example, in a cool, northern area, early seedlings might include alder and cottonwood trees. As the soil grows older and richer, these trees might be replaced by spruce and hemlock. Eventually, succession may lead to a community of organisms that does not change unless the ecosystem is disturbed. Reaching this stable community can take centuries.

✓ *Checkpoint* *What are some pioneer species?*

Figure 26 Primary succession occurs in an area where no ecosystem previously existed. **A.** After a volcanic eruption, the ground surface consists of ash and rock. **B.** The first organisms to appear are lichens and moss. **C.** Weeds and grasses take root in the thin layer of soil. **D.** Eventually, tree seedlings and shrubs sprout. *Applying Concepts What determines the particular species that appear during succession?*

Figure 27 Secondary succession occurs following a disturbance to an ecosystem, such as clearing a forest for farmland. When the farm is abandoned, the forest gradually returns. **A.** After two years, weeds and wildflowers fill the field. **B.** After five years, pine seedlings and other plants populate the field. **C.** After 30 years, a pine forest has grown up. **D.** After 100 years, a mixed forest of pine, oak, and hickory is developing in the field.

Secondary Succession

The changes following the Yellowstone fire were an example of secondary succession. **Secondary succession** is the series of changes that occur after a disturbance in an existing ecosystem. Natural disturbances that have this effect include fires, hurricanes, and tornadoes. Human activities, such as farming, logging, or mining, may also disturb an ecosystem. **Unlike primary succession, secondary succession occurs in a place where an ecosystem has previously existed.**

Secondary succession occurs somewhat more rapidly than primary succession. Consider, for example, an abandoned field in the southeastern United States. Follow the process of succession in such a field in Figure 27. After a century, a hardwood forest is developing. This forest is very stable and will remain for a long time. Of course, the particular species that come and go in the process of succession depend on the biome.

Section 5 Review

1. How are primary and secondary succession different?
2. What is a pioneer species?
3. Give two examples of natural disturbances and two examples of human disturbances that can result in secondary succession.
4. **Thinking Critically Classifying** Grass poking through the cracks in a sidewalk is an example of succession. Is this primary or secondary succession? Explain.

Science at Home

Interview an older family member or neighbor who has lived in your neighborhood for a long time. Ask the person to describe how the neighborhood has changed over time. Have areas that were formerly grassy been paved or developed? Have any farms, parks, or lots returned to a wild state? Write a summary of your interview. Can you classify any of the changes as examples of succession?

SECTION 1 — Energy Flow in Ecosystems

Key Ideas

◆ The energy role of an organism is that of a producer, consumer, or decomposer.

◆ Producers are the source of all the food in an ecosystem. Most producers use sunlight to make food molecules through photosynthesis.

◆ Consumers include herbivores, carnivores, omnivores, and scavengers.

◆ Decomposers return nutrients to the environment where they can be used again.

◆ A food web shows the feeding relationships that exist in an ecosystem.

◆ At each level in an energy pyramid, there is less available energy than at the level below.

Key Terms

producer	omnivore	food chain
consumer	scavenger	food web
herbivore	decomposer	energy pyramid
carnivore		

SECTION 2 — Cycles of Matter

INTEGRATING CHEMISTRY

Key Ideas

◆ Matter, such as water, carbon dioxide, oxygen, and nitrogen, cycles through an ecosystem. Energy must be supplied constantly.

◆ The processes of evaporation, condensation, and precipitation form the water cycle.

◆ Producers use carbon dioxide to produce other carbon-containing molecules.

◆ Free nitrogen in the atmosphere cannot be used by most living things. Nitrogen must be fixed by certain types of bacteria.

Key Terms

water cycle	condensation	nitrogen fixation
evaporation	precipitation	nodules

SECTION 3 — Biogeography

Key Ideas

◆ Means of dispersal of organisms include continental drift, wind, water, and living things.

◆ Three factors that limit dipersal are physical barriers, competition, and climate.

Key Terms

biogeography	native species
continental drift	exotic species
dispersal	climate

SECTION 4 — Earth's Biomes

Key Ideas

◆ Temperature and precipitation mostly determine the type of ecosystem found in an area.

◆ Land biomes include rain forests, deserts, grasslands, deciduous forests, boreal forests, and tundras.

◆ There is only enough sunlight for photosynthesis to occur near the surface or in shallow areas of water biomes.

Key Terms

biome	savanna	permafrost
canopy	deciduous trees	estuary
understory	hibernation	intertidal zone
desert	coniferous trees	neritic zone
grassland	tundra	

SECTION 5 — Succession

Key Idea

◆ Primary succession occurs where no previous ecosystem exists. Secondary succession occurs after a disturbance.

Key Terms

succession	pioneer species
primary succession	secondary succession

USING THE INTERNET

www.science-explorer.phschool.com

Reviewing Content

For more review of key concepts, see the Interactive Student Tutorial CD-ROM.

Multiple Choice

Choose the letter of the best answer.

1. A diagram that shows how much energy is available at each feeding level in an ecosystem is a(n)
   a. food chain.
   b. food web.
   c. succession.
   d. energy pyramid.
2. Which of the following organisms are typical decomposers?
   a. grasses and ferns
   b. bacteria and mushrooms
   c. mice and deer
   d. lions and snakes
3. Which of the following is *not* recycled in an ecosystem?
   a. carbon
   b. nitrogen
   c. water
   d. energy
4. Organisms may be dispersed in all the following ways *except* by
   a. wind.
   b. water.
   c. temperature.
   d. other organisms.
5. Much of Canada is covered in pine and spruce forests. The winter is cold and long. What is this biome?
   a. tundra
   b. boreal forest
   c. deciduous forest
   d. grassland

True or False

If the statement is true, write true. If it is false, change the underlined word or words to make the statement true.

6. An organism that eats the remains of dead organisms is called a(n) <u>herbivore</u>.
7. The step of the water cycle is which liquid water changes to water vapor is <u>evaporation</u>.
8. The study of the past and present distribution of species on Earth is called <u>succession</u>.
9. <u>Precipitation</u> and temperature are the two major abiotic factors that determine what types of plants can grow in an area.
10. The land biome that gets the highest average amount of precipitation is the tropical <u>grassland</u> biome.

Checking Concepts

11. Name and briefly define each of the three energy roles organisms can play in an ecosystem.
12. How are food chains and food webs different?
13. What is the source of energy for most ecosystems?
14. Describe the role of nitrogen-fixing bacteria in the nitrogen cycle.
15. Explain the difference between a native species and an exotic species.
16. How has continental drift affected the distribution of species on Earth?
17. What organisms are the producers in most marine ecosystems?
18. **Writing to Learn** Choose any of the biomes described in this chapter. Imagine that you are a typical animal found in that biome. Write a paragraph describing the conditions and other organisms in your animal's biome.

Thinking Visually

19. **Flowchart** Copy the flowchart below on a separate sheet of paper. Complete the flowchart to show how carbon cycles through an ecosystem. (For more on flowcharts, see the Skills Handbook.)

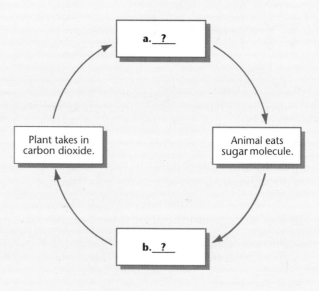

Applying Skills

Use the diagram of a food web below to answer Questions 20–22.

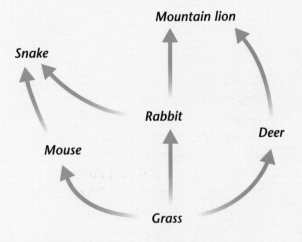

20. Classifying Identify the energy role of each organism in this food web. For consumers, specify whether they are first-level, second-level, or third-level.

21. Inferring Which level of the food web contains the greatest amount of available energy?

22. Predicting If a disease were to kill most of the rabbits in this area, predict how the snakes, deer, and mountain lions would be affected.

Thinking Critically

23. Relating Cause and Effect Every few years, a farmer plants clover in a wheatfield. Explain this practice.

24. Comparing and Contrasting How are the desert biome and the tundra biome similar? How are they different?

25. Inferring Polar bears are very well adapted to life around the Arctic Ocean. Their white fur camouflages them in the snow. They can swim and hunt in very cold water. Is the distribution of polar bears limited by physical barriers, competition, or climate? Explain your answer.

26. Predicting A volcano has just erupted in the ocean near Hawaii, forming a new island. How might succession change this island over time?

Performance Assessment

CHAPTER PROJECT 2 Wrap Up

Present Your Project Check over your report, poster, or other product. It should clearly present your data and conclusions about the effect of your variable on the decomposition process.

Reflect and Record In your notebook, compare your results to your predictions about the different waste materials in the compost mixture. Were you surprised by any of your results? Based on what you have learned from your project and those of your classmates, make a list of the ideal conditions for decomposition.

Getting Involved

In Your School With your classmates, take a group of younger students on a "sock walk" to learn about seed dispersal. Give the students thick white socks to wear over their shoes. Lead the students on a short walk through a field, woods, or park near your school. Back at school, the students can remove the socks and observe how many seeds they collected. Help them plant the socks in pans of soil. Place the pans in a sunny spot and water them regularly. How many species did the students successfully disperse?

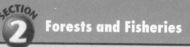

WHAT'S AHEAD

Variety Show

The colors in this meadow show that many different types of organisms live here. In other places, life's variety is less obvious. In this chapter's project, you will become an ecologist as you study the diversity of life in a small plot of land. Keep in mind that the area you will study has just a small sample of the huge variety of organisms that live on Earth.

Your Goal To observe the diversity of organisms in a plot of land.

To complete this project you must
- ◆ stake out a 1.5 meter-by-1.5 meter plot of ground
- ◆ keep a record of your observations of the abiotic conditions
- ◆ identify the species of organisms you observe
- ◆ follow the safety guidelines in Appendix A

Get Started Read over the project and prepare a notebook in which to record your observations. Include places to record the date, time, air temperature, and other weather conditions during each observation. Leave space for drawings or photographs of the organisms in your plot.

Check Your Progress You'll be working on this project as you study this chapter. To keep your project on track, look for Check Your Progress boxes at the following points.

Section 1 Review, page 89: Stake out your plot, and begin to observe it.

Section 4 Review, page 108: Identify the organisms in your plot. Begin to prepare your presentation.

Wrap Up At the end of the chapter (page 111), you will present your findings to the class. You will describe your observations and share the diversity of life in your plot.

A woodchuck feasts on wildflowers in a meadow exploding with color. Black-eyed Susans, Queen Anne's lace, and butterflyweed are part of the meadow's diversity.

SECTION
4
Integrating Health
The Search for New Medicines

Discover How Are Plant Chemicals Separated?

SECTION
① Environmental Issues

DISCOVER ·································ACTIVITY···

How Do You Decide?

1. On a sheet of paper, list the three environmental issues you think are most important.

2. Form a group with three other classmates. Share your lists. As a group decide which one of the issues is the most important.

Think It Over
Forming Operational Definitions
Based on your group's discussion, how would you define the term *environmental issue?*

GUIDE FOR READING

◆ What are the main types of environmental issues?

◆ What is environmental science?

◆ How do decision makers balance different needs and concerns?

Reading Tip Before you read, make a list of ways that humans depend on the environment. As you read, add examples from the text.

Figure 1 This leopard seal's habitat could be affected if oil drilling is allowed in Antarctica. This tradeoff is an example of an environmental issue.

Here's a puzzle for you: What is bigger than the United States and Mexico combined; is covered with two kilometers of ice; is a source of oil, coal, and iron; and is a unique habitat for many animals? The answer is Antarctica. People once thought of Antarctica as a useless, icy wasteland. But when explorers told of its huge populations of seals and whales, hunters began going to Antarctica. Then scientists set up research stations to study the unique conditions there. They soon discovered valuable minerals beneath the thick ice.

Now the puzzle is what to do with Antarctica. Many people want its rich deposits of minerals and oil. Others worry that mining will harm the delicate ecosystems there. Some people propose building hotels, parks, and ski resorts. But others feel that Antarctica should remain undisturbed. It is not even obvious who should decide Antarctica's fate.

In 1998, 26 nations agreed to ban mining and oil exploration in Antarctica for at least 50 years. As resources become more scarce elsewhere in the world, the debate will surely continue. What is the best use of Antarctica?

Types of Environmental Issues

People have always used Earth's resources. But as the human population has grown, so has its effect on the environment. People compete with each other and with other living things for Earth's limited resources. Disposing of wastes created by people can change ecosystems. And while people are continuing to take resources from the environment, many resources cannot be replaced. These resources could eventually run out.

Figure 2 Cherries are a renewable resource. After they are harvested, new cherries will grow in their place. In contrast, the aluminum and iron used to make these kitchen tools are nonrenewable resources.

The three main types of environmental issues are resource use, population growth, and pollution. These issues are all connected, making them very difficult to solve.

Resource Use Anything in the environment that is used by people is a natural resource. Some natural resources, called **renewable resources,** are naturally replaced in a relatively short time. Renewable resources include sunlight, wind, and trees. But it is possible to use up some renewable resources. For example, if people cut down trees faster than they can grow back, the supply of this resource will decrease.

Natural resources that are not replaced as they are used are called **nonrenewable resources.** Most nonrenewable resources, such as coal and oil, exist in a limited supply. As nonrenewable resources are used, the supply may eventually be depleted.

Figure 3 If two's company, six billion is certainly a crowd! The human population has grown rapidly in the last few centuries. *Calculating How much has the population grown since 1650?*

Population Growth Figure 3 shows how the human population has changed in the last 3,000 years. You can see that the population grew very slowly until about A.D. 1650. Around that time, improvements in medicine, agriculture, and sanitation enabled people to live longer. The death rate decreased. But as the population has continued to grow, the demand for resources has also grown.

Pollution Any change to the environment that has a negative effect on living things is called **pollution.** Pollution is an issue because it is often the result of an activity that benefits humans. For example, generating electricity by burning coal can result in air pollution. Some pesticides used to kill insects that eat crops are harmful to other animals.

☑ *Checkpoint* *What is a natural resource?*

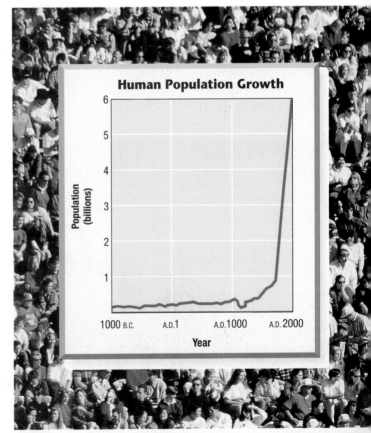

Human Population Growth

(Population (billions) graphed from 1000 B.C. through A.D. 2000)

Approaches to Environmental Issues

Dealing with environmental issues means making choices. These choices can be made at personal, local, national, or global levels. Whether to ride in a car, take a bus, or ride your bicycle to the mall is an example of a personal choice. Whether to build a landfill or an incinerator for disposing of a town's wastes is a local choice. Whether the United States should allow oil drilling in a wildlife refuge is a national choice. How to protect Earth's atmosphere is a global choice.

Choices that seem personal are often part of much larger issues. Choices of what you eat, what you wear, and how you travel all affect the environment in a small way. When the choices made by millions of people are added together, each person's actions can make a difference.

SCIENCE & History

Making a Difference

Can one individual change the way people think? The leaders featured in this time line have influenced the way that many people think about environmental issues.

1892
California writer John Muir founds the Sierra Club. The group promotes the setting aside of wild areas as national parks. Muir's actions lead to the establishment of Yosemite National Park.

1905
Forestry scientist Gifford Pinchot is appointed the first director of the United States Forest Service. His goal is to manage forests scientifically to meet current and future lumber needs.

1875   **1900**   **1925**

1903
President Theodore Roosevelt establishes the first National Wildlife Refuge on Pelican Island, Florida, to protect the brown pelican.

Theodore Roosevelt (left) and John Muir (right)

The first step in making environmental decisions is to understand how humans interact with the environment. **Environmental science is the study of the natural processes that occur in the environment and how humans can affect them.**

When people make decisions about environmental issues, the information provided by environmental scientists is a starting point. The next step is to decide what to do with the information. But environmental decisions also involve discussions of values, not just facts and figures. Environmental decisions usually require considering many different points of view. Most of these viewpoints fall into one of these three categories: development, preservation, or conservation.

☑ *Checkpoint* *What is an example of a local choice about an environmental issue?*

In Your Journal

Find out more about one of the people featured in this time line. Write a short biography of the person's life explaining how he or she became involved in environmental issues. What obstacles did the person overcome to accomplish his or her goal?

1949

Naturalist Aldo Leopold publishes *A Sand County Almanac.* This classic book links wildlife management to the science of ecology.

1969

At the age of 79, journalist Marjory Stoneman Douglas founds Friends of the Everglades. This grassroots organization is dedicated to preserving the unique Florida ecosystem. She continues to work for the Everglades until her death in 1998.

1950	1975	2000

1962

Biologist Rachel Carson writes *Silent Spring,* which describes the harmful effects of pesticides on the environment. The book raises awareness of how human activities can affect the environment.

1977

Biologist Wangari Maathai founds the Green Belt Movement. This organization encourages restoring forests in Kenya and other African nations.

Economic value

The hills are a source of resources such as lumber and minerals.

Scenic value

The river valley is a beautiful and peaceful area.

Recreational value

The river is a good place to canoe and raft. Hikers can enjoy the surrounding hills.

Ecological value

The river valley is home to many plants, animals, and other organisms.

Health value

The river is a source of clean drinking water.

Figure 4 The environment is valued for many different reasons. *Applying Concepts In what other ways might this area be valuable?*

Development The belief that humans should be able to freely use and benefit from all of Earth's resources is referred to as the **development viewpoint.** This viewpoint considers the environment in terms of economics. Economics involves business, money, and jobs. According to the development viewpoint, the most valuable parts of the environment are those resources that are most useful to human beings.

Preservation The belief that all parts of the environment are equally important, no matter how useful they are to humans, is the **preservation viewpoint.** This viewpoint considers humans to be the caretakers of nature. Preservationists feel that Earth and its resources should be a source of beauty, comfort, and recreation. The preservation viewpoint is that living things and ecosystems should not be disturbed for the benefit of people.

Conservation The **conservation viewpoint** is the belief that people should use resources from the environment as long as they do not destroy those resources. Conservationists feel that people must balance development and preservation. The conservation viewpoint is that people should manage Earth's resources for the future, not just for today.

☑ *Checkpoint* *What are three viewpoints about how humans should interact with the environment?*

Weighing Costs and Benefits

Lawmakers work with many different government agencies to make environmental decisions. Together they must consider the needs and concerns of people with many different viewpoints. **To help balance these different opinions, decision makers weigh the costs and benefits of a proposal.**

Costs and benefits are often economic. Will a proposal provide jobs? Will it cost too much money? But costs and benefits are not only measured in terms of money. For example, building an incinerator might reduce the beauty of a natural landscape (a scenic cost). But the incinerator might be safer than an existing open dump site (a health benefit). It is also important to consider short-term and long-term effects. A proposal's short-term costs might be outweighed by its long-term benefits.

Consider the costs and benefits of drilling for oil in Antarctica. Drilling for oil would have many costs. It would be very expensive to set up a drilling operation in such a cold and distant place. Transporting the oil would be difficult and costly. An oil spill in the seas around Antarctica could harm the fish, penguins, and seals there.

On the other hand, there would be many benefits to drilling in Antarctica. A new supply of oil would provide fuel for heat, electricity, and transportation. The plan would create many new jobs. There would be a greater opportunity to study Antarctica's ecosystems. Do the benefits of drilling outweigh the costs? This is the kind of question lawmakers ask when they make environmental decisions.

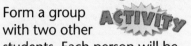

Communicating

Form a group with two other students. Each person will be assigned a different viewpoint toward the environment. Hold a panel discussion in which each person proposes how the continent of Antarctica should be used. What similarities and differences are there among your responses?

Section 1 Review

1. List the three main types of environmental issues.
2. Define environmental science.
3. What is one way to balance different viewpoints on an environmental issue?
4. How has the growth of the human population affected the environment?
5. List three costs and three benefits of drilling for oil on Antarctica.
6. **Thinking Critically Comparing and Contrasting** Compare renewable and nonrenewable resources. Give an example of each type of resource.

Check Your Progress

CHAPTER PROJECT 3

Stake out a square plot measuring 1.5 meters on each side. Record the date, time, temperature, and weather. Observe the organisms in your plot, and record them with notes and drawings. Include enough detail so that you can identify any unfamiliar organisms later. (*Hint:* Also note evidence such as feathers or footprints that shows that other organisms may have visited the plot.)

Is Paper a Renewable Resource?

Recycling is a common local environmental issue. In this lab, you will explore how well paper can be recycled.

Problem

What happens when paper is recycled?

Skills Focus

observing, designing experiments

Materials

newspaper microscope water
eggbeater square pan screen
plastic wrap mixing bowl heavy book
microscope slide

Procedure

1. Tear off a small piece of newspaper. Place the paper on a microscope slide and examine it under a microscope. Record your observations.

2. Tear a sheet of newspaper into pieces about the size of postage stamps. Place the pieces in the mixing bowl. Add enough water to cover the newspaper. Cover the bowl and let the mixture stand overnight.

3. The next day, add more water to cover the paper if necessary. Use the eggbeater to mix the wet paper until it is smooth. This thick liquid is called paper pulp.

4. Place the screen in the bottom of the pan. Pour the pulp onto the screen, spreading it out evenly. Then lift the screen above the pan, allowing most of the water to drip into the pan.

5. Place the screen and pulp on several layers of newspaper to absorb the rest of the water. Lay a sheet of plastic wrap over the pulp. Place a heavy book on top of the plastic wrap to press more water out of the pulp.

6. After 30 minutes, remove the book. Carefully turn over the screen, plastic wrap, and pulp. Remove the screen and plastic wrap. Let the pulp sit on the newspaper for one or two more days to dry. Replace the newspaper layers if necessary.

7. When the pulp is dry, observe it closely. Record your observations.

Analyze and Conclude

1. What kind of structures did you observe when you examined torn newspaper under a microscope? What are these structures made of? Where do they come from?

2. What do you think happens to the structures you observed when paper is recycled?

3. Based on your results, predict how many times a sheet of newspaper can be recycled.

4. **Apply** Should paper be classified as a renewable or nonrenewable resource? Explain.

Design an Experiment

Using procedures like those in this lab, design an experiment to recycle three different types of paper, such as shiny magazine paper, paper towels, and cardboard. Find out how the resulting papers differ. Obtain your teacher's approval for your plans before you try your experiment.

2 Forests and Fisheries

DISCOVER · ACTIVITY · · ·

What Happened to the Tuna?

1. Use the data in the table to make a line graph. Label the axes of the graph and add a title. (To review graphing, see the Skills Handbook.)

2. Mark the high and low points on the graph.

Think It Over

Inferring How did the tuna population change during this period? Can you suggest a possible reason for this change?

Year	Western Atlantic Bluefin Tuna Population
1970	240,000
1975	190,000
1980	90,000
1985	60,000
1990	45,000
1994	60,000

A
t first glance, a bluefin tuna and a pine tree may not seem to have much in common. One is an animal and the other is a plant. One lives in the ocean and the other lives on land. However, tuna and pine trees are both living resources. Tuna are a source of food for people. People don't eat pine trees, but they do use them to make lumber, paper, and turpentine. People also use pine needles as mulch in gardens.

Every day you use many different products that are made from living organisms. In this section, you will read about two major types of living resources: forests and fisheries. As you read, think about how they are similar and how they are different.

Forest Resources

Forests are a resource because they contain valuable materials. Many products are made from the flowers, fruits, seeds, and other parts of forest plants. Some of these products, such as maple syrup, rubber, and nuts, come from living trees. Other products, such as lumber and pulp for paper, require cutting trees down. Conifers, including pine and spruce, are used for construction and for making paper. Hardwoods, such as oak, cherry, and maple, are used for furniture because of their strength and beauty.

Trees and other plants produce oxygen that other organisms need to survive. They also absorb carbon dioxide and many pollutants from the air. Trees also help prevent flooding and control soil erosion. Their roots absorb rainwater and hold the soil together.

GUIDE FOR READING

◆ How can forests and fisheries be managed?

Reading Tip As you read, make a list of ways to conserve forests and fisheries.

Figure 5 One important use of forest resources is for building housing.

Figure 6 Clear-cutting has left large portions of these hillsides bare. *Interpreting Photographs* What problems might clear-cutting cause?

Social Studies
CONNECTION

Many of the world's living resources are owned by no one—they are shared by everyone. A word that is sometimes used to describe such a shared resource is a "commons." This word comes from a time when villages were built around common areas of open land. All the town's residents grazed their cattle on the commons. This worked well as long as there weren't too many people. But as more and more people brought their cattle to the commons, the area would become overgrazed. There would not be enough pasture to feed even one cow—the "tragedy of the commons."

In Your Journal

Suppose you live in a farming community with a central commons. Propose a solution that will allow residents to use the commons while protecting it from overuse.

Managing Forests

There are about 300 million hectares of forests in the United States. That's nearly a third of the nation's area! Many forests are located on publicly owned land. Others are owned by private timber and paper companies or by individuals. Forest industries provide jobs for 1.5 million people.

Because new trees can be planted to replace trees that are cut down, forests can be renewable resources. The United States Forest Service and environmental organizations work with forestry companies to conserve forest resources. They try to develop logging methods that maintain forests as renewable resources.

Logging Methods There are two major methods of logging: clear-cutting and selective cutting. **Clear-cutting** is the process of cutting down all the trees in an area at once. Cutting down only some trees in a forest and leaving a mix of tree sizes and species behind is called **selective cutting.**

Each logging method has advantages and disadvantages. Clear-cutting is usually quicker and cheaper than selective cutting. It may also be safer for the loggers. In selective cutting, the loggers must move the heavy equipment and logs around the remaining trees in the forest. But selective cutting is usually less damaging to the forest environment than clear-cutting. When an area of forest is clear-cut, the habitat changes. Clear-cutting exposes the soil to wind and rain. Without the protection of the tree roots, the soil is more easily blown or washed away. Soil washed into streams may harm the fish and other organisms that live there.

Sustainable Forestry Forests can be managed to provide a sustained yield. A **sustainable yield** is a regular amount of a renewable resource such as trees that can be harvested without reducing the future supply. This works sort of like a book swap: as long as you donate a book each time you borrow one, the total supply of books will not be affected. Planting a tree to replace one being cut down is like donating a book to replace a borrowed one.

Part of forest management is planning how frequently the trees must be replanted to keep a constant supply. Different species grow at different rates. Trees with softer woods, such as pines, usually mature faster than trees with harder woods, such as hickory, oak, and cherry. Forests containing faster-growing trees can be harvested and replanted more often. For example, pine forests may be harvested every 20 to 30 years. On the other hand, some hardwood forests may be harvested only every 40 to 100 years. One sustainable approach is to log small patches of forest. This way, different sections of forest can be harvested every year.

Certified Wood Forests that are managed in a sustainable way can be certified by the Forest Stewardship Council. Once a forest is certified, all wood logged from that forest may carry a "well-managed" label. This label allows businesses and individuals to select wood from forests that are managed for sustainable yields.

☑ *Checkpoint* *What is a sustainable yield?*

Figure 7 Two logging methods are clear-cutting and selective cutting. **A.** After clear-cutting, the new trees are usually all the same age and species. **B.** Selective cutting results in a more diverse forest.

Original forest   *Clear-cutting*   *Replanted growth*

Original forest   *Selective cutting*   *Diverse regrowth*

Sharpen your Skills

Calculating

ACTIVITY

In a recent year, the total catch of fish in the world was 112.9 million metric tons. Based on the data below, calculate the percent of this total each country caught.

Country	Catch (millions of metric tons)
China	24.4
Japan	6.8
United States	5.6
Peru	8.9

Figure 8 A fishing boat returns to harbor at the end of a long day. Overfishing has forced the crews of many boats to find other work until the fisheries recover.

Fisheries

Until recently, the oceans seemed like an unlimited resource. The waters held such huge schools of fish, it seemed impossible that they could ever disappear. And fish reproduce in incredible numbers. A single codfish can lay as many as nine million eggs in a single year! But people have discovered that this resource has limits. After many years of big catches, the number of sardines off the California coast suddenly declined. The same thing happened to the huge schools of cod off the New England coast. What caused these changes?

An area with a large population of valuable ocean organisms is called a **fishery.** Some major fisheries include the Grand Banks off Newfoundland, Georges Bank off New England, and Monterey Canyon off California. Fisheries like these are valuable renewable resources. But if fish are caught at a faster rate than they can breed, the population decreases. This situation is known as overfishing.

Scientists estimate that 70 percent of the world's major fisheries have been overfished. But if those fish populations are allowed to recover, a sustainable yield of fish can once again be harvested. **Managing fisheries for a sustainable yield includes setting fishing limits, changing fishing methods, developing aquaculture techniques, and finding new resources.**

Fishing Limits Laws can help protect individual fish species. Laws may also limit the amount that can be caught or require that fish be at least a certain size. This ensures that young fish

survive long enough to reproduce. Also, setting an upper limit on the size of fish caught ensures that breeding fish remain in the population. But if a fishery has been severely overfished, the government may need to completely ban fishing until the populations can recover.

Fishing Methods Today fishing practices are regulated by laws. Some fishing crews now use nets with a larger mesh size to allow small, young fish to escape. Some methods have been outlawed. These methods include poisoning fish with cyanide and stunning them by exploding dynamite underwater. These techniques kill all the fish in an area rather than selecting certain fish.

Aquaculture The practice of raising fish and other water-dwelling organisms for food is called **aquaculture.** The fish may be raised in artificial ponds or bays. Salmon, catfish, and shrimp are farmed in this way in the United States.

However, aquaculture is not a perfect solution. The artificial ponds and bays often replace natural habitats such as salt marshes. Maintaining the farms can cause pollution and spread diseases into wild fish populations.

New Resources Today about 9,000 different fish species are harvested for food. More than half the animal protein eaten by people throughout the world comes from fish. One way to help feed a growing human population is to fish for new species. Scientists and chefs are working together to introduce people to deep-water species such as monkfish and tile fish, as well as easy-to-farm freshwater fish such as tilapia.

Figure 9 As fishing limits become stricter, aquaculture is playing a larger role in meeting the worldwide demand for fish. This fish farm in Hawaii raises tilapia.

Section 2 Review

1. Describe one example of a sustainable forestry practice.
2. What are three ways fisheries can be managed so that they will continue to provide fish for the future?
3. Why are forests considered renewable resources?
4. **Thinking Critically Comparing and Contrasting** Describe the advantages and disadvantages of clear-cutting and selective cutting.

Science at Home

With a family member, conduct a "Forest and Fishery" survey of your home. Make a list of all the things that are made from either forest or fishery products. Then ask other family members to predict how many items are on the list. Are they surprised by the answer?

Tree Cookie Tales

Tree cookies aren't snacks! They're slices of a tree trunk that contain clues about the tree's age, past weather conditions, and fires that occurred during its life. In this lab, you'll interpret the data hidden in a tree cookie.

Problem

What can tree cookies reveal about the past?

Materials

tree cookie
colored pencils
metric ruler
calculator (optional)
hand lens

Procedure

1. Use a hand lens to examine your tree cookie. Draw a simple diagram of your tree cookie. Label the bark, tree rings, and center, or pith.

2. Notice the light-colored and dark-colored rings. The light ring results from fast springtime growth. The dark ring, where the cells are smaller, results from slower summertime growth. Each pair of light and dark rings represents one year's growth, so the pair is called an annual ring. Observe and count the annual rings.

3. Compare the spring and summer portions of the annual rings. Identify the thinnest and thickest rings.

4. Measure the distance from the center to the outermost edge of the last summer growth ring. This is the radius of your tree cookie. Record your measurement.

5. Measure the distance from the center to the outermost edge of the 10th summer growth ring. Record your measurement.

6. Examine your tree cookie for any other evidence of its history, such as damaged bark or burn marks. Record your observations.

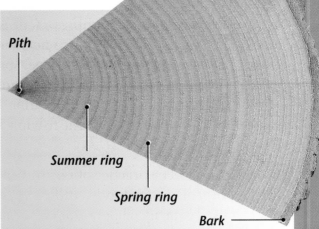

Pith

Summer ring

Spring ring

Bark

Analyze and Conclude

1. How old was your tree? How do you know?

2. What percent of the tree's growth took place during the first 10 years of its life? (*Hint:* Divide the distance from the center to the 10th growth ring by the radius. Then multiply by 100. This gives you the percent of growth that occurred during the tree's first 10 years.)

3. How did the spring rings compare to the summer rings for the same year? Suggest a reason.

4. Why might the annual rings be narrower for some years than for others?

5. Using evidence from your tree cookie, summarize the history of the tree.

6. **Think About It** Suppose you had cookies from two other trees of the same species that grew near your tree. How could you verify the interpretations you made in this lab?

More to Explore

Examine and compare several tree cookies. Record any similarities and differences you observe. Do you think any of the tree cookies came from trees growing in the same area? Support your answer with specific evidence.

DISCOVER · ACTIVITY

How Much Variety Is There?

1. You will be given two cups of seeds and a paper plate. The seeds in Cup A represent the trees in a section of tropical rain forest. The seeds in Cup B represent the trees in a section of deciduous forest.

2. Pour the seeds from Cup A onto the plate. Sort the seeds by type. Count the different types of seeds. This number represents the number of different kinds of trees in that type of forest.

3. Pour the seeds back into Cup A.

4. Repeat Steps 2 and 3 with the seeds in Cup B.

5. Share your results with your class. Use the class results to calculate the average number of different kinds of seeds in each type of forest.

Think It Over

Inferring How does the variety of trees in the tropical rain forest compare with the variety of trees in a deciduous forest? Can you suggest any advantages of having a wide variety of species?

No one knows exactly how many species live on Earth. So far, more than 1.7 million species have been identified. The number of different species in an area is called its **biodiversity.** It is difficult to estimate the total biodiversity on Earth because many areas of the planet have not been thoroughly studied. Some experts think that the deep oceans alone could contain 10 million new species! Protecting this diversity is a major environmental issue today.

> ### GUIDE FOR READING
>
> ◆ What factors affect an area's biodiversity?
>
> ◆ Which human activities threaten biodiversity?
>
> ◆ How can biodiversity be protected?
>
> *Reading Tip* Before you read, use the headings to make an outline on biodiversity.

Factors Affecting Biodiversity

Biodiversity varies from place to place on Earth. **Factors that affect biodiversity in an ecosystem include area, climate, and diversity of niches.**

Area Within an ecosystem, a large area will contain more species than a small area. For example, suppose you were counting tree species in a forest. You would find far more tree species in a 10-square-meter area than in a 1-square-meter area.

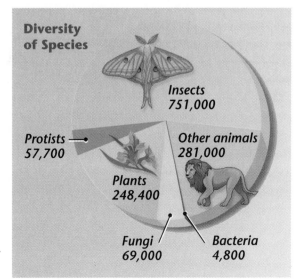

Figure 10 Organisms of many kinds are part of Earth's biodiversity.
Interpreting Graphs Which group of organisms has the greatest number of species?

Diversity of Species

Insects 751,000

Protists 57,700

Other animals 281,000

Plants 248,400

Fungi 69,000

Bacteria 4,800

In Costa Rica, which is half the size of Tennessee, there are 850 species of birds—200 more than in all the rest of North America.

A 10-hectare area of forest in Borneo contains 700 species of trees, as many as all of North America.

A single river in Brazil contains more species than all of the rivers in the United States combined.

Figure 11 Tropical ecosystems tend to be more diverse than those further from the equator.

Figure 12 Coral reefs are the second most diverse ecosystems. *Applying Concepts What is one reason why coral reefs are so diverse?*

Climate In general, the number of species increases from the poles toward the equator. The tropical rain forests of Latin America, southeast Asia, and central Africa are the most diverse ecosystems in the world. These forests cover about 7 percent of Earth's land surface and contain over half of the world's species.

The reason for the great biodiversity in the tropics is not fully understood. Many scientists hypothesize that it has to do with climate. For example, tropical rain forests have fairly constant temperatures and large amounts of rainfall throughout the year. Many plants in these regions have year-round growing seasons. This means that food is available for other organisms year-round.

Niche Diversity Coral reefs make up less than 1 percent of the oceans' area. But reefs are home to 20 percent of the world's saltwater fish species. Coral reefs are the second most diverse ecosystems in the world. Found only in shallow, warm waters, coral reefs are often called the rain forests of the sea. A reef provides many different niches for organisms that live under, on, and among the coral. This enables more species to live in the reef than in a more uniform habitat such as a flat sandbar.

✓ *Checkpoint What is one possible reason that tropical regions have the greatest biodiversity?*

The Value of Biodiversity

Perhaps you are wondering how biodiversity is important. Does it matter whether there are 50 or 5,000 species of ferns in some faraway rain forest? Is it necessary to protect every one of these species?

There are many reasons why preserving biodiversity is important. The simplest reason is that wild organisms and ecosystems are a source of beauty and recreation.

Economic Value Many plants, animals, and other organisms are essential for human survival. In addition to providing food and oxygen, these organisms supply raw materials for clothing, medicine, and other products. No one knows how many other useful species have not yet been identified.

Ecosystems are economically valuable, too. For example, many companies now run wildlife tours in rain forests, savannas, mountain ranges, and other locations. This ecosystem tourism, or "ecotourism," is an important source of jobs and money for nations such as Brazil, Costa Rica, and Kenya.

Value to the Ecosystem All the species in an ecosystem are connected to one another. Species may depend on each other for food and shelter. A change that affects one species will surely affect all the others.

Some species play a particularly important role. A species that influences the survival of many other species in an ecosystem is called a **keystone species.** If a keystone species disappears, the entire ecosystem may change. For example, the sea stars in Figure 14 are a keystone species in their ecosystem. The sea stars prey mostly on the mussels that live in tide pools. When researchers removed the sea stars from an area, the mussels began to outcompete many of the other species in the tide pool. The sea star predators had kept the population of mussels in check, allowing other species to live. When the keystone species disappeared, the balance in the ecosystem was destroyed.

Figure 13 Ecosystem tours such as safaris can provide income for local people. These tourists are observing giraffes in Botswana.

Figure 14 These sea stars on the Washington coast are an example of a keystone species. By preying on mussels, the sea stars keep the mussels from taking over the ecosystem.

Gene Pool Diversity

The organisms in a healthy population have a diversity of traits. These traits are determined by genes. **Genes** are the structures in an organism's cells that carry its hereditary information. Every organism receives a combination of genes from its parents. Genes determine the organism's characteristics, from its size and appearance to its ability to fight disease. The organisms in one species share many genes. But each organism also has some genes that differ from those of other individuals. These individual differences make up the total gene "pool" of that species.

Species that lack a diverse gene pool are less able to adapt to disease, parasites, or drought. For example, most agricultural crops, such as wheat and corn, have very little diversity. These species are bred to be very uniform. If a disease or parasite attacks, the whole population could be affected. A fungus once wiped out much of the corn crop in the United States in this way. Fortunately, there are many wild varieties of corn that have slightly different genes. At least some of these plants contain genes that make them more resistant to the fungus. Scientists were able to breed corn that was not affected by the fungus. Keeping a diverse gene pool helps ensure that crop species can survive such problems.

✓ *Checkpoint* *What do an organism's genes determine?*

Figure 15 Just as diversity of species is important to an ecosystem, diversity of genes is important within a species. Diverse genes give these potatoes their rainbow of colors.

Extinction of Species

The disappearance of all members of a species from Earth is called **extinction.** Extinction is a natural process. Many species that once lived on Earth, from dinosaurs to dodos, are now extinct. But in the last few centuries, the number of species becoming extinct has increased dramatically.

Once a population drops below a certain level, the species may not be able to recover. For example, millions of passenger pigeons once darkened the skies in the United States. People hunted the birds for sport and food, killing many hundreds of thousands. This was only part of the total population of passenger pigeons. But at some point, there were not enough birds to reproduce and increase the population. Only after the birds disappeared did people realize that the species could not survive without its enormous numbers.

Species in danger of becoming extinct in the near future are considered **endangered species.** Species that could become endangered in the near future are considered **threatened species.**

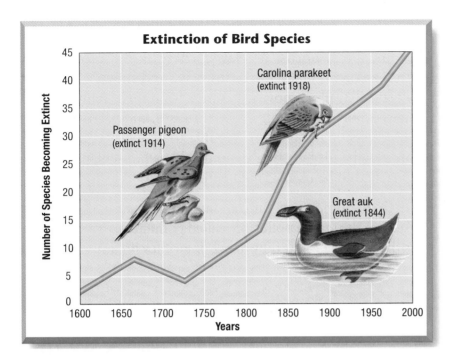

Extinction of Bird Species

Number of Species Becoming Extinct (y-axis: 0 to 45)
Years (x-axis: 1600 to 2000)

Passenger pigeon (extinct 1914)

Carolina parakeet (extinct 1918)

Great auk (extinct 1844)

Figure 16 This graph shows the rate of extinction of bird species in the last 400 years.
Interpreting Graphs How many bird species became extinct in 1750? In 1850? In 1950?

Threatened and endangered species are found on every continent and in every ocean. Some are well-known animals such as Africa's black rhinoceros. Others are little known, such as hutias, rodents that live on only a few Caribbean islands. Ensuring that these species survive is one way to protect Earth's biodiversity.

Causes of Extinction

A natural event, such as an earthquake or volcano, can damage an ecosystem, wiping out populations or even some species. **Human activities can also threaten biodiversity. These activities include habitat destruction, poaching, pollution, and introduction of exotic species.**

Habitat Destruction The major cause of extinction is **habitat destruction,** the loss of a natural habitat. This can occur when forests are cleared to build towns or create grazing land. Plowing grasslands or filling in wetlands greatly changes those ecosystems. Some species may not be able to survive such changes to their habitats.

Breaking larger habitats into smaller, isolated pieces, or fragments, is called **habitat fragmentation.** For example, building a road through a forest disrupts habitats. This makes trees more vulnerable to wind damage. Plants may be less likely to successfully disperse their seeds. Habitat fragmentation is also very harmful to large mammals. These animals usually need large areas of land to find enough food to survive. They may not be able to obtain enough resources in a small area. They may also be injured trying to cross to another area.

Figure 17 Building this subdivision caused the habitats in the area to change. Open land was replaced by houses, streets, and yards.
Inferring How would these changes affect species in this area?

Poaching The illegal killing or removal of wildlife species is called **poaching.** Many endangered animals are hunted for their skin, fur, teeth, horns, or claws. These things are used for making medicines, jewelry, coats, belts, and shoes.

People illegally remove organisms from their habitats to sell them as exotic pets. Tropical fish, tortoises, and parrots are very popular pets, making them valuable to poachers. Endangered plants may be illegally dug up and sold as houseplants. Others are poached to be used as medicines.

Pollution Some species are endangered because of pollution. Substances that cause pollution, called pollutants, may reach animals through the water they drink or air they breathe. Pollutants

EXPLORING *Endangered Species*

A broad range of species and habitats are represented on the endangered list in the United States.

Grizzly bear ▷ This omnivore needs a large area to obtain food. Shrinking wilderness areas have limited its numbers.

Piping plover The ▷ population of this tiny, active coastal bird is recovering as a result of increased protection of its sand dune nesting sites.

◁ **Eureka valley evening primrose** This flower, which blooms for only one night, must compete for water with exotic plants.

may also settle in the soil. From there they are absorbed by plants, and build up in other organisms through the food chain. Pollutants may kill or weaken organisms or cause birth defects.

Exotic Species Introducing exotic species into an ecosystem can threaten biodiversity. When European sailors began visiting Hawaii hundreds of years ago, rats from their ships escaped onto the islands. Without any predators in Hawaii, the rats multiplied quickly. They ate the eggs of the nene goose. To protect the geese, people brought the rat-eating mongoose from India to help control the rat population. Unfortunately, the mongooses preferred eating eggs to rats. With both the rats and the mongoose eating its eggs, the nene goose is now endangered.

◀ **Steller's sea lion** This mammal competes with fishermen for its prey along the Pacific coast.

Schaus swallowtail ▶ butterfly Threatened by habitat loss and pesticide pollution in the Florida Keys, this butterfly was nearly wiped out by Hurricane Andrew.

▲ **Whooping crane** Threatened by habitat destruction and disease, half of the remaining population of this wading bird is in captivity. The species seems to be recovering well since its lowest point in the 1940s.

◀ **New Mexico ridgenose rattlesnake** Illegal collectors have reduced the population of this rare snake, the largest known group of which lives in a single canyon.

Protecting Biodiversity

Many people are working to preserve the world's biodiversity. Some focus on protecting individual endangered species, such as the giant panda or the gray whale. Others try to protect entire ecosystems, such as the Great Barrier Reef in Australia. **Many programs to protect biodiversity combine scientific and legal approaches.**

Captive Breeding One scientific approach to protecting severely endangered species is captive breeding. **Captive breeding** is the mating of animals in zoos or wildlife preserves. Scientists care for the young to increase their chance of survival. These offspring are then released back into the wild.

A captive breeding program was the only hope for the California condor. California condors are the largest birds in North America. They became endangered as a result of habitat destruction, poaching, and pollution. By the mid-1980s there were fewer than ten California condors in the wild. Fewer than 30 were in zoos. Scientists captured all the wild condors and brought them to the zoos. Soon afterward, the first California condor chick was successfully bred in captivity. Today, there are more than 100 California condors in zoos. Some condors have even been returned to the wild. Though successful, this program has cost more than $20 million. It is not possible to save many species in this costly way.

Laws and Treaties Laws can help protect individual species. Some nations have made it illegal to sell endangered species or products made from them. In the United States, the Endangered Species Act of 1973 prohibits importing or trading products made from threatened or endangered species. This law also requires the development of plans to save endangered species.

Figure 18 Captive breeding programs use a scientific approach to protect endangered species.
A. California condor chicks raised in captivity need to learn what adult condors look like. Here, a scientist uses a puppet to feed and groom a chick.
B. These young green turtles were hatched in the laboratory. Now a researcher is releasing the turtles into their natural ocean habitat.

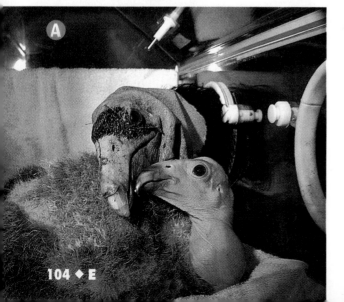

American alligators, Pacific gray whales, and green sea turtles are just a few of the species that have begun to recover as a result of legal protection.

The most important international treaty protecting wildlife is the Convention on International Trade in Endangered Species. Eighty nations signed this treaty in 1973. This treaty lists nearly 700 threatened and endangered species that cannot be traded for profit. Laws like these are difficult to enforce. Even so, they have helped to reduce the poaching of many endangered species, including African elephants, snow leopards, sperm whales, and mountain gorillas.

Habitat Preservation The most effective way to preserve biodiversity is to protect whole ecosystems. Preserving whole habitats saves not only endangered species, but also other species that depend on them.

Beginning in 1872 with Yellowstone National Park, the world's first national park, many countries have set aside wildlife habitats as parks and refuges. In addition, private organizations have purchased millions of hectares of endangered habitats throughout the world. Today, there are about 7,000 nature parks, preserves, and refuges in the world.

To be most effective, reserves must have the characteristics of diverse ecosystems. For example, they must be large enough to support the populations that live there. The reserves must contain a variety of niches. And of course, it is still necessary to keep the air, land, and water clean, remove exotic species, and control poaching.

Figure 19 Preserving whole habitats is probably the most effective way to protect biodiversity.

Section 3 Review

1. What are three factors that affect biodiversity?
2. List four possible causes of extinction.
3. Give an example of a legal approach and a scientific approach to preventing extinction.
4. Which are the most diverse ecosystems on Earth?
5. Identify three ways in which biodiversity is important.
6. **Thinking Critically** **Making Generalizations** Explain how the statement "In the web of life, all things are connected" relates to keystone species.

Science at Home

Obtain a map of your community or state. With a family member, identify any city, state, or national parks, reserves, or refuges in your area. Create a travel brochure highlighting one of these areas. Describe the habitats there. Find out whether any endangered or threatened species live in the park. Include their pictures in your brochure.

SECTION 4 The Search for New Medicines

How Are Plant Chemicals Separated?

1. Using a black marking pen, draw a dot about 2 centimeters from the end of a strip of filter paper.

2. Pour a few centimeters of water into a clear plastic cup.

3. Tape the top edge of the filter paper strip to a pencil. Place the pencil across the top of the cup so that the ink dot hangs just below the water surface. If necessary, turn the pencil to adjust the length of the paper.

4. Observe what happens to the black dot.

Think It Over

Observing How many different colors of ink did you separate from the black ink? This process models one method of separating individual chemicals contained in plants.

GUIDE FOR READING

◆ Why are many rain forest plants sources of medicines?

Reading Tip As you read, identify statements that show how biodiversity is related to human health.

Pacific yew tree

You lace up your hiking boots, and sling your collecting bag over your shoulder. It's time to head out for another day of searching in the cool, damp forest. Stepping carefully to avoid mud, you walk beneath the giant evergreens. Their needle-covered branches form a thick roof above your head. Rotting logs covered with ferns, seedlings, and brightly colored fungi line your path. You scan the ground for telltale signs of the object of your search. What are you looking for in this forest? A plant that can save lives!

This ancient forest is the temperate rain forest of the Pacific Northwest. Many of its giant trees are more than 200 years old. Like tropical rain forests, temperate rain forests are diverse ecosystems. They contain many species that are found nowhere else. Some of these species are threatened or endangered, including the bull trout, Olympic salamander, and the life-saving plant you are looking for—the Pacific yew tree.

Plants and Medicines

People have always valued plants for their ability to heal wounds and fight diseases. For example, aspirin was originally made from the bark of the willow tree. The active chemical in aspirin can now be made in a laboratory.

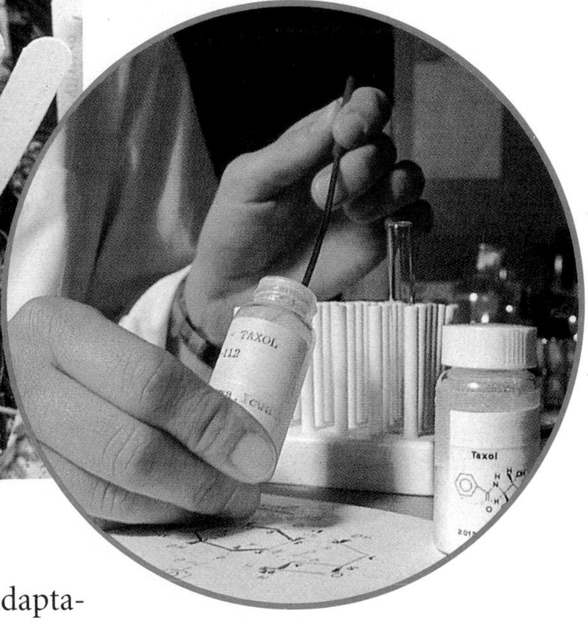

Figure 20 Scientists studied Pacific yew tree seedlings to learn more about the cancer-fighting substance taxol. In the closeup, a researcher examines taxol crystals.

The ability to fight disease is a result of the plants' adaptations to their environment. Plants in many ecosystems produce chemicals that protect them from predators, parasites, and diseases. This is particularly true in rain forests, where so many organisms make their living by eating plants. **Some chemicals that rain forest plants produce to protect their leaves and bark can also be used to fight human diseases.**

The Story of Taxol

The Pacific yew tree is very resistant to diseases and insects. Scientists began studying the bark of the Pacific yew to find out why it was so hardy. They separated chemicals from the bark. During this analysis, the scientists discovered unusual crystals in the bark. These crystals are made from a chemical called **taxol,** the substance that protects the Pacific yew tree.

Scientists next experimented with taxol in the laboratory. They discovered that taxol crystals affect cancer cells in an unusual way. Typically, cancer cells grow and divide very rapidly. This quick growth forms a mass of cells called a tumor. When cancer cells are exposed to taxol, the taxol forms structures that look like tiny cages around each cancer cell. These structures prevent the cancer cells from dividing. As a result, the cancer cannot grow and spread.

After more research, doctors were ready to test taxol on cancer patients. The taxol treatments often were able to shrink certain types of tumors. Sometimes they even stopped the cancer from spreading in the body. Taxol is now used to treat more than 12,000 cancer patients each year.

☑ *Checkpoint* *How is taxol helpful to Pacific yew trees?*

A Threatened Supply of Taxol

The demand for taxol as a cancer treatment has grown rapidly. Now many scientists have become concerned about the supply of Pacific yew trees. It takes the bark of three Pacific yew trees to produce enough pure taxol for one cancer patient's treatment. If the bark is removed from a yew tree, the tree cannot survive. And by the time researchers discovered taxol's value as a cancer-fighting drug, a large portion of the yew trees' temperate rain forests were gone.

Taxol has a very complex chemical structure. Chemists have been working for many years to reproduce this structure. In 1996, chemists successfully created taxol in the laboratory for the first time. This discovery could help protect the remaining Pacific yew trees for future generations.

Figure 21 This researcher is pressing leaves as part of a species survey in a forest reserve.

Biodiversity and Medicine

Almost half of all medicines sold today contain chemicals originally found in wild organisms. What other medicines are growing undiscovered in the forests of the world? So far, only about 2 percent of the world's known plant species have been studied for possible medical use. In 1995 the American Medical Association called for the protection of Earth's biodiversity. Their goal was to preserve the undiscovered medicines that may exist in nature. Governments, scientists, and private companies are working together to find new species all over the world. Perhaps they will find new sources of cancer-fighting drugs.

Section 4 Review

1. What adaptations of rain forest plants make them a likely source of medicines?
2. Describe the ecosystem in which Pacific yew trees are found.
3. How does taxol affect cancer cells?
4. **Thinking Critically** Inferring Suppose a group of scientists is planning an expedition to identify new species in the South American rain forest. Why might a company that manufactures medicines be interested in supporting their expedition?

Check Your Progress

CHAPTER PROJECT 3

Visit your plot regularly to make observations. Use field guides to identify the plants, animals, and other organisms you observe. Record their locations within your plot along with their common and scientific names. By now you should also be planning how to present your findings. Consider using a series of drawings, a flip chart, a computer presentation, or a video of your plot with closeups of the species you have identified. (*Hint:* Be sure to include the data you collected on abiotic factors.)

SECTION 1 Environmental Issues

Key Ideas

◆ Three types of environmental issues are resource use, population growth, and pollution.

◆ Environmental science is the study of the natural processes that occur in the environment and how humans can affect them.

◆ Making environmental decisions requires balancing different viewpoints and weighing the costs and benefits of proposals.

Key Terms

renewable resources
nonrenewable resources
pollution
development viewpoint
preservation viewpoint
conservation viewpoint

SECTION 2 Forests and Fisheries

Key Ideas

◆ Because new trees can be planted to replace those that are cut down, forests can be renewable resources.

◆ Managing fisheries involves setting fishing limits, changing fishing methods, developing aquaculture techniques, and finding new resources.

Key Terms

clear-cutting   fishery
selective cutting   aquaculture
sustainable yield

SECTION 3 Biodiversity

Key Ideas

◆ Factors that affect biodiversity include area, climate, and diversity of niches.

◆ Tropical rain forests are the most diverse ecosystems in the world. Coral reefs are the second most diverse ecosystems in the world.

◆ Diversity of organisms is a source of beauty, inspiration, and recreation. Many species and ecosystems also have economic value. Some species play critical roles in their ecosystems.

◆ Human activities that threaten biodiversity include habitat destruction, poaching, pollution, and introduction of exotic species.

◆ Three techniques for protecting biodiversity are regulating capture and trade, captive breeding, and habitat preservation.

Key Terms

biodiversity   threatened species
keystone species   habitat destruction
genes   habitat fragmentation
extinction   poaching
endangered species   captive breeding

SECTION 4 The Search for New Medicines

INTEGRATING HEALTH

Key Ideas

◆ Many plants make chemicals that protect them from predators, parasites, and disease. These chemicals may fight human diseases.

◆ The cancer-fighting drug taxol comes from Pacific yew trees, which have been affected by logging of the forests where they grow.

◆ The possible discovery of other medicines is one reason to protect biodiversity.

Key Term

taxol

USING THE INTERNET

ACTIVITY

www.science-explorer.phschool.com

Reviewing Content

For more review of key concepts, see the Interactive Student Tutorial CD-ROM.

Multiple Choice

Choose the letter of the best answer.

1. The viewpoint that humans should be able to benefit from all of Earth's resources is the
   a. conservation viewpoint.
   b. development viewpoint.
   c. scientific viewpoint.
   d. preservation viewpoint.
2. The most diverse ecosystems in the world are
   a. coral reefs.   b. deserts.
   c. grasslands.   d. tropical rain forests.
3. If all members of a species disappear from Earth, that species is
   a. extinct.   b. endangered.
   c. nonrenewable.   d. threatened.
4. The illegal removal from the wild or killing of an endangered species is called
   a. habitat destruction.
   b. poaching.
   c. pollution.
   d. captive breeding.
5. Taxol, which comes from Pacific yew trees, is a medicine that is used to fight
   a. heart disease.   b. cancer.
   c. lung disease.   d. diabetes.

True or False

If the statement is true, write true. If it is false, change the underlined word or words to make the statement true.

6. The three main types of environmental issues today are resource use, pollution, and <u>population growth</u>.
7. Forests and fisheries are examples of <u>nonrenewable</u> resources.
8. A <u>sustainable yield</u> is a number of trees that can be regularly harvested without affecting the health of the forest.
9. A species that influences the survival of many other species in an ecosystem is called a(n) <u>endangered</u> species.
10. The most effective way to protect biodiversity is through habitat <u>fragmentation</u>.

Checking Concepts

11. Give an example of a personal or local environmental issue and an example of a national or global environmental issue.
12. How are environmental decisions made?
13. Compare the effects of clear-cutting and selective cutting on forest ecosystems.
14. Describe one way to prevent overfishing.
15. Explain how habitat destruction affects species.
16. **Writing to Learn** You are a member of the county land use commission. Hundreds of people are moving to your county every day. You must make a decision regarding how to manage a 5,000-hectare woodland area in your county. Choose one point of view: development, preservation, or conservation. Write an editorial for a newspaper explaining your position.

Thinking Visually

17. **Concept Map** Copy the biodiversity concept map below onto a sheet of paper. Complete it and add a title. (For more on concept maps, see the Skills Handbook.)

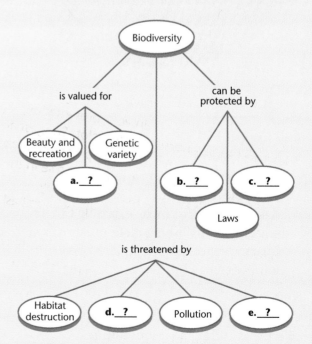

Applying Skills

One study identifies the reasons that mammal and bird species are endangered or threatened. Use the table to answer Questions 18–20.

Reason	Mammals	Birds
Poaching	31%	20%
Habitat loss	32%	60%
Exotic species	17%	12%
Other causes	20%	8%

18. **Graphing** Make a bar graph comparing the reasons that mammals and birds are endangered and threatened. Show percents for each animal group on the vertical axis and reasons on the horizontal axis.

19. **Interpreting Data** What is the major reason that mammals become endangered or threatened? What mainly endangers or threatens birds?

20. **Developing Hypotheses** Suggest explanations for the differences between the data for mammals and birds.

Thinking Critically

21. **Relating Cause and Effect** Explain how human population growth affects other species on Earth.

22. **Making Generalizations** Describe how an exotic species can threaten other species in an ecosystem.

23. **Predicting** How could the extinction of a species today affect your life 20 years from now?

24. **Relating Cause and Effect** Explain why many human medicines are made from chemicals that come from plants.

25. **Making Judgments** Suppose you were given $1 million toward saving an endangered turtle species. You could use the money to start a captive breeding program for the turtles. Or you could use the money to purchase and protect part of the turtle's habitat. How would you spend the money? Explain your answer.

Performance Assessment

CHAPTER PROJECT 3 Wrap Up

Present Your Project In your presentation, describe the biodiversity in your plot. Suggest an explanation for any patterns you observed. Make sure each person in your group has a role in the presentation. Before the presentation day, brainstorm questions your classmates might ask. Then prepare answers for them.

Reflect and Record In your journal, write what you learned from observing a single location. Which of your findings were surprising? What was the hardest part of this project? What would you do differently if you did this project again?

Getting Involved

In Your Community Use references from your library, or environmental organizations, to discover what threatened and endangered species live in your state. With your classmates, develop a brochure featuring pictures and facts about these species. With your teacher's permission, distribute your brochure at stores or libraries in your area.

Land and Soil Resources

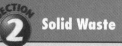

PROJECT 4

What's in a Package?

The next time you're in the supermarket, take a look at all the different kinds of packages. There are glass bottles, plastic bottles, metal cans, cardboard boxes, plastic bags, paper wrappers, and more! Different kinds of packages are used for different kinds of products.

Many of these packages are opened and then thrown away. But where is "away"? In this chapter, you will read about what happens to wastes after they are discarded. While you study the chapter, you will be analyzing the anatomy of a package.

Your Goal To analyze and display information about a product package.

Your display must

◆ Include a cutaway portion of the package with the different materials labeled.
◆ Identify the purpose of each part of the package.
◆ Describe what happens to each part of the package after it is thrown away in your community.

Get Started Obtain a product package to study. Empty the package and clean it out.

Check Your Progress You'll be working on this project as you study this chapter. To keep your project on track, look for Check Your Progress boxes at the following points.

Section 1 Review, page 119: Cut the package open and identify the materials from which it is made.

Section 3 Review, page 134: Investigate what happens to the materials that make up the package.

Wrap Up At the end of the chapter (page 137), you will assemble your product display and present it to your class.

A bulldozer climbs a giant pile of trash at a landfill site. Waste disposal is a growing environmental concern.

SECTION 1 Conserving Land and Soil

DISCOVER ··· ACTIVITY····

How Does Mining Affect the Land?

1. You will be given a pan filled with sand and soil representing a mining site. There are at least 10 deposits of "ore" (sunflower seeds) buried in your mining site.

2. Your goal is to locate and remove the ore from your site. You may use a pencil, a pair of tweezers, and a spoon as mining tools.

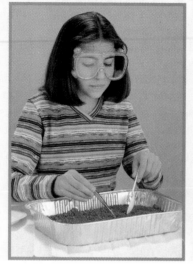

3. After you have extracted the chunks of ore, break them open to remove the "minerals" inside. **CAUTION:** Do not eat the sunflower seeds.

4. Observe your mining site and the surrounding area after your mining operations are finished.

Think It Over
Predicting How did mining change the land at your mining site? Predict whether it would be easy or difficult to restore the land to its original state. Explain.

GUIDE FOR READING

◆ How do people use land?

◆ What kinds of problems occur when soil is not properly managed?

Reading Tip Before you read, use the section headings to make an outline about land and soil conservation. Leave space in the outline to take notes.

Less than a quarter of Earth's surface is dry land. Except for a small amount formed when volcanoes erupt, new land cannot be created. All the people on Earth must share this limited amount of land to produce their food, build shelter, and obtain other resources. Land is a precious resource. As the American author Mark Twain once said about land, "They don't make it anymore."

Types of Land Use

People use land in many ways. **Three uses that change the land are agriculture, development, and mining.** Examples of these land uses are shown in Figure 1.

Agriculture Land is the source of most food. Crops such as wheat, rice, and potatoes require large areas of fertile land. But less than a third of Earth's land can be farmed. The rest is too dry, too wet, too salty, or too mountainous. To provide food for the growing population, new farmland must be created by clearing forests, draining wetlands, and irrigating deserts. When people make these changes, organisms that depended on the natural ecosystem must find new homes.

Many crops are grown to feed livestock such as hogs, chicken, and cattle. Other land serves as pasture or rangeland for grazing animals.

Development People settled the first villages in areas that had good soil and were near a source of fresh water. As population grew, these settlements became towns and cities. People built more houses and paved roads. The construction of buildings, roads, bridges, dams, and other structures is called **development.**

In the United States, about a million hectares of farmland (an area half the size of New Jersey) are developed each year. Development not only reduces the amount of farmland, but can also destroy wildlife habitats.

Mining Mining is the removal of nonrenewable resources such as iron, copper, and coal from the land. Resources just below the surface are strip mined. Strip mining involves removing a strip of land to obtain the minerals and then replacing the strip. Strip mines expose the soil. It can then be blown or washed away more easily. Strip-mined areas may remain barren for years before the soil becomes rich enough to support the growth of plants again.

For resources located deep underground, it is necessary to dig a tunnel, or shaft. The minerals are carried up through the shafts. This process is called underground mining.

✓ *Checkpoint* *Why isn't all land suitable for farming?*

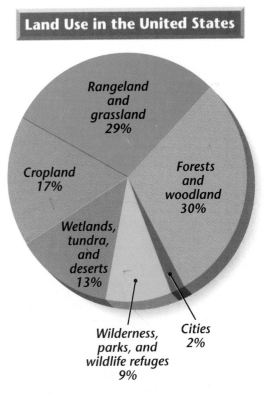

Land Use in the United States

Rangeland and grassland 29%

Forests and woodland 30%

Cropland 17%

Wetlands, tundra, and deserts 13%

Wilderness, parks, and wildlife refuges 9%

Cities 2%

Figure 1 Land in the United States is used in many ways. *Classifying Which of these land uses change the natural ecosystems of the land?*

Figure 2 Three major uses of land are agriculture, development, and mining.

Protecting the Soil

INTEGRATING EARTH SCIENCE Do you think of soil only as something that has to be washed off your hands or swept off the floor? Then you may not realize how much you depend on soil! Soil is a complex system made up of living and nonliving things. It contains the minerals and nutrients that plants need to grow. Soil also absorbs, stores, and filters water. Bacteria, fungi, and other organisms that live in soil break down the wastes and remains of living things. These decomposers recycle the chemical substances that are necessary for life.

Figure 3 shows the structure of fertile soil. Notice that it is composed of several layers. The very top layer of dead leaves and grass is called **litter.** The next layer, **topsoil,** is a mixture of rock fragments, nutrients, water, air, and decaying animal and plant matter. The water and nutrients are absorbed by the many plant roots located in this layer. Below the topsoil is the **subsoil.** The subsoil also contains rock fragments, water, and air, but has less animal and plant matter than the topsoil.

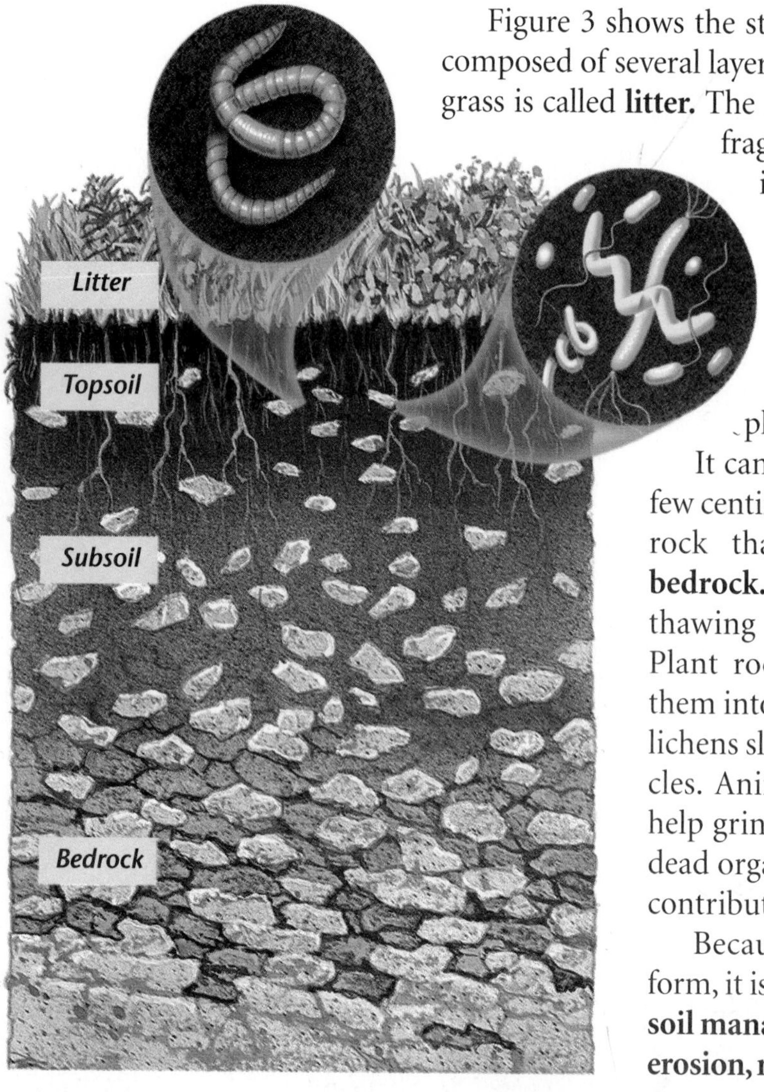

It can take hundreds of years to form just a few centimeters of new soil. All soil begins as the rock that makes up Earth's crust, called **bedrock.** Natural processes such as freezing and thawing gradually break apart the bedrock. Plant roots wedge between rocks and break them into smaller pieces. Chemicals released by lichens slowly break the rock into smaller particles. Animals such as earthworms and moles help grind rocks into even smaller particles. As dead organisms break down, their remains also contribute to the mixture.

Because rich topsoil takes a long time to form, it is important to protect Earth's soil. **Poor soil management can result in three problems: erosion, nutrient depletion, and desertification.**

Figure 3 Soil consists of several layers. *Applying Concepts In which layer are most plant roots located? What do the roots absorb there?*

Erosion The process by which water, wind, or ice moves particles of rocks or soil is called **erosion.** Normally, plant roots hold soil in place. But when soil is exposed to wind and water, erosion occurs more rapidly. Many uses of land, including logging, mining, and farming, expose the soil and can cause erosion. Some farming methods that help reduce erosion are described in *Exploring Soil Conservation.*

Nutrient Depletion Plants make their own food through photosynthesis. But plants also require a variety of nutrients from the soil. Just as your body needs iron, zinc, and calcium to grow and function properly, plants need nitrogen, potassium, phosphorus, and other nutrients. Decomposers supply these nutrients to the soil as they break down the remains of dead organisms.

Sometimes, a farmer plants the same crops in a field year after year. As a result, the plants use more nutrients than the decomposers can replace. The soil becomes less fertile, a situation that is called **nutrient depletion.**

One way to prevent nutrient depletion is to periodically leave fields **fallow,** or unplanted with crops. A second way to prevent nutrient depletion is to leave the unused parts of crops, such as cornstalks and watermelon vines, in the fields rather than

EXPLORING *Soil Conservation*

These farming practices can help reduce soil erosion.

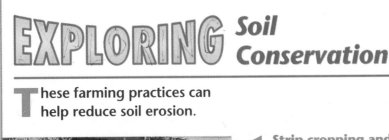

◀ Strip cropping and contour plowing
Farmers alternate strips of tall crops, such as corn, with short crops, such as squash. The short crops prevent soil from washing out of the tall crop rows, which are less protected. Crops are planted in curving rows that follow the slope, or contour, of the land. Contour plowing can reduce soil erosion as much as 50 percent on gently sloping land.

▲ Windbreaks
Rows of trees are planted along the edges of fields. These windbreaks block the wind and also trap eroding soil. Using fruit or nut trees as windbreaks provides an extra benefit for the farmer and wildlife.

Conservation plowing ▼
Rather than plowing fields and leaving them bare, farmers use machines that break up only the subsoil. This method leaves the dead stalks and weeds from the previous year's crop in the ground to hold the topsoil in place.

Terracing ▶
Steep hillsides are built up into a series of flat "terraces." The ridges of soil at the edges of the terraces slow down runoff and catch eroding soil.

clearing them away. The stalks and vines decompose in the fields, adding nutrients to the soil.

Another method of preventing nutrient depletion is crop rotation. In **crop rotation,** a farmer plants different crops in a field each year. Different types of plants absorb different amounts of nutrients from the soil. Some crops, such as corn and cotton, absorb large amounts of nutrients. The next year, the farmer plants crops that use fewer soil nutrients, such as oats, barley, or rye. The year after that, the farmer sows legumes such as alfalfa or beans to restore the nutrient supply. Another benefit of crop rotation is that it limits the growth of pest populations from year to year.

✓ *Checkpoint* *What causes nutrient depletion?*

Desertification Plants cannot grow without the moisture and nutrients in fertile soil. The advance of desertlike conditions into areas that previously were fertile is called **desertification.** In the past 50 years, desertification has occurred on about five billion hectares of land.

One cause of desertification is climate. During periods of drought, crops fail. Without plant cover, the exposed soil easily blows away. Overgrazing of grasslands by cattle and sheep also exposes the soil. Cutting down trees for firewood can also cause desertification.

Desertification is a very serious problem. People cannot grow crops and graze livestock where desertification has occurred. People may face famine and starvation as a result. In central Africa, where desertification is severe, millions of rural people are moving to the cities because they can no longer support themselves on the land.

Figure 4 Large areas of the world are at risk of desertification. One cause is overgrazing. Without grass to hold the soil in place, the Senegal plain is becoming a barren desert. *Interpreting Maps In which biome are most of the areas at risk of desertification located? (Hint: Refer to Chapter 2.)*

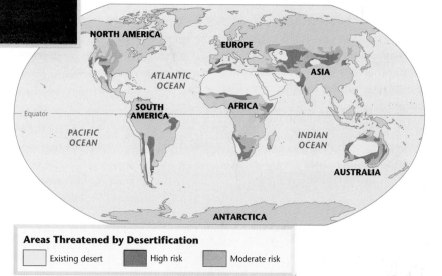

Areas Threatened by Desertification

Existing desert | High risk | Moderate risk

Figure 5 It's hard to believe that cows now graze on the same hillside that used to be an open mine. Thanks to land reclamation practices, many mining areas are being restored for other uses.

Restoring the Land

Fortunately, it is often possible to restore land damaged by erosion or mining. The process of restoring an area of land to a more natural, productive state is called **land reclamation.** In addition to restoring lands for agriculture, land reclamation can restore habitats for wildlife. Many different types of land reclamation projects are currently underway all over the world. But it is generally more difficult and expensive to restore damaged land and soil than it is to protect them in the first place.

Figure 5 shows an example of land reclamation. When the mining operation in the first scene was completed, the mine operators smoothed out the sides of the mining cuts. Then they carefully replaced the subsoil and topsoil that had been removed before mining. Finally, they planted grass. The former mine is now agricultural land.

Section 1 Review

1. List three ways that people use land.
2. What are three problems that can occur when topsoil is not properly managed?
3. Describe the effects of strip mining on the land.
4. Why is it important to protect topsoil?
5. Describe two methods for reducing soil erosion.
6. **Thinking Critically** **Relating Cause and Effect** How may human activities be related to desertification?

Check Your Progress

CHAPTER PROJECT 4

Cut your package open so that you can observe its construction. Create a data table identifying each part of the package, the material it is made of, and its purpose. What properties of these materials make them desirable as packaging? (*Hint:* Packaging benefits include protecting a product from breakage, preventing spoilage, making it more attractive, or making it easier to use. Can you think of other benefits of the materials in your package?)

Skills Lab

Save That Soil

In this lab, you'll decide how to control variables as you investigate the way rainfall causes soil erosion.

Problem

How are different types of land surfaces affected by rainfall?

Materials

newspaper	2 unbreakable pans
2 blocks	sod
loose soil	"rainmaker"
water	

Procedure

1. Cover a table with newspaper. Obtain two pans. Insert a block under one end of each pan to raise the two ends to the same height.
2. Read over the rest of the lab. Write a hypothesis that you will test. Pay careful attention to the variables you must control.
3. Place loose soil in the raised end of one pan. Place a small square of sod (soil with grass growing in it) in the raised end of the second pan. One variable is the amount of soil in each pan. Find a way to make the two amounts of soil the same. Record your procedures.
4. Create a "rainmaker" that controls the amount of water and the way it falls on the two soil samples. Then use your rainmaker to test the effect of the same amount of "rain" on the two kinds of soil. Record the results.
5. Review your experiment and your results. Do you see any procedure you wish to change? If so, get your teacher's permission to try the lab again with your revised procedures.

Analyze and Conclude

1. What effects did the "rainwater" produce on each type of soil you tested?
2. This experiment models soil erosion. What can you conclude about actual soil erosion caused by rain? How could a farmer use the information gained from this experiment to conserve topsoil?
3. **Think About It** Why was it essential for you to control the amounts of soil and "rainfall" in the two pans?

Design an Experiment

How does soil erosion caused by a gentle, steady rain compare with that caused by a heavy downpour? Design an experiment to find out. Be sure to control the way you imitate the two types of rain. Obtain your teacher's permission before conducting this experiment.

DISCOVER ··· ACTIVITY

What's in the Trash?

Your teacher will give you a trash bag. The items in the bag represent the most common categories of household waste in the United States.

1. Before you open the bag, predict what the two most common categories are.

2. Put on some plastic gloves. Open the bag and sort the trash items into categories based on what they are made of.

3. Count the number of trash items in each category. Construct a bar graph showing the number of pieces of trash in each category.

Think It Over
Interpreting Data Based on your graph, what are the two most common types of household waste? Was your prediction correct?

How much trash does your family throw away in a year? If it's your job to take the trash out, you might say that it's a large amount. But the amount of trash produced in the United States may be even greater than you think. Consider these facts:

◆ The average person produces about 2 kilograms of trash daily.

◆ Every hour, people throw away 2.5 million plastic bottles.

◆ Every two weeks, people throw away enough glass bottles and jars to fill the World Trade Center towers in New York City.

◆ Every year, people throw away enough white paper to build a wall 4 meters high that stretches from coast to coast.

◆ Every year, people throw away 1.6 billion pens, 2.9 million tons of paper towels, and 220 million automobile tires.

You can see why people call the United States a "throw-away society"! Disposable products can be cheap and convenient. But they have created a big problem—what to do with all the trash.

GUIDE FOR READING

◆ What can be done with solid waste?

◆ What are the four major types of waste that can be recycled?

◆ What are the "three R's"?

Reading Tip Before you read, preview *Exploring a Landfill* on page 122. Make a list of any unfamiliar words in the diagram. Look for the meanings of these words as you read.

The Problem of Waste Disposal

In their daily activities, people generate many types of waste, including used paper, empty packages, and food scraps. The waste materials produced in homes, businesses, schools, and other places in a community are called **municipal solid waste.** Other sources of solid waste include construction debris and certain agricultural and industrial wastes. **Three methods of handling solid waste are to bury it, to burn it, or to recycle it.** Each method has advantages and disadvantages.

EXPLORING *a Landfill*

A well-designed sanitary landfill contains the waste and prevents it from polluting the surrounding land and water.

Leachate treatment
The collected leachate is pumped into holding tanks and treated with chemicals. Any leftover solids are collected and hauled to a safe disposal site.

Gas recovery
Bacteria break down wastes in a landfill, producing methane and carbon dioxide. These gases could build up pressure in the landfill and cause an explosion. To avoid that, vent pipes collect the gases and release them. The gases are sometimes burned off in a flare.

Solid waste layers
Compacting the waste reduces its volume and keeps the landfill from settling. Each layer of compacted waste is covered with a layer of clean soil or plastic.

Monitoring wells
Testing wells surround the landfill. The wells are monitored to detect any wastes polluting the groundwater.

Leachate collection
Water moving through the landfill dissolves substances from the waste material, forming leachate, which collects at the bottom.

Liners
Layers of clay and plastic line the bottom and sides of the landfill. The liners keep liquids from leaking into the soil.

Landfills Until fairly recently, people usually disposed of waste in open holes in the ground. But these open dumps were dangerous and unsightly. Rainwater falling on the wastes dissolved chemicals from the waste, forming a polluted liquid called **leachate.** Leachate could run off into streams and lakes, or trickle down into the groundwater below the dump.

In 1976, the government banned open dumps. Now much solid waste is buried in landfills that are constructed to hold the wastes more safely. A **sanitary landfill** holds municipal solid waste, construction debris, and some types of agricultural and industrial waste. *Exploring a Landfill* shows the parts of a well-designed sanitary landfill. Once a landfill is full, it is covered with a clay cap to keep rainwater from entering the waste.

However, even well-designed landfills still pose a risk of polluting groundwater. And while capped landfills can be reused in certain ways, including as parks and sites for sports arenas, they cannot be used for other needs, such as housing or agriculture.

Incineration The burning of solid waste is called **incineration** (in sin ur AY shun). Incineration has some advantages over the use of landfills. The burning facilities, or incinerators, do not take up as much space. They do not pose a risk of polluting groundwater. The heat produced by burning solid waste can be used to generate electricity. These "waste-to-energy" plants supply electricity to many homes in the United States.

Unfortunately, incinerators do have drawbacks. Even the best incinerators release some pollution into the air. And although incinerators reduce the volume of waste by as much as 90 percent, some waste still remains. This waste needs to be disposed of somewhere. Finally, incinerators are much more expensive to build than sanitary landfills. Many communities cannot afford to replace an existing landfill with an incinerator.

✓ *Checkpoint* *What is a waste-to-energy plant?*

Graphing

What happens to trash? Use the data in the table below to construct a circle graph of methods of municipal solid waste disposal in the United States. Give your circle graph a title. (For help making a circle graph, see the Skills Handbook.)

Method of Disposal	Percentage of Waste
Landfills	56%
Recycling	27%
Incineration	17%

Figure 6 This waste-to-energy plant generates electricity while disposing of municipal solid waste.

Figure 7 Metal and glass are two frequently recycled materials.
A. Crumpled aluminum cans ride up a conveyor belt in a recycling center. **B.** A giant mound of crushed glass awaits recycling.
Predicting *Without recycling, what might eventually happen to the supply of aluminum?*

Recycling

INTEGRATING TECHNOLOGY The process of reclaiming raw materials and reusing them is called **recycling.** Recycling reduces the volume of solid waste. Recycling enables people to use the materials in wastes again, rather than discarding those materials. As you know, matter in ecosystems is naturally recycled through the water cycle, carbon cycle, and other processes. A substance that can be broken down and recycled by bacteria and other decomposers is **biodegradable** (by oh dih GRAY duh bul).

Unfortunately, many of the products people use today are not biodegradable. Plastic containers, metal cans, rubber tires, and glass jars are examples of products that do not naturally decompose. Instead, people have developed techniques to recycle the raw materials in these products.

A wide range of materials, including motor oil, tires, and batteries, can be recycled. **Most recycling focuses on four major categories of products: metal, glass, paper, and plastic.**

Metal In your classroom, you are surrounded by metal objects that can be recycled. Your desk, scissors, staples, and paper clips are probably made of steel. Another very common metal, aluminum, is used to make soda cans, house siding, window screens, and many other products.

Metals such as iron and aluminum can be melted and reused. Recycling metal saves money and causes less pollution than making new metal. With recycling, no ore needs to be mined, transported to factories, or processed. In addition, recycling metals helps conserve these nonrenewable resources.

Glass Glass is made from sand, soda ash, and limestone mixed together and heated. Glass is one of the easiest products to recycle because glass pieces can be melted down over and over to make new glass containers. Recycled glass is also used to make fiberglass, bricks, tiles, and the reflective paints on road signs.

Recycling glass is less expensive than making glass from raw materials. Because the recycled pieces melt at a lower temperature than the raw materials, less energy is required. Recycling glass also reduces the environmental damage caused by mining for sand, soda, and limestone.

☑ *Checkpoint* *Why is it easy to recycle glass?*

Paper It takes about 17 trees to make one metric ton of paper. Paper mills turn wood into a thick liquid called pulp. Pulp is spread out and dried to produce paper. Pulp can also be made from used paper such as old newspapers. The newspapers must be washed to remove the inks and dyes. The paper is then mixed with more water and other chemicals to form pulp.

Most paper products can only be recycled a few times. Recycled paper is not as smooth or strong as paper made from wood pulp. Each time paper is recycled to make pulp, the new paper is rougher, weaker, and darker.

Plastic When oil is refined to make gasoline and other petroleum products, solid materials called **resins** are left over. Resins can be heated, stretched, and molded into plastic products. Have you ever noticed a symbol like the ones in Figure 8 on a plastic container? This number indicates what type of plastic a container is made of. For example, plastics labeled with a *1* or a *2* are made from plastics that are often recycled. Common products made from these types of plastic include milk jugs, detergent containers, and soda bottles.

It's in the Numbers

Sort pieces of plastic prod- **ACTIVITY** ucts into groups according to their recycling numbers. Compare and contrast the pieces in each group with each other and with those in other groups.

Classifying Write a sentence describing characteristics of the plastics in each group.

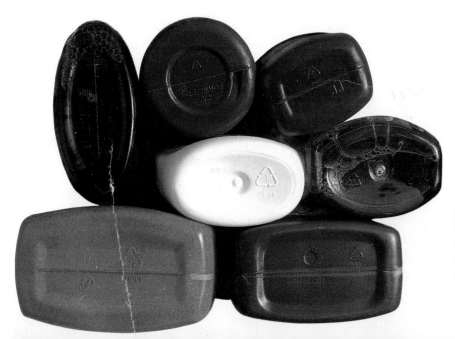

Figure 8 These plastic bottles have numbers indicating the type of plastic they are made of. Plastics must be sorted by type before they are recycled.

Energy Savings in Manufacturing	
Material	**Using Recycled Rather Than Raw Materials**
Aluminum	90–97 %
Glass	4–32 %
Paper	23–74 %

Figure 9 As this table shows, some kinds of recycling save more energy than others. *Interpreting Data Which type of recycling saves the most energy?*

When they are recycled, they take on very different forms: as fiber filling for sleeping bags and jackets, carpeting, park benches, shower stalls, floor tiles, trash cans, or dock pilings!

Is Recycling Worthwhile? In addition to conserving resources, recycling saves energy. Figure 9 shows how much energy can be saved by using recycled materials instead of raw materials.

Recycling is not a complete answer to the solid waste problem. Many materials can be recycled. But scientists have not found good ways to recycle other materials, such as plastic-coated paper and plastic foam. There are not enough uses for some recycled products, such as low-quality recycled newspaper. Finally, all recycling processes require energy and create some pollution.

✓ *Checkpoint* **What are some advantages and disadvantages of recycling?**

Solid Waste Management

In the past few decades, people have become more aware of the solid waste problem. Many communities now collect recyclable items along with other household trash. Many supermarkets recycle paper and plastic grocery bags. Many states charge deposit fees on certain glass, metal, and plastic containers. When people return the containers to be recycled, they get their deposit back. This return system encourages people to recycle the containers instead of throwing them away. You might have seen recycling bins for metal and glass drink containers in movie theaters, parks, and other public areas. Consumers can also choose to buy products made with recyclable materials.

Figure 10 These students are sorting materials for a school recycling project.

As a result of these efforts, the amount of municipal solid waste that is recycled has increased. But most municipal solid waste in the United States still goes to landfills. Yet as usable land becomes more scarce, it will be even more critical to reduce the need for landfills.

What Can You Do?

The good news is that there are lots of ways individuals can help control the solid waste problem. **These are sometimes called the "three R's"—reduce, reuse, and recycle.** *Reduce* refers to creating less waste in the first place. For example, you can use a cloth shopping bag rather than a disposable paper or plastic bag. *Reuse* refers to finding another use for an object rather than discarding it. For example, you could refill plastic drink bottles with drinking water or juice you mix instead of buying drinks in new bottles. And *recycle* refers to reclaiming raw materials to create new products. You can make sure you recycle at home, and you can also encourage others to recycle. How about starting a used paper collection and recycling program at your school?

One way to significantly reduce the amount of solid waste your family produces is to start a compost pile. **Composting** is the process of helping the natural decomposition processes break down many forms of waste. Compost piles can be used to recycle yard trash such as grass clippings and raked leaves, and food waste such as fruit and vegetable scraps, eggshells, and coffee grounds. Some farms use compost piles to naturally recycle animal manure. Compost is an excellent natural fertilizer for plants.

Figure 11 Many communities have neighborhood compost bins like this one in Brooklyn, in New York City. *Applying Concepts How does composting help solve the solid waste problem?*

Section 2 Review

1. What happens to most solid waste in the United States?
2. List the four major categories of solid waste that are most often recycled.
3. Name and define the "three R's" of solid waste management.
4. Give an example of a way in which communities can reduce their solid waste.
5. What is composting?
6. **Thinking Critically** Comparing and Contrasting Compare the recycling of metal and paper. How are they similar? How are they different?

Science at Home

For one week, have your family collect their household trash in large bags. Do not include food waste. At the end of the week, hold a trash weigh-in. Multiply the total amount by 52 to show how much trash your family produces in a year. Together, can you suggest any ways to reduce your family trash load?

Waste, Away!

About two thirds of municipal solid waste ends up in a landfill. In this lab, you'll investigate how landfills are constructed to be most effective and safe.

Problem

How do different kinds of landfills work?

Skills Focus

making models, drawing conclusions

Materials

measuring cup	metric ruler	soil
small pebbles	cheesecloth	scissors
plastic wrap	water	newspaper
5 rubber bands	red food coloring	tweezers

heavy-duty plastic bag
12 small sponge cubes
3 transparent, wide-mouthed jars

Procedure

1. Read over the rest of the procedure to preview the three landfill systems you will model. Determine which parts of the models represent potential drinking water, rainfall, solid waste, leachate, and the landfill systems themselves. Write a prediction about the way each system will respond to the test you'll conduct in Part 2.

Part 1 Modeling Three Landfill Systems

2. Obtain 3 identical jars. Label them *System 1, System 2,* and *System 3.* Pour clean, clear water into each jar to a depth of 5 cm.

3. Add equal amounts of small pebbles to each jar. The pebbles should be just below the surface of the water.

4. For System 1, cover the pebble and water mixture with 2.5 cm of soil.

5. For System 2, suspend a piece of cheesecloth in the jar about 5 cm above the water line, as shown in the photograph. Hold the cheesecloth in place with a rubber band around the outside mouth of the jar. Gently pour a handful of small pebbles into the cheesecloth.

6. For System 3, suspend a plastic bag in the jar about 5 cm above the water line. Hold the bag in place with a rubber band around the outside mouth of the jar. Gently pour a handful of small pebbles into the plastic bag.

7. Observe the water and pebbles at the bottom of each system. Record your observations.

Part 2 Testing the Systems

8. Soak 12 identical sponge cubes in water tinted with red food coloring. Use tweezers to place four soaked sponge cubes onto the top surface in each jar.

9. Cover the sponge cubes in Systems 2 and 3 with a thin layer of soil. Leave the sponge cubes in System 1 uncovered.

10. Make a labeled drawing of each system. Explain what each part of the model represents.

11. Pour 150 mL of water over each system. Then cover each jar with plastic wrap, and hold the wrap in place with a rubber band. Let the systems stand overnight.

12. Observe each landfill system. Note especially any changes in the color or clarity of the "groundwater." Record your observations.

Analyze and Conclude

1. Explain how your models represent three common types of landfills: a well-designed, or sanitary, landfill; a landfill with a poor design; and an open dump. Compare the way the three systems work.

2. Which part of the model represented the leachate? How well did each landfill system protect the groundwater from the leachate?

3. Do you think a community's water supply is protected when waste is placed in landfills that are not immediately above groundwater sources? Explain.

4. **Apply** Based on your results, which landfill system is safest for the environment? Explain your answer.

Design an Experiment

Solid waste can be compacted (crushed into smaller pieces) and have liquid removed before it is placed in a landfill. Does preparing the waste in this way make it safer for the environment? Write a hypothesis, then use the ideas and procedures from this lab to test your hypothesis. Obtain your teacher's permission before trying your experiment.

SECTION 3 Hazardous Wastes

DISCOVER ⸱⸱ ACTIVITY

What's Hazardous?

1. Your teacher will give you labels from some common hazardous household products.

2. Read the information on each label. Identify the word or words that tell why the product is hazardous.

Think It Over

Forming Operational Definitions Based on your observations of the product labels, write a definition of the term *hazardous*.

GUIDE FOR READING

◆ What are the categories of hazardous wastes?

◆ How can hazardous wastes affect human health?

◆ What techniques can be used to manage hazardous wastes?

Reading Tip Before you read, rewrite the headings in each section as *how, what,* or *where* questions. As you read, look for answers to these questions.

In the early 1950s, the city of Niagara Falls, New York, bought an area of land around an old canal. The canal had been filled with chemical wastes from nearby industries. On top of this land, the city built a new neighborhood and elementary school. The neighborhood was named Love Canal.

Then strange things began to happen. Children playing in muddy fields developed skin rashes. Wooden fence posts rotted and turned black. People reported colored liquid seeping into their basements. Babies were born with birth defects. Adults developed epilepsy, liver disease, and nerve disorders. The neighborhood was finally declared a federal emergency disaster area. More than two hundred families were moved away.

What was behind these strange events at Love Canal? Building the neighborhood had caused the clay cover on the old canal dump site to crack. Rainwater seeped into the buried wastes through the cracks. The construction caused chemicals to leak from the underground storage containers. Over time, water mixed with the chemicals to form a dangerous leachate. This leachate polluted the soil and the groundwater and leaked into people's basements.

The Love Canal problem was the first time a federal emergency was declared in an area because of hazardous wastes. It helped people realize that certain chemicals can remain dangerous in soil and water for many years. As a result, new laws were passed to find and clean up other dangerous waste sites.

Figure 12 This school in Love Canal was abandoned because of pollution.

Types of Hazardous Wastes

Many people picture hazardous wastes as bubbling chemicals, thick fumes, or oozing slime. But even some harmless-looking, common materials such as window cleaner, radio batteries, and nail polish remover can become hazardous wastes. **Hazardous waste** is any material that can be harmful to human health or the environment if it is not properly disposed of.

Hazardous wastes are created during the manufacture of many household products. Many more are produced as a result of agriculture, industry, military operations, and research at hospitals and scientific laboratories.

Hazardous wastes are classified into four categories: toxic, explosive, flammable, and corrosive. Figure 13 gives some examples of these types of waste. **Toxic** wastes, or poisonous wastes, are wastes that can damage the health of humans and other organisms. **Explosive** wastes are wastes that react very quickly when exposed to air or water, or that explode when they are dropped. Explosive wastes are also called reactive wastes. **Flammable** wastes catch fire easily and can begin burning at fairly low temperatures. **Corrosive** wastes are wastes that dissolve or eat through many materials.

Other wastes that require special disposal are radioactive wastes. **Radioactive** wastes are wastes that contain unstable atoms. These unstable atoms give off radiation that can cause cancer and other diseases. There are two types of radioactive wastes: high-level waste and low-level waste. An example of high-level radioactive waste is the used fuel from nuclear reactors. Low-level radioactive wastes are produced when radioactive minerals such as uranium are mined. They are also produced at some medical and scientific research sites. Radioactive waste can remain dangerous for thousands of years.

Figure 13 Vehicles transporting dangerous materials must use signs like these to alert people of the potential dangers of their loads.

Category: Radioactive
Examples: Uranium, plutonium

Category: Flammable
Example: Kerosene

Category: Toxic
Examples: Chlorine, PCBs, mercury

Category: Explosive
Example: Nitroglycerin

Category: Corrosive
Examples: Hydrochloric acid, sodium hydroxide

Health Effects of Hazardous Wastes

INTEGRATING HEALTH A person can be exposed to hazardous wastes by breathing, eating or drinking, or touching them. Many factors determine the effects of a hazardous substance on a person. One factor is how harmful the substance is. Another factor is how much of the substance a person is exposed to. A third factor is how long the exposure lasts. A person may be exposed for a short time, such as a child accidentally drinking antifreeze. Or a person may be exposed for many years, as were the residents of Love Canal. Finally, a person's age, weight, and health all influence how a substance affects that person.

In general, short-term exposure to hazardous wastes may cause irritation or more severe health problems. These health problems can include breathing difficulties, internal bleeding, paralysis, coma, and even death. **Long-term exposure to hazardous wastes may cause diseases, such as cancer, and may damage body organs, including the brain, liver, kidneys, and lungs.** These effects may eventually be life threatening.

Disposal of Hazardous Wastes

It is hard to safely dispose of hazardous wastes. Burying them can pollute the soil or groundwater. Releasing wastes into lakes or rivers can pollute surface water. Burning hazardous wastes can pollute the air. You can see the problem!

Methods of hazardous waste disposal include burial in land-fills, incineration, and breakdown by living organisms. Another method involves storing liquid wastes in deep rock layers.

Figure 14 Hazardous wastes can pollute the soil, water, and air. The chemical drums on the left were illegally dumped in a field. Below, environmental scientists in protective gear test the contents of an old storage tank.

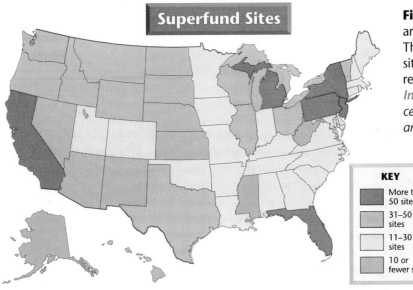

Superfund Sites

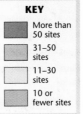

KEY

- More than 50 sites
- 31–50 sites
- 11–30 sites
- 10 or fewer sites

Figures 15 Superfund sites are located all over the country. This map shows the number of sites in different states in a recent year.
Inferring Why do you think certain states have many sites and others have few?

Hazardous wastes are most often disposed of in carefully designed landfills. These landfills are lined with clay and plastic to keep chemicals from leaking into the soil and groundwater. A clay and plastic cover prevents rainwater from seeping into the wastes.

Scientists have developed some other methods for disposing of hazardous waste. For example, wastes can be incinerated at very high temperatures. Incineration often breaks down harmful compounds into less harmful ones. Bacteria, algae, and fungi can break down some hazardous chemicals. Another disposal method involves pumping liquid wastes into a layer of sandstone or limestone thousands of meters underground. The wastes spread throughout this soft rock layer. But the wastes cannot move through the thicker, harder layers of rock above and below. A few types of hazardous waste, such as motor oil and lead-acid car batteries, can even be recycled.

Scientists have not been able to develop completely safe methods for disposing of radioactive waste. Some techniques used today are mixing the waste with concrete or sealing it in abandoned mine shafts. High-level radioactive wastes are currently stored in vaults dug hundreds of meters underground or in concrete and steel containers above ground. But these storage areas are temporary. Scientists are still searching for methods that will provide safe, permanent disposal of radioactive wastes.

✓ *Checkpoint* **How are most hazardous wastes disposed of?**

Locating Disposal Sites

Besides deciding how to dispose of hazardous wastes, communities must also decide *where* to dispose of them. Should there be fewer, larger disposal sites, or many smaller ones? Each answer has costs and benefits.

Social Studies
CONNECTION

In 1980, Congress passed a law creating a hazardous waste site cleanup program called the Superfund. The law determines who should pay for the cleanup. This can include any businesses or people that have ever owned or operated the property, or have ever contributed wastes to it.

In Your Journal

Most industries did not purposely pollute the air, land, and water. In the past, people were largely unaware that some industrial wastes were hazardous, and that these substances could have serious effects many years later. Should these industries still be responsible for paying for the cleanup? If not, where should this money come from? Write a paragraph explaining your opinion.

Figure 16 The scent of these citronella candles naturally repels insects and creates less hazardous waste than bug spray.

Most people don't want to live or work near a hazardous waste disposal facility. In general, people would prefer to have a single large facility located in an area where few people live. A central facility could treat many different types of hazardous wastes. It would be easier to monitor than many scattered sites. However, transporting hazardous wastes to a distant central facility can be costly, difficult, and dangerous. The greater travel distances increase the risk of an accident that could release hazardous wastes into the environment. It may be safer, cheaper, and easier to transport wastes to small local facilities instead.

Reducing Hazardous Waste

The best way to manage hazardous wastes is to produce less of them in the first place. Industries are eager to develop safe alternatives to harmful chemicals. For example, some brands of furniture polishes are now made from lemon oil and beeswax instead of petroleum oils. Many products such as air fresheners, plastic dishes and countertops, carpets, and curtains used to be made with the chemical formaldehyde, which gradually leaked out of these products into the air. Companies have developed alternatives to formaldehyde to use in their products. For instance, the next time you are in a supermarket or hardware store, look for air fresheners that are labeled "formaldehyde-free."

At home, you can find substitutes for some hazardous household chemicals. For example, instead of using insect spray, use harmless materials that naturally repel insects, such as the citronella candles shown in Figure 16. Many household cleaners also now come in biodegradable forms.

Section 3 Review

1. List and define the four categories of hazardous waste.
2. Describe the short-term and long-term effects of hazardous substances on human health.
3. Describe one method used to dispose of hazardous wastes.
4. What was the significance of the events at Love Canal?
5. Explain why radioactive wastes are particularly difficult to manage.
6. **Thinking Critically   Making Judgments** Do you think hazardous wastes should be treated and disposed of at one central facility or at many small local facilities? Give reasons for your answer.

Check Your Progress   CHAPTER PROJECT 4
By now you should be investigating what happens to the different materials in your package when it is thrown away. You will need to find out what types of waste your community recycles, and how it handles other solid waste. (*Hint:* The town engineer or Department of Public Works may be a good source of this information. Be sure to check with your teacher before contacting anyone.)

SECTION 1 How Land is Used

Key Ideas

◆ Land is a nonrenewable resource. All the people on Earth must share this limited resource for agriculture, development, mining, and other uses.

◆ Soil is a complex system that takes a very long time to form.

◆ Poor soil management can cause erosion, nutrient depletion, and desertification.

◆ There are many farming techniques to help prevent erosion and nutrient depletion.

Key Terms

development	nutrient depletion
litter	fallow
topsoil	crop rotation
subsoil	desertification
bedrock	land reclamation
erosion	

SECTION 2 Solid Waste

Key Ideas

◆ Wastes are produced in the making and using of many products.

◆ Three ways of handling solid waste are to bury it, to burn it, or to recycle it.

◆ Most municipal solid waste in the United States is buried in sanitary landfills.

◆ The main types of municipal solid waste that are recycled are metal, glass, paper, and plastic.

◆ Recycling can conserve both resources and energy. However, there are not always many ways to use recycled materials.

◆ One way to help solve the solid waste problem is to practice the "three R's"— reduce, reuse, and recycle.

Key Terms

municipal solid waste	recycling
leachate	biodegradable
sanitary landfill	resins
incineration	composting

SECTION 3 Hazardous Wastes

INTEGRATING CHEMISTRY

Key Ideas

◆ Hazardous wastes are materials that can threaten human health and safety or can be harmful to the environment if they are not properly disposed of.

◆ Hazardous wastes include toxic, explosive, flammable, and corrosive wastes. Radioactive wastes also require special disposal.

◆ How a person is affected by a hazardous substance depends on several factors, including the amount of the substance, the length of time the person is exposed, and how the substance enters the person's body.

◆ It is very difficult to find safe ways to dispose of hazardous wastes and good places to store them. A good way to manage hazardous wastes is to produce less of them.

Key Terms

hazardous waste	flammable
toxic	corrosive
explosive	radioactive

USING THE INTERNET

ACTIVITY

www.science-explorer.phschool.com

Reviewing Content

For more review of key concepts, see the Interactive Student Tutorial CD-ROM.

Multiple Choice
Choose the letter of the best answer.

1. The advance of desertlike conditions into areas that previously were fertile is called
   a. desertification.
   b. crop rotation.
   c. nutrient depletion.
   d. land reclamation.

2. Water containing dissolved chemicals from a landfill is called
   a. resin.
   b. litter.
   c. leachate.
   d. compost.

3. Solid wastes are burned in the process of
   a. incineration.
   b. composting.
   c. erosion.
   d. recycling.

4. Which of the following is a biogradable waste?
   a. a glass jar   b. a metal can
   c. an apple core   d. a plastic bag

5. Wastes that contain unstable atoms are called
   a. corrosive.   b. flammable.
   c. radioactive.   d. explosive.

True and False
If the statement is true, write true. If it is false, change the underlined word or words to make the statement true.

6. Three major types of land use are agriculture, development, and <u>mining</u>.
7. The layer of soil that contains the most animal and plant matter is the <u>subsoil</u>.
8. Fields that are left unplanted with crops are called <u>fallow</u>.
9. Most of the municipal solid waste generated in the United States is disposed of in <u>landfills</u>.
10. Liners prevent the waste in landfills from polluting the <u>air</u>.

Checking Concepts

11. List two living things and two nonliving things that are found in topsoil.
12. Choose one of the following techniques and explain how it can reduce soil erosion: contour plowing, terracing, conservation plowing, or windbreaks.
13. Give examples of two techniques for preventing nutrient depletion.
14. What does the number on a plastic container indicate?
15. Describe one way communities can encourage residents to produce less solid waste.
16. What is composting? What kinds of materials can be composted?
17. Explain how a person might be exposed to a hazardous substance that was buried underground many years ago.
18. **Writing to Learn** Write a public service announcement to inform people about household hazardous wastes. Begin with a "hook" to catch your listener's attention. Be sure to explain what makes a waste hazardous. Also give examples of household hazardous wastes, and tell people what to do with these substances.

Thinking Visually

19. **Compare/Contrast Table** On a separate sheet of paper, copy the table below about ways to dispose of municipal solid waste. Then complete it and add a title. (For more on compare/contrast tables, see the Skills Handbook.)

	Landfill	Incinerator
Cost		
Pollution		
Attractiveness		
Usefulness to Community		

Applying Skills

Use the following data on municipal solid waste in the United States to answer Questions 20–22.

Type of Waste	Percent of Total
Paper and cardboard	38%
Food wastes	10%
Yard wastes	13%
Metals	8%
Plastics	9%
Glass	6%
Other wastes	16%

20. Graphing Use the data to create a circle graph. (To review circle graphs, see the Skills Handbook.)

21. Classifying Which of the types of waste shown are recyclable? Which include wastes that can be composted?

22. Developing Hypotheses Why do you think paper makes up the largest percent of solid waste?

Thinking Critically

23. Making Judgments Suppose you go to the store to buy some juice. You can choose from juice sold in an aluminum, glass, or plastic container, all for the same price. Which would you choose? Explain your answer.

24. Applying Concepts If you owned a large farm on a hill, how would you prevent soil erosion? Explain your answer.

25. Problem Solving In strip mining, a layer of soil is removed to expose a resource, such as coal, underneath. What methods could be used to restore this damaged land?

26. Predicting Suppose that hundreds of years in the future, people dig into a landfill from around the year 2000. What types of materials might they find? What types of materials might not be present? Explain your answers.

27. Applying Concepts Why is it unsafe to bury or incinerate radioactive waste?

Performance Assessment

CHAPTER PROJECT 4 — Wrap Up

Present Your Project As you finish work on your project, share it with one or more of your classmates. Ask them for feedback on the following: Does your display clearly explain what the product package is made of? Are the benefits of the package identified? Does the display describe what happens to each material in the package? If you need to make any revisions to your display, do so now.

Reflect and Record In your project notebook, describe the most surprising information you learned during this project. What questions might you ask before purchasing a product like the one you studied?

Getting Involved

In Your Community With your teacher's permission, work with your class to hold a "Solid Waste Day." This might include a field trip to a local incinerator, recycling facility, or public works department. Your class could also invite a guest speaker, or make an exhibit for younger students on waste disposal and recycling.

CHAPTER
5
Air and Water Resources

WHAT'S AHEAD

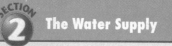

SECTION
1 Air Pollution

Discover How Does the Scent Spread?
Sharpen Your Skills Communicating
Try This How Acid Is Your Rain?
Real-World Lab How Does the Garden Grow?

SECTION
2 The Water Supply

Discover How Does the Water Change?
Try This Getting Clean
Skills Lab Concentrate on This!

Integrating Technology
SECTION
3 Finding Pollution
Solutions

Discover Can You Remove the Tea?
Sharpen Your Skills Graphing

Pollution vs. Purity

Pollution is a change to the environment that has a harmful effect on humans and other living things. Pollution can come from a single smokestack or from many different sources all over the world.

As you study this chapter, your project is to help communicate the importance of preventing pollution and protecting air or water quality.

Your Goal To create a book, game, or video that educates younger students about air or water quality.

Your product should
- present facts about the causes and effects of a form of pollution
- engage your audience while informing them about the topic
- include steps that the students can take to be part of the "pollution solution"

Get Started Survey the chapter to see what types of pollution are discussed. Begin thinking about which topic you would like to study. Discuss with your teacher what age group your product should be designed for. Decide which form your product will take.

Check Your Progress You'll be working on the project as you study this chapter. To keep your project on track, look for Check Your Progress boxes at the following points.

Section 2 Review, page 153: Gather information on your topic and organize it.

Section 3 Review, page 158: Design and create your product.

Wrap Up At the end of the chapter (page 161), you will present your product to younger students and get their feedback.

Smoke billows from a row of smokestacks at an automobile plant.

SECTION 1 Air Pollution

DISCOVER
ACTIVITY

How Does the Scent Spread?

1. Choose a place to stand so that you and your classmates are evenly spread around the room.
2. Your teacher will open a bottle of perfume in one corner of the room.
3. Raise your hand when you first smell the perfume.

Think It Over

Inferring Describe the pattern you observed as people raised their hands. How do you think the smell traveled across the room?

GUIDE FOR READING

◆ What causes photochemical smog?

◆ How is the ozone layer important?

◆ What are climate predictions based on?

Reading Tip As you read, make a list of different types of air pollution. Write a sentence about the effect of each type.

Figure 1 The air supply aboard the space station *Mir* was threatened by a collision during docking.

June 25, 1997, began as an ordinary day aboard the Russian space station *Mir*. The three crew members were busy with their usual tasks. One checked on the various scientific experiments. Another was exercising. The third cosmonaut was skillfully guiding a supply ship as it docked with *Mir*.

Suddenly, the crew members heard a frightening sound—the crumpling of collapsing metal. The space station jolted from side to side. The pressure gauges indicated an air leak! One crew member hurried to prepare the emergency evacuation vehicle. Meanwhile, the other two managed to close the airtight door between the damaged area and the rest of the space station. Fortunately, the pressure soon returned to normal. A disaster had been avoided. There was no need to abandon ship.

Closing the door preserved the most valuable resource on *Mir*—the air. Although you probably don't think about the air very often, it is just as important on Earth as it is on a space station. Air is a resource you use every minute of your life.

What's in the Air?

Though you can't see, taste, or smell it, you are surrounded by air. Air is a mixture of nitrogen, oxygen, carbon dioxide, water vapor, and other gases. Almost all living things depend on these gases to carry out their life processes.

Nitrogen, oxygen, and carbon dioxide cycle between the atmosphere and living things. These cycles ensure that the air supply on Earth will not run out. But they don't guarantee that the air will always be clean. A change to the atmosphere that has harmful effects is called **air pollution.** Substances that cause pollution are called pollutants. Pollutants can be particles, such as ash, or gases, such as chlorine. Air pollution can affect the health of humans and other living things. Pollution can even impact the climate of the whole planet.

What causes air pollution? If you're like many people, you probably picture a factory smokestack, belching thick black smoke into the sky. Until the mid-1900s, factories and power plants that burned coal produced most of the air pollution in the United States. Particles and gases that are released into the air are called **emissions.** Today, there is an even larger source of emissions that cause air pollution: motor vehicles such as cars, trucks, and airplanes. The engines of these vehicles release gases such as carbon monoxide, an invisible toxic gas.

Though most air pollution is the result of human activities, there are some natural causes as well. For example, an erupting volcano sends an enormous load of soot, ash, sulfur, and nitrogen oxide gases into the atmosphere.

☑ *Checkpoint* **What are some examples of air pollutants?**

Smog

Have you ever heard a weather forecaster talk about a "smog alert"? A smog alert is a warning about a type of air pollution called photochemical smog. **Photochemical smog** is a thick, brownish haze formed when certain gases in the air react with sunlight. When the smog level is high, it settles as a haze over a city. Smog can make people's eyes burn and irritate their throats.

The major sources of photochemical smog are the gases emitted by automobiles and trucks. Burning gasoline in a car engine releases some gases into the air. These gases include hydrocarbons (compounds containing hydrogen and carbon) and nitrogen oxides. The gases react in the sunlight and produce a form of oxygen called **ozone.** Ozone, which is toxic, is the major chemical found in smog.

 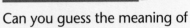
Figure 2 A haze of photochemical smog hangs over this city's skyline. *Interpreting Photographs What is the source of the smog?*

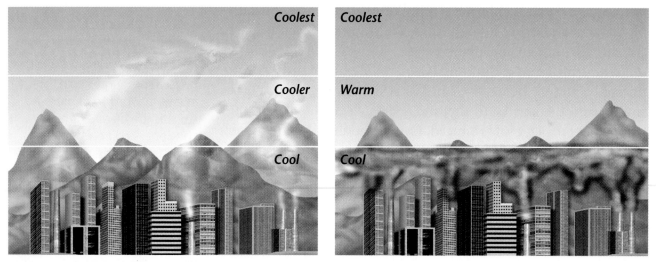

Coolest

Coolest

Cooler

Warm

Cool

Cool

Figure 3 Normally, pollutants rise high in the air and blow away (left). But during a temperature inversion, a layer of warm air traps pollutants close to the ground (right).

Temperature Inversion Pollutants usually blow away from the place where they are produced. Normally, air close to the ground is heated by Earth's surface. As the air warms, it rises into the cooler air above it. The pollutants are carried higher into the atmosphere where they blow away. But certain weather conditions cause a condition known as a temperature inversion. During a **temperature inversion,** a layer of warm air prevents the rising air from escaping. The polluted air is trapped and held close to Earth's surface. The smog becomes more concentrated and dangerous.

Health Effects of Smog The effects of smog can be more

INTEGRATING
HEALTH

serious than itchy, watery eyes and a scratchy throat. The ozone in smog can cause lung problems and harm the body's defenses against infection. When smog levels reach a certain point, a city issues a smog alert. During a smog alert, you should avoid exercising outdoors. People who have asthma or other conditions that affect their breathing should be particularly careful.

☑ *Checkpoint* *What happens during a temperature inversion?*

Acid Rain

Another type of air pollution is caused by power plants and factories that burn coal and oil. These fuels produce nitrogen oxides and sulfur oxides when they are burned. These gases react with water vapor in the air, forming nitric acid and sulfuric acid. The acids return to Earth's surface dissolved in precipitation. Precipitation that is more acidic than normal is called **acid rain.** Acid rain can be in the form of snow, sleet, or fog as well as rain.

As you can imagine, acid falling from the sky has some negative effects. When acid rain falls into a pond or lake, it changes the conditions there. Many fish, and particularly their eggs, cannot survive in more acidic water. Acid rain that falls on the ground can damage plants by affecting the nutrient levels in the soil. Whole forests have been destroyed by acid rain. Fortunately, some of the effects of acid rain are reversible. Badly damaged lakes have been restored by adding substances such as lime that neutralize the acid.

Acid rain doesn't just affect living things. The acid reacts with stone and metal in buildings and statues. Automobiles rust more quickly in areas with acid rain. These effects are not reversible.

Indoor Air Pollution

You might think that you could avoid air pollution by staying inside. But in fact, the air inside buildings can be polluted, too. Many substances can cause indoor air pollution. Some, such as dust, pet hair, and air fresheners, bother only those people who are allergic to them. Other pollutants have more widespread effects. Asbestos, a building material common in older buildings, can cause lung disease. Products such as oil-based paints, glues, and cleaning supplies may give off toxic fumes. Read the label whenever you use any of these products. You may need to open a window or use the chemical outdoors.

If you have been near someone smoking a cigarette, you know how the smell stays in your clothes and hair even after you leave the room. The smoke reached your lungs every time you inhaled near the smoking person. Research has shown that cigarette smoke can damage the lungs and heart. Now smoking is banned in many places such as restaurants, airports, and stadiums.

How Acid Is Your Rain?

In this activity you will test whether rain in your area is more or less acidic than lemon juice (citric acid).

1. Collect some rainwater in a clean plastic cup.

2. Indoors, dip a piece of pH paper into the cup. Compare the color of the paper to the chart on the package to find the pH. (The lower the pH of a substance, the more acidic it is.)

3. Pour a little lemon juice into a plastic cup. Repeat Step 2 with the lemon juice.

Measuring What is the pH of the rainwater? How does it compare to the pH of the lemon juice?

Figure 4 Air inside buildings can be polluted, too. *Observing How many sources of pollution can you spot in this room?*

Figure 5 Installing a carbon monoxide detector in a home can save lives. Because carbon monoxide has no color or odor, it cannot be detected by sight or smell.

Carbon Monoxide One particularly dangerous type of indoor air pollution is carbon monoxide. Carbon monoxide is a colorless, odorless gas that forms when wood, coal, oil, or gas are incompletely burned. When carbon monoxide builds up in an enclosed space such as a basement, apartment, or house, it can be deadly. Because carbon monoxide cannot be detected by sight or smell, its victims have no warning that the level is dangerously high. Any home heated by wood, coal, oil, or gas should have a carbon monoxide detector. The detector sounds a warning alarm when the gas is present.

Radon Another type of pollution that is difficult to detect is radon. Radon is a colorless, odorless gas that is radioactive. It is formed naturally by certain types of rocks underground. Radon can enter homes through cracks in basement walls or floors. Research indicates that breathing radon gas over many years may cause lung cancer and other health problems. But the level of radon necessary to cause these effects is unknown. To be safe, many homeowners have installed ventilation systems to prevent radon from building up in their homes.

✓ *Checkpoint* *Why is it important to install carbon monoxide detectors in homes?*

The Ozone Layer

If you have ever had a sunburn, you have experienced the painful effects of the sun's ultraviolet radiation. But did you know that such burns would be even worse without the protection of the ozone layer? The **ozone layer** is a layer of the upper atmosphere about 30 kilometers above Earth's surface. Actually, the concentration of ozone in this layer is very low—only a few parts per million.

Communicating

Write a radio public service announcement to inform people about either carbon monoxide or radon. Think about how the announcement could catch your listeners' attention. Describe the source and effects of the pollutant. Suggest how listeners can protect themselves.

Yet even the small amount of ozone in the ozone layer protects people from the effects of too much ultraviolet radiation. These effects include sunburn, eye diseases, and skin cancer.

Since you read earlier that ozone is a pollutant, the fact that ozone can be helpful may sound confusing. The difference between ozone as a pollutant and ozone as a helpful gas is its location. Ozone close to Earth's surface in the form of smog is harmful. Higher in the atmosphere, where people cannot breathe it, ozone protects us.

The Source of Ozone   Ozone is constantly being made and destroyed. When sunlight strikes an ozone molecule, the energy of the ultraviolet radiation is partly absorbed. This energy causes the molecule to break apart into an oxygen molecule and an oxygen atom, as shown in Figure 6. The oxygen atom soon collides with another oxygen molecule. They react to form a new ozone molecule. Each time this cycle occurs, some ultraviolet energy is absorbed. That energy does not reach Earth's surface.

The Ozone Hole   In the late 1970s, scientists observed that the amount of ozone in the ozone layer seemed to be decreasing. What was to blame for this loss of ozone?

One problem was a group of gases containing chlorine and fluorine, called **chlorofluorocarbons,** or "CFCs." CFCs had been used instead of smelly, toxic ammonia in refrigerators and air conditioners. CFCs were also used in fire extinguishers and aerosol spray cans. Then scientists discovered that CFCs react with ozone molecules. The CFCs block the cycle that absorbs ultraviolet radiation. In 1990, many nations signed an agreement to ban the use of almost all CFCs by the year 2000. Unfortunately, the CFC molecules are very stable. They have remained in the atmosphere for a long time. But scientists predict that if the ban is maintained, the ozone layer will gradually recover.

Concentration

Levels of pollutants are often written as concentrations. A concentration is a ratio that compares the amount of one substance to a certain amount of another substance. For example, suppose that the concentration of ozone in a part of the atmosphere is 3 parts per million. This means that there are 3 molecules of ozone in 1,000,000 molecules of air. This ratio can also be written in three other ways:

3 : 1,000,000 or

3 to 1,000,000 or

$$\frac{3}{1,000,000}$$

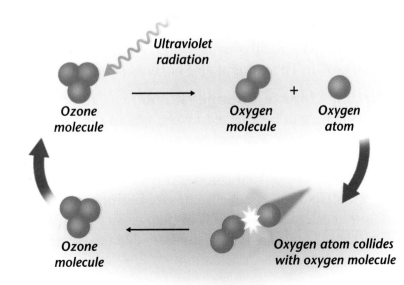

Ultraviolet radiation

Ozone molecule → Oxygen molecule + Oxygen atom

Ozone molecule ← Oxygen atom collides with oxygen molecule

Figure 6 When ultraviolet radiation from the sun strikes an ozone molecule, some energy is absorbed by the ozone molecule. This energy causes the ozone molecule to split into an oxygen molecule and a free oxygen atom. *Interpreting Diagrams* What happens when the free oxygen atom collides with an oxygen molecule?

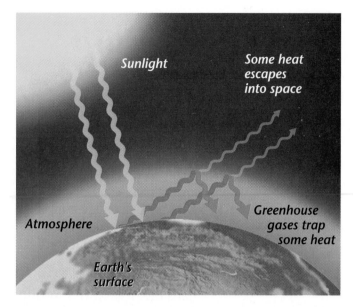

Figure 7 When energy in the form of sunlight strikes Earth's surface, it changes to heat. Certain gases in the atmosphere trap some of the heat, preventing it from escaping back into space. This trapping of heat is known as the greenhouse effect.
Applying Concepts What gases in the atmosphere trap heat near Earth's surface?

Global Climate Change

Some changes to the atmosphere affect the climate of the whole planet. To understand why, you need to know more about the atmosphere.

The Greenhouse Effect Think about the INTEGRATING EARTH SCIENCE sun shining through a window on a cool day. The window lets light enter the room. The light strikes objects in the room and is converted to heat. But the closed windows trap the warm air inside, so the room becomes warmer.

In the atmosphere, water vapor, carbon dioxide, and certain other gases act like windows. These gases allow sunlight to reach Earth's surface, but they prevent the heat from escaping back into space. The trapping of heat near Earth's surface is called the **greenhouse effect**. Without the greenhouse effect, Earth would be much colder—about 33°C colder on average.

Global Warming Since the 1800s, coal and oil have been the main sources of energy in most of the world. As you have read, burning these substances produces carbon dioxide. During this time, the amount of carbon dioxide in the atmosphere has increased from 280 parts per million to 350 parts per million. This amount is increasing more quickly every year.

Does increasing carbon dioxide cause the greenhouse effect to become stronger? One theory, called **global warming,** predicts that the increase in carbon dioxide will cause the average temperature to continue to rise. Scientists have estimated that the increase in the next century could be as much as 3 to 8 Celsius degrees. Although that may not sound like a big change, it could have a huge impact. Parts of the Antarctic ice cap would melt, raising the level of the oceans. The temperature change would affect climate patterns all over the world. This would affect where crops are grown. There might also be more severe storms.

Predicting Climate Change It is difficult to predict how Earth's climate will be affected by changes in the atmosphere. The systems that create climate are very complex. Scientists have studied these systems for less than a century, a very short time to learn about processes that can occur over thousands of years. **Most scientists base their climate predictions on computer models that calculate the effects of changes in the atmosphere.** As *Exploring Climate Predictions* shows, making these predictions requires many types of information.

EXPLORING Climate Predictions

Many factors affect the complex systems that create climate. Good predictions must consider as many of these factors as possible.

Emissions
Power plants, factories, and vehicles produce gases that increase the greenhouse effect. Will there be more emissions in the future, or will ways be found to reduce them? Will people change their habits to use less energy?

Oceans
Carbon dioxide cycles between the atmosphere and the oceans, where it dissolves in the water. If ocean temperatures change, will more or less carbon dioxide be dissolved?

Forests
Plants take in carbon dioxide during photosynthesis. As forests are cut down, more carbon dioxide stays in the atmosphere. But if Earth continues to get warmer, more plants may grow. They will remove more carbon dioxide from the air. Which effect will be greater?

Clouds
If Earth gets warmer, more water will evaporate. More water vapor in the air would increase the greenhouse effect. But there would also be more clouds, which reflect sunlight away from Earth's surface. Will the result be warmer or cooler air?

Section 1 Review

1. How does photochemical smog form?
2. How does the ozone layer protect people?
3. How do scientists make climate predictions?
4. Give three examples of indoor air pollutants and list their sources.
5. **Thinking Critically** Predicting One possible result of global warming is that melting ice could cause ocean levels to rise. What effects might this have?

Science at Home

What particles are in your air? With a family member, set up two particle collectors. Smear petroleum jelly on the inside of two clean, empty glass jars. Place one inside your home and the other outside. Make sure both jars are in locations where they will not be disturbed. Predict what you will find if you leave the jars in place for a few days. Compare the particles in each jar. How similar are they? Can you identify any of the particles?

Outside Wed. 11/5

HOW DOES THE GARDEN GROW?

Air pollution doesn't just affect the air. It can affect rain, which then falls on the land, harming organisms living there. In this lab you will investigate how pollutants affect plants.

Problem

How do pollutants affect seed growth?

Skills Focus

controlling variables, measuring, interpreting data

Materials

2 plastic petri dishes with lids wax pencil
potting soil acid solution
20 radish seeds oil solution
detergent solution salt solution
day-old tap water masking tape
metric ruler

Procedure

1. Read all the steps of the lab. Choose a pollutant to investigate. Write a hypothesis about the effect of this pollutant. Then copy the data table into your notebook. Write the name of the pollutant in the data table.
2. Write your initials on the lids of the petri dishes. Then write "Control" on one lid. Label the other lid with the name of your pollutant.
3. Fill each dish with potting soil. Do not pack down the soil.

4. Pour 10 mL of water into the control dish. Pour 10 mL of the pollutant solution into the pollutant dish. Lightly scatter 10 seeds on the soil surface in each dish.
5. Cover each dish with the correct lid. Tape the lids firmly in place. Store the dishes where they will receive light and will not be moved. Wash your hands with soap.
6. Once a day for the next five days, observe the seeds (do not open the lids). Record your observations in the data table. Use a metric ruler to measure the length of any roots or shoots that develop. If you do not observe any change, record that observation.

Analyze and Conclude

1. How many seeds germinated each day in the control dish? In the pollutant dish? How many seeds total germinated in each dish?
2. Did the seedlings grown under the two conditions differ? If so, how?
3. Did your results support your hypothesis? Explain.
4. **Apply** Predict what the effect would be if the pollutant you investigated reached a vegetable garden or farm.

Design an Experiment

Do you think the pollutant you studied has the same effect on all types of plants? Write a hypothesis, and design an experiment to test it. With your teacher's approval, carry out your plan.

DATA TABLE				
Date	Number of Seeds That Germinated		Condition of Seedlings	
	Control	Pollutant	Control	Pollutant

SECTION
2 The Water Supply

DISCOVER •• ACTIVITY

How Does the Water Change?

1. Shine a flashlight through a clear plastic cup of water.
2. Add 6 drops of milk to the water and stir.
3. Shine the flashlight through the cup again. Note any differences.

Think It Over
Observing Where in the cup of water is the milk located? Could you easily separate the milk from the water?

Most of Earth's surface is covered by some form of water. Oceans cover nearly three fourths of Earth's surface. Around the poles are vast sheets of ice. From space you cannot even see many parts of Earth because they are hidden behind clouds of tiny water droplets. It's hard to believe that water is a scarce resource in much of the world.

A Limited Supply

How can water be scarce when there is so much of it on Earth's surface? **The reason is that most of the water on Earth—about 97 percent—is salt water. Salt water cannot be used for drinking or watering crops.** People need fresh water for these purposes.

In addition, about three quarters of the fresh water on Earth is in the form of ice. This water is not available for people to use. Finally, the supplies of liquid fresh water that do exist are not always close to where people live. For example, many cities in the southwestern United States draw their drinking water from rivers hundreds of kilometers away. About half the people in the United States use **groundwater,** water stored in layers of soil and rock beneath Earth's surface.

GUIDE FOR READING

◆ Why is fresh water a limited resource?

◆ What are the major sources of water pollution?

Reading Tip As you read, identify sentences that support this statement: *Water is a scarce resource that must be protected.*

Figure 8 A view from space shows the abundance of water on Earth.

Figure 9 People obtain and store water in many ways. At left, a tower holds the water supply of a community in Bucks County, Pennsylvania. At right, women in the Yucatán in Mexico draw water from a well.

Getting Clean

In this activity you will see how Earth's fresh water is purified in the water cycle.

1. Pour 15 mL of water into a plastic cup.

2. Add a few drops of food coloring and half a teaspoon of sugar. Stir until the sugar is dissolved.

3. Put the cup in the sunlight in a place where it will not be disturbed.

4. Check on the cup twice a day until all the water has evaporated. Observe what remains in the cup.

Making Models What do the sugar and food coloring represent? What happens to the water in this activity?

Renewing the Supply Fortunately, Earth's supply of fresh water is renewable. Water continually moves between the atmosphere and Earth's surface in the water cycle. Water evaporates from oceans, lakes, and rivers, becoming water vapor in the atmosphere. As the water evaporates, any dissolved substances are left behind. The pure water vapor condenses into tiny droplets which form clouds. When the droplets become large and heavy enough, they fall as precipitation.

Water Shortages Water shortages occur when people use water in an area faster than the water cycle can replace it. This is more likely to happen during a **drought,** a period when less rain than normal falls in an area. During a drought, people have to limit their water use. All unnecessary water uses may be banned. If the drought is severe, crops may die from lack of water.

Due to growing populations, many places in the world never receive enough rain to meet their water needs. They must obtain water from distant sources or by other means. For example, the desert nation of Saudi Arabia obtains more than half its fresh water by removing salt from ocean water.

☑ *Checkpoint* *What is a drought?*

Water Pollution

When fresh water supplies are scarce, pollution can be devastating. Any change to water that has a harmful effect on people or other living things is called **water pollution.** Some pollutants, such as iron and copper, make water unpleasant to drink or wash in. Other pollutants, such as mercury or benzene, can cause sickness or even death.

Most pollution is the result of human activities. Many activities—including agriculture, industry, construction, and mining—produce wastes that can end up in water.

If you did the Discover activity, you saw that a few drops of milk quickly spread throughout a cup of water. You could not tell where the milk first entered the water. In the same way, pollutants dissolve and move throughout a body of water. This is how pollution can affect areas far from its source.

Sewage The water and human wastes that are washed down sinks, toilets, and showers are called **sewage.** If sewage is not treated to kill disease-causing organisms, they quickly multiply. If untreated sewage mixes with water used for drinking or swimming, these organisms can make people very ill.

Even treated sewage can pollute. The wastes in the sewage can feed bacteria living in the water. As the bacteria multiply, they use up the oxygen in the water. Other organisms that need the oxygen, such as fish, cannot survive.

Agricultural Wastes Animal wastes and farm chemicals are also sources of pollution. Two examples are fertilizers and pesticides. **Fertilizers** are chemicals that provide nutrients to help crops grow better. But rain can wash fertilizers into ponds, where they cause algae to grow quickly. The algae soon cover the pond, blocking light from reaching plants in the pond. **Pesticides** are chemicals that kill crop-destroying organisms such as beetles or worms. However, pesticides can also harm other animals such as birds that feed in the sprayed fields.

Because agricultural chemicals are usually spread over a large, open area, it is hard to keep them from polluting nearby water. Even low levels of chemicals in the water can build up to harmful concentrations as they move through the food chain.

Figure 10 This plane is spraying crops with pesticides. *Relating Cause and Effect How might pesticides sprayed on a field affect fish that live in a nearby pond?*

Figure 11 Industrial processes and mining are two sources of chemical pollutants. At left, a chemical plant spills wastes into a river. At right, dissolved copper from a mine turns a stream turquoise.

Industry and Mining Chemical plants, paper and textile mills, and factories that use metals produce wastes that can pollute water. Mining sites are another source of metal wastes. Chemicals and metals can harm the living things in the polluted bodies of water. In addition, humans that drink the water or feed on these organisms are exposed to the pollution.

Sediments When water runs off bare ground, it turns a muddy brown color. This color is due to particles of rock, silt, and sand called **sediments.** Water that flows through places where the ground is disturbed, such as building sites and mines, can pick up large loads of sediments.

As sediments wash into bodies of water, the particles cover up the food sources, nesting sites, and eggs of organisms. By blocking sunlight in the water, the sediments prevent algae and plants from growing. This affects other organisms that rely on the algae and plants for food.

Oil and Gasoline One of the most dramatic forms of water pollution is an oil spill. You may have seen news reports showing beaches covered with tarry black oil, or of volunteers cleaning globs of oil from the feathers of birds. It can take many years for an area to recover from such a spill.

Another pollution problem is caused by oil and gasoline that leak out of underground storage tanks. Think of how many gas stations there are in your area. Each one has storage tanks below the street level to hold the gasoline. In the past, these tanks were often made of steel. Over time, they rusted and developed small holes. As the gasoline leaked out, it soaked into the soil and polluted the groundwater. The pollution was sometimes carried very far away from the leaking tank. Controlling this type of pollution has been difficult because the sources are hidden underground.

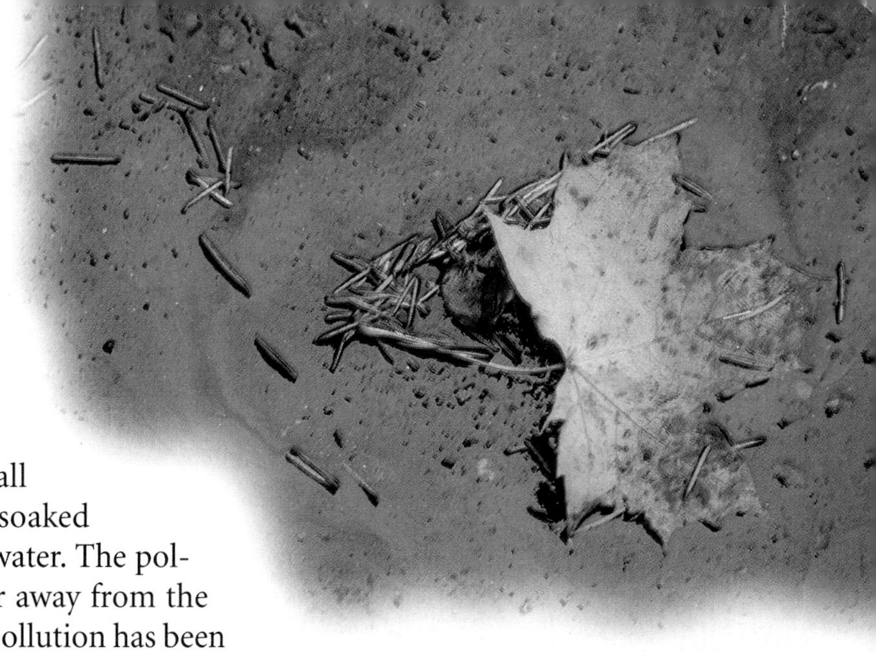

Heat Pollution is usually thought of as a substance added to water. But the addition of heat can also have a negative effect on a body of water. Sometimes factories or power plants release water that has been used to cool machinery. This heated water changes the temperature of the stream or lake into which it is released. This temperature change can kill plants, animals, and other organisms in the body of water. If you have ever kept an aquarium, you know that fish can only survive within a small temperature range. Today most power plants have cooling towers that release steam rather than hot water. In the next section, you will read about some other methods of preventing both water and air pollution.

Figure 12 A sheen of oil swirls around a maple leaf in a puddle. *Observing* What characteristics of oil make it difficult to clean up?

Section 2 Review

1. Why isn't most of the water on Earth's surface available for people to use?
2. Name four types of human activities that can be sources of water pollution.
3. Explain why finding the source of water pollution can be difficult.
4. What is sewage? Why should sewage be treated before being released to the environment?
5. **Thinking Critically Relating Cause and Effect** In what way can heat pollute a body of water?

Check Your Progress

CHAPTER PROJECT 5

By now you should be gathering information to include in your product. Consider including the story of a historical event related to your topic in order to get your audience's interest. As you collect information, begin putting it in a logical order. Using an outline or a storyboard can help you organize your thoughts. (*Hint:* Be sure to keep your topic well focused. Air and water quality are very broad topics! Focusing your topic will help you stay on task and manage your time.)

Skills Lab

Concentrate on This!

Many pollutants have harmful effects even at very low concentrations. In this lab you will compare different concentrations of a pollutant in water.

Problem

Can you detect a pollutant in water at a very low concentration?

Materials

9 small test tubes   test tube rack
marker   food coloring
plastic dropper   water

Procedure

1. Read through the entire procedure. Write a prediction about the results you expect. Then copy the data table into your notebook.
2. Label nine test tubes 1 through 9.
3. Use a plastic dropper to add 9 drops of water to each test tube. Try to make all the drops about the same size.
4. Add 1 drop of food coloring to Test Tube 1. Record the total number of drops now in the test tube. Swirl the test tube gently to mix.
5. The concentration of food coloring in Test Tube 1 is 1 drop in 10 drops, or 1 part per 10. Record that concentration in the data table.
6. Now use the dropper to transfer 1 drop of the mixture from Test Tube 1 into Test Tube 2. Swirl Test Tube 2 to mix its contents.

7. Record the concentration in Test Tube 2. [*Hint:* The drop you just added had a concentration of 1 part per 10. When you dilute (water down) that drop to 1/10 of its strength, the new concentration is 1 part per (10 × 10).]
8. For test tubes 3 through 9, add 1 drop from the previous test tube. Record each new concentration in the data table.
9. Observe the water in each test tube. Record your observation. If you do not observe any color in a test tube, write "colorless."

Analyze and Conclude

1. How does the appearance of the water change from test tubes 1 through 9?
2. Food coloring consists of molecules of dye. Are there any food coloring molecules remaining in Test Tube 9? Explain.
3. What is meant by a "part" in this lab?
4. Which test tube has a concentration of 1 part per million? Which test tube has a concentration of 1 part per billion?
5. **Think About It** Why is parts per million a useful form of measurement when discussing environmental issues?

Design an Experiment

Which is more concentrated, a mixture with 5 parts per million, or 10 parts per 10 million? How different do the two mixtures appear? Use the ideas from this lab to design a plan to find out. Check your plan with your teacher.

		DATA TABLE		
Test Tube	Total Drops Added	Concentration of Food Coloring	Color	
1				
2				

SECTION 3 Finding Pollution Solutions

DISCOVER

Can You Remove the Tea?

1. Pour some cooled herbal tea into a plastic cup. Observe the color of the tea.

2. Place a paper filter in a funnel. Fill it halfway with crushed charcoal. Put the funnel on top of another plastic cup.

3. Slowly pour the tea through the funnel so that it collects in the cup.

4. Observe the filtered liquid.

Think It Over

Developing Hypotheses Suggest an explanation for any changes you observe in the tea after pouring it through the funnel.

O nly 50 years ago, the French Broad River in North Carolina was a river to avoid. Its color changed daily, depending on the dyes being used at a nearby blanket factory. Towns dumped raw sewage into the water. Sediment and fertilizers from farms washed into the river with every rainfall. The few fish were unhealthy and covered with sores. Mostly, the river was a home for wastes and bacteria—certainly not a place for people to play. Today, however, the river is a popular white-water rafting spot. Fish thrive in the clear water. The blanket factory and other plants have stopped releasing wastes into the river. The towns have sewage treatment plants. And ponds catch the runoff from farm fields before it reaches the river.

This story shows that pollution problems can be solved. People near the river still carry out the same activities—farming, building houses, and even making blankets. But by changing the way they do these things, they have stopped the pollution.

In the United States, laws regulate the amount of certain pollutants that can be released into the environment. Laws also state how these pollutants must be handled. The major federal laws that control air and water quality are the Clean Air Act and the Clean Water Act. These laws also encourage the development of new technology to reduce pollution.

GUIDE FOR READING

◆ How can technology help control air pollution?

◆ How can technology help control water pollution?

Reading Tip Before you read, use the section headings to make an outline. Leave space in your outline to take notes.

Rafters enjoying the clean water of the French Broad River

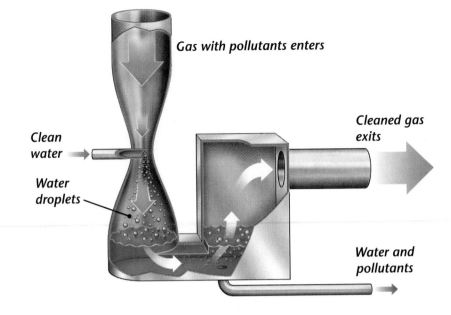

Figure 13 A smokestack scrubber removes pollutants such as sulfur dioxide from emissions. The dirty gas passes through a tube containing water droplets. Pollutants dissolve in the water, leaving clean gas to flow out of the chamber. The dirty water still must be properly disposed of.

Gas with pollutants enters

Cleaned gas exits

Clean water

Water droplets

Water and pollutants

Reducing Air Pollution

The Clean Air Act has resulted in the development of technology to control air pollution. **The major role of technology in controlling air pollution is to reduce emissions.**

Emissions Controls At one time, industries dealt with emissions by building tall smokestacks. The stacks released wastes high in the air, where they could blow away. But the pollutants still ended up somewhere. Now factories place devices in the stacks to treat emissions. For example, a filter can trap particles of ash. The device in Figure 13, called a **scrubber,** removes pollutants from emissions using a stream of water droplets. Pollutants dissolve in the water and fall into a container.

Cars and trucks now contain pollution control devices. For example, a **catalytic converter** is a device that reduces emissions of carbon monoxide, hydrocarbons, and nitrogen oxides. This device causes the gases to react, forming less harmful carbon dioxide and water.

Laws can ensure that people use pollution-control devices. For example, in many states, cars must pass emissions tests. The state of California's strict emissions-testing laws have helped reduce the smog problem in Los Angeles in recent years.

CFC Substitutes When a pollutant is banned by law, people must find substitutes for the banned substance. For example, in 1990 many nations agreed to stop using most CFCs by the year 2000. Scientists immediately began to search for substitutes for these chemicals. Refrigerators and air conditioners were redesigned to use less harmful substances. Researchers developed new ways to make products such as plastic foam without using CFCs. As a result of this work, fewer CFCs should enter the atmosphere after 2000 than in the past.

Graphing

The table below shows a scientist's predictions of chlorine levels in the atmosphere with and without the ban on CFCs. Make a line graph of the data, using two different colors. Write a short paragraph describing the results.

Year	Chlorine Level (parts per billion)	
	With Ban	Without Ban
1985	2.5	2.5
1990	3.5	4.0
1995	3.8	5.0
2000	3.6	7.5
2005	3.4	10.0

Cleaning Up the Water

Technology can also help control water pollution. **Two ways to reduce water pollution are to treat wastes so that they are less harmful, and to find substitutes for pollutants.**

Sewage Treatment   Most communities treat wastewater before returning it to the environment. A typical sewage plant handles the waste in several steps. **Primary treatment** removes solid materials from the wastewater. During primary treatment, the water passes through filters. Then it is held in tanks where heavy particles settle out. **Secondary treatment** involves using bacteria to break down wastes. Finally, the water is treated with chlorine to kill disease-causing organisms.

The town of Arcata, California, treats sewage in a creative way. Wastewater flows into ponds containing algae that begin to break down the sewage. Then the water flows into artificial marshes lined with cattails and bulrushes. These plants and the bacteria in the marsh filter and clean the water. These marshes are also habitats for many mollusks, fish, and birds. Trails for walking and biking encourage people to enjoy the marshes as well. After two months in this system, the wastewater is cleaner than the bay into which it is released!

Oil and Gasoline   Oil is a pollutant that nature can handle in small amounts. Bacteria that break down oil live in the ocean. When oil is present, the bacteria multiply quickly as they feed on it. As the oil disappears, the bacteria population dies down. But in the case of a very large spill, many organisms are affected before the balance in the ecosystem is restored.

Gasoline or oil that leaks from an underground tank is hard to clean up. If the pollution has not spread far, the soil around the tank can be removed. But pollution that reaches groundwater may be carried far away. Groundwater can be pumped to the surface, treated, and then returned underground. This can take many years.

Figure 14 A bicyclist in Arcata, California, may not even be aware that this peaceful marsh is also a sewage treatment system.
Applying Concepts What are the two major sewage treatment steps?

Figure 15 Workers struggle to clean oil from a rocky beach.

Industrial and Agricultural Chemicals Instead of releasing wastes to the environment, industries can recycle their wastes to recover useful materials. Once such programs are underway, companies often find they save money as well as reduce pollution. Others change their processes to produce less waste or less harmful waste. For example, some industries use natural fruit acids as cleaning agents rather than toxic solvents. Likewise, many farmers are finding alternatives to toxic pesticides and fertilizers for their crops.

What Can You Do?

You may not think there is much you can do to reduce air and water pollution. But in fact, some small changes in people's behavior can make a big difference.

You can help reduce air pollution by reducing certain types of energy use. Much air pollution is a result of fuels that are burned to provide electricity and transportation. Using less energy conserves fuel resources and also reduces pollution. When you take public transportation, walk, or ride a bicycle, there is one fewer car on the road. This means there are fewer emissions that contribute to smog and the greenhouse effect. In the next chapter, you will read how you can use less energy for these purposes.

It is also easy to prevent water pollution at home. Some common household water pollutants are paint and paint thinner, motor oil, and garden chemicals. You can avoid causing water pollution by never pouring these chemicals down the drain. Instead, save these materials for your community's next hazardous household waste collection day.

Figure 16 These teens are planting trees in a park in Austin, Texas. Planting trees is one way to improve air quality. Trees absorb carbon dioxide from the air and produce oxygen.

Section 3 Review

1. What role does technology usually play in controlling air pollution?
2. In what two basic ways can technology help control water pollution?
3. Describe one smokestack device that can help reduce emissions from factories.
4. Explain how small oil spills can be cleaned up naturally.
5. **Thinking Critically** **Making Generalizations** Explain how laws can play a part in reducing pollution.

Check Your Progress
CHAPTER PROJECT 5
Now you are ready to make your finished product using the information you have gathered. Keep in mind the age group of your audience when you are considering word choice, number and style of pictures, music, and other parts of your product. (*Hint:* Don't forget to include steps that members of your audience can take to be part of the solution. Make sure these suggestions are appropriate for their age.)

SECTION 1 Air Pollution

Key Ideas

- Air pollutants can be in the form of particles or gases.
- The major sources of photochemical smog are the gases emitted by motor vehicles.
- Sources of indoor air pollution include smoke, dust, pet hair, asbestos, and other substances. Two dangerous pollutants that are very difficult to detect are carbon monoxide and radon.
- Certain gases in Earth's atmosphere prevent heat from escaping back into space.
- The ozone layer protects people and other living things from the effects of too much ultraviolet radiation.
- Most scientists base their climate predictions on computer models that calculate the effects of changes in the atmosphere.

Key Terms

air pollution	acid rain
emissions	ozone layer
photochemical smog	chlorofluorocarbons
ozone	greenhouse effect
temperature inversion	global warming

SECTION 2 The Water Supply

Key Ideas

- Most of Earth's water—about 97 percent— is salt water.
- People and many other organisms require fresh water to carry out their life processes.
- Although there are some natural sources of water pollution, most pollution is the result of human activities. Agriculture, industry, construction, and mining all produce wastes that can end up in water.

Key Terms

groundwater	fertilizer
drought	pesticide
water pollution	sediments
sewage	

SECTION 3 Finding Pollution Solutions

INTEGRATING TECHNOLOGY

Key Ideas

- The major role of technology in controlling air pollution is to reduce emissions.
- Two basic ways to reduce water pollution are to treat wastes so that they are less harmful, and to find substitutes for pollutants.

Key Terms

scrubber	primary treatment
catalytic converter	secondary treatment

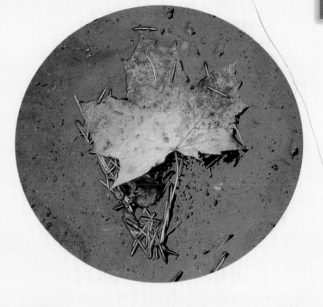

ACTIVITY

USING THE INTERNET

www.science-explorer.phschool.com

Reviewing Content

For more review of key concepts, see the Interactive Student Tutorial CD-ROM.

Multiple Choice
Choose the letter of the best answer.

1. Particles and gases released into the air are
   a. sewage.   b. emissions.
   c. scrubbers.   d. acid rain.
2. A deadly gas formed when fuels are incompletely burned is
   a. ozone.
   b. carbon monoxide.
   c. photochemical smog.
   d. CFCs.
3. Which gas is thought to be the cause of global warming?
   a. radon   b. ozone
   c. carbon dioxide d. carbon monoxide
4. The water and waste materials washed down toilets and sinks are called
   a. pesticides.
   b. sewage.
   c. industrial chemicals.
   d. fertilizers.
5. A technology that reduces carbon monoxide emissions from vehicles is a
   a. scrubber.
   b. catalytic converter.
   c. filter.
   d. CFC substitute.

True or False
If the statement is true, write true. If it is false, change the underlined word or words to make the statement true.

6. Most photochemical smog is produced by <u>motor vehicles</u>.
7. The presence of a layer of warm air that traps pollutants close to Earth's surface is called a <u>temperature inversion</u>.
8. Ozone in the <u>lower</u> atmosphere protects people from ultraviolet radiation.
9. About 97 percent of Earth's water is <u>fresh</u> water.
10. Oil in the ocean will eventually be broken down by <u>fish</u>.

Checking Concepts

11. Describe some possible health effects of photochemical smog.
12. How does acid rain form?
13. What role do water vapor and carbon dioxide play in the greenhouse effect?
14. What is a drought? What effects could a drought have on people?
15. Explain how fertilizers from a farm might pollute a nearby river.
16. What is one way to reduce emissions from cars and trucks?
17. How can a small oil spill in the ocean be naturally cleaned up?
18. **Writing to Learn** Write a television newscast explaining how one of the following factors is related to climate predictions: clouds, forests, oceans, emissions.

Thinking Visually

19. **Concept Map** Copy the concept map below about air pollution onto a separate sheet of paper. Then complete it and add a title. (For more on concept maps, see the Skills Handbook).

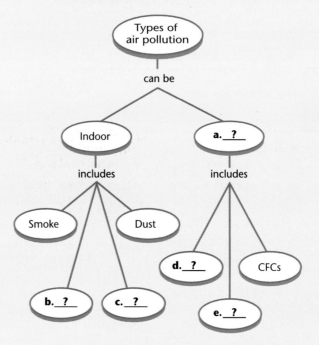

Applying Skills

Use the graph to answer Questions 20–22.

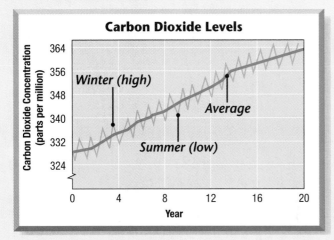

Carbon Dioxide Levels

Winter (high)

Average

Summer (low)

Carbon Dioxide Concentration (parts per million)

364
356
348
340
332
324

0   4   8   12   16   20

Year

20. Interpreting Data What was the average level of carbon dioxide in the atmosphere at the beginning of the study? What was the average level of carbon dioxide in Year 20 of the study?

21. Calculating How much did the average level of carbon dioxide increase during the study period?

22. Developing Hypotheses In each year of the study, the winter level of carbon dioxide was higher than the summer level. Suggest an explanation for this.

Thinking Critically

23. Comparing and Contrasting How are radon and carbon monoxide alike? How are they different?

24. Predicting What effect might a sudden increase in the amount of ozone in the ozone layer have?

25. Making Generalizations Would you expect the levels of photochemical smog to be worse in cities or in rural areas? Explain your answer.

Performance Assessment

CHAPTER PROJECT 5 Wrap Up

Present Your Project Share your finished project with a group of younger students. As the children view or play with the product, notice what parts they find most interesting. After they are finished, ask them what they liked and didn't like about the product. What do they remember most?

Reflect and Record In your project notebook, write a short evaluation of your product. What parts of the product do you feel worked best? Which ones were most difficult? What challenges did you face in communicating information in the form you chose to work with?

Getting Involved

In Your School Conduct a school air-quality audit. With your classmates, create a plan for evaluating your school's air quality. Check your plan with your teacher before beginning. You might survey the school for possible sources of pollutants, including dangerous gases and substances that could cause allergies. You could also measure the air temperature in different areas at different times of the day. Prepare a summary of your findings.

WHAT'S AHEAD

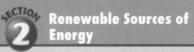

Energy Audit

The Los Angeles skyline comes alive with electric lights as the sun goes down. It takes a lot of energy to keep a city running. Energy keeps the people of Los Angeles cool, provides them with electricity, and helps them move from place to place. Energy is also needed to make the products that clothe, feed, inform, and entertain them.

How much energy does it take to keep your school running? Throughout the chapter, you will work in a group to study energy use in your school.

Your Goal To write a report on a type of energy use in your school including your suggestions for saving energy.

To complete the project, you must
- ◆ Survey the types and amount of energy used in the area
- ◆ Identify ways to conserve energy in that area
- ◆ Prepare a written report summarizing your observations and proposing your suggestions

Get Started With your group, select an area of the school to study, such as a classroom, the cafeteria, or the school grounds. You could also consider the school's heating or cooling system or transportation to and from school. Brainstorm a list of the ways in which you think energy is used in and around your school.

Check Your Progress You'll be working on this project as you study this chapter. To keep your project on track, look for Check Your Progress boxes at the following points.

Section 1 Review, page 170: Observe the area and record the types of energy used.
Section 2 Review, page 178: Collect data on the amount of energy used and look for ways to reduce it.
Section 3 Review, page 185: Write a draft of your report.

Wrap Up At the end of the chapter (page 193), you will present your group's proposal to make your school more energy-efficient.

Electricity makes downtown Los Angeles sparkle at dusk.

SECTION
1 Fossil Fuels

DISCOVER ···························· ACTIVITY····

What's in a Piece of Coal?

1. Observe a chunk of coal. Record your observations in as much detail as possible, including color, texture, and shape.

2. Now use a hand lens to observe the coal more closely.

3. Examine your coal for fossils, imprints of plant or animal remains.

Think It Over
Observing What did you notice when you used the hand lens compared to your first observations? What do you think coal is made of?

GUIDE FOR READING

◆ How do fuels provide energy?

◆ What are the three major fossil fuels?

◆ Why are fossil fuels considered nonrenewable resources?

Reading Tip As you read, make a table comparing coal, oil, and natural gas. Describe each fuel and note how it is obtained and used.

The blackout happened on a November afternoon in 1965, just as evening rush hour was beginning. One small part in one power plant stopped working. To replace the lost power, the automatic controls shifted electricity from another source. This overloaded another part of the system, causing it to shut down. The problem kept growing. Within minutes, much of the Northeast was without electricity! Lights went out, plunging buildings into darkness. Thousands of people were trapped in dark elevators. Traffic signals stopped working, causing huge traffic jams. Electric stoves, radios, clocks—nothing worked. It took 13 hours to restore the power. During that time, more than 30 million people were reminded just how much their lives depended on electricity.

Producing electricity is an important use of energy resources. Other uses include transportation and heating. As you read about Earth's energy resources, think about how each is used to meet people's energy needs.

Fuels and Energy

INTEGRATING PHYSICS How did you travel to school today? Whether you traveled in a car or a bus, walked, or rode your bike, you used some form of energy. The source of that energy was a fuel. **A fuel is a substance that provides a form of energy— such as heat, light, electricity, or motion— as the result of a chemical change.**

◀ Electric power lines stretch against the evening sky.

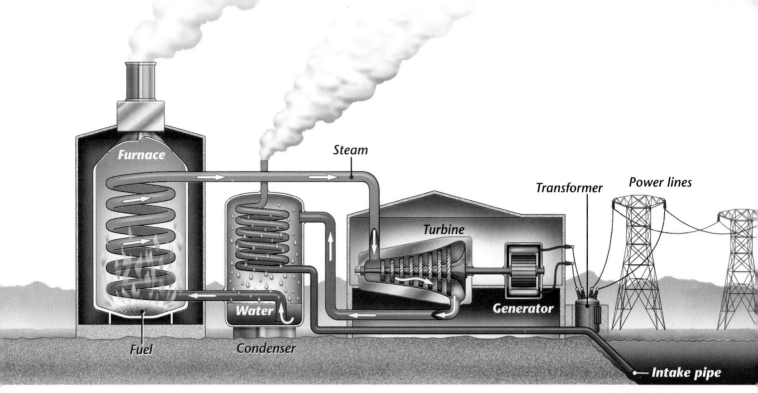

Figure 1 Electric power plants generate electricity by converting energy from one form to another. In the furnace, fuel is burned, releasing thermal energy. This energy is used to boil water and make steam. The mechanical energy of the moving steam turns the blades of a turbine. The turbine turns the shaft of the generator, producing an electric current.

Energy can be converted from one form to another. To see how, rub your hands together quickly for several seconds. Did you feel them become warmer? When you moved your hands, they had mechanical energy, the energy of motion. The friction of your hands rubbing together converted some of this mechanical energy to thermal energy, which you felt as heat.

Combustion Fuels contain stored chemical energy, which can be released by burning. The process of burning a fuel is called **combustion.** For example, the fuel used by most cars is gasoline. When gasoline is burned in a car engine, it undergoes a chemical change. The gasoline combines with oxygen, producing carbon dioxide and water. The combustion of gasoline also converts some of the stored chemical energy into thermal energy. This thermal energy is converted to mechanical energy that moves the car.

Production of Electricity The energy stored in fuels can be used to generate electricty. In most power plants, the thermal energy produced by burning fuel is used to boil water, making steam, as shown in Figure 1. The mechanical energy of the steam turns the blades of a turbine. The shaft of the turbine is connected to a generator. The generator consists of powerful magnets surrounded by coils of copper wire. As the shaft rotates, the magnets turn inside the wire coil, producing an electric current. The electric current flows through power lines to homes and industries.

✓ *Checkpoint* *What are three energy conversions that might occur in a power plant?*

Graphing ACTIVITY

Use the data in the table below to make a circle graph showing the uses of energy in the United States. (To review circle graphs, see the Skills Handbook.)

End Use of Energy	Percent of Total Energy
Transportation	26.5
Industry	38.1
Homes and businesses	35.4

What Are Fossil Fuels?

Most of the energy used today comes from organisms that lived hundreds of millions of years ago. As these plants, animals, and other organisms died, their remains piled up. Layers of sand, rock, and mud buried the dead organisms. Over time, heat and pressure changed the material into other substances. **Fossil fuels** are the energy-rich substances formed from the remains of once-living organisms. **The three major fossil fuels are coal, oil, and natural gas.**

Fossil fuels are made of hydrocarbons. **Hydrocarbons** are energy-rich chemical compounds that contain carbon and hydrogen atoms. During combustion, the carbon and hydrogen combine with oxygen in the air to form carbon dioxide and water. This process releases energy in the forms of heat and light.

Fossil fuels have more hydrocarbons per kilogram than most other fuels. For this reason, they are an excellent source of energy. Combustion of one kilogram of coal, for example, provides twice as much heat as burning one kilogram of wood. Oil and natural gas provide three times the energy of wood.

☑ *Checkpoint* *Why do fossil fuels yield more energy than other fuels?*

Coal

Coal is a solid fossil fuel formed from plant remains. People have burned coal to produce heat for thousands of years. But coal was only a minor source of energy compared to wood until the 1800s. As Europe and the United States entered the Industrial Revolution, the need for fuel increased rapidly.

Figure 2 Coal is formed from the remains of trees and other plants that grew in swamps hundreds of millions of years ago.

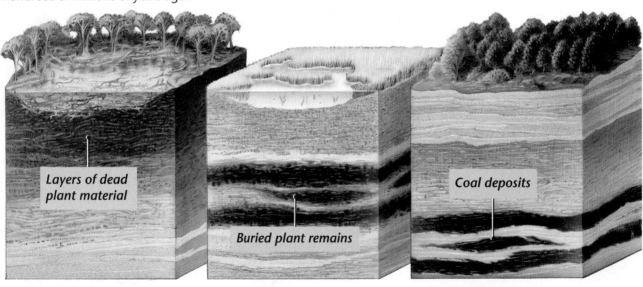

Layers of dead plant material

Buried plant remains

Coal deposits

200 million years ago   **50 million years ago**   **Present**

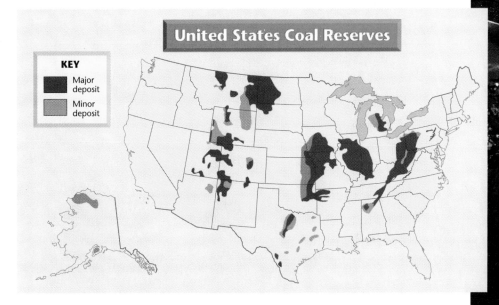

United States Coal Reserves

KEY
Major deposit
Minor deposit

Figure 3 The map shows the locations of coal reserves in the United States. In the photograph, a miner obtains hard coal from a shaft deep underground. *Interpreting Maps Which states have major deposits of coal?*

As forests were cut down, firewood became more expensive. It became worthwhile to find, mine, and transport coal. Coal fueled the huge steam engines that powered trains, ships, and factories during the Industrial Revolution.

Today, coal provides 23 percent of the energy used in the United States. The major use of coal is to fuel electric power plants.

Coal Mining Before it can be used to produce energy, coal has

INTEGRATING TECHNOLOGY

to be removed from the ground, or mined. Some coal is located very deep underground or is mixed with other materials, making it too difficult to obtain. Known deposits of coal (and other fossil fuels) that can be obtained using current technology are called **reserves.**

A century ago, miners had to break the coal apart with hand tools. Today they use machines to chop the coal into chunks and lift it to the surface. The coal is then cleaned to remove rocks, sand, and other materials that do not burn. Removing them also makes the coal lighter, reducing the cost of transporting it.

Coal as an Energy Source Coal is the most plentiful fossil fuel in the United States. It is fairly easy to transport, and provides a lot of energy when burned. But coal also has some disadvantages. Coal mining can increase erosion. Runoff from mines can cause water pollution. Finally, burning most types of coal results in more air pollution than other fossil fuels.

In addition, coal mining can be a dangerous job. Thousands of miners have been killed or injured in accidents in the mines. Many more suffer from "black lung," a disease caused by years of breathing coal dust. Fortunately, the mining industry has been working hard to improve conditions. New safety procedures and better equipment, including robots and drills that produce less coal dust, have made coal mining safer.

Figure 4 A farmer in Ireland turns over blocks of soft peat. Peat is formed in the early stages of the process of coal formation.

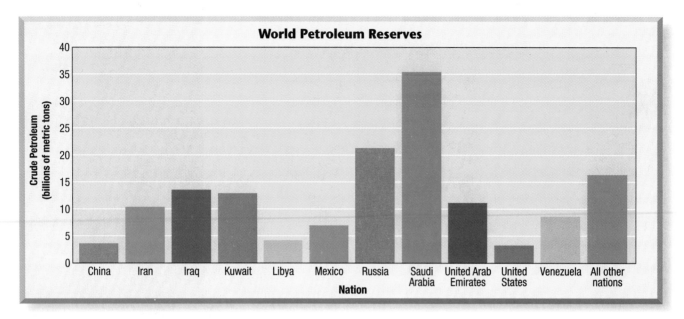

World Petroleum Reserves

(Bar graph showing Crude Petroleum (billions of metric tons) on the y-axis from 0 to 40, and Nation on the x-axis)

China ~3.5, Iran ~10.5, Iraq ~13.5, Kuwait ~13, Libya ~4, Mexico ~7, Russia ~21, Saudi Arabia ~35.5, United Arab Emirates ~11, United States ~3, Venezuela ~8.5, All other nations ~16

Figure 5 Known petroleum deposits, called reserves, are located in many parts of the world. *Interpreting Graphs Which two nations have the largest reserves?*

Oil

Oil is a thick, black, liquid fossil fuel. It formed from the remains of small animals, algae, and protists that lived in oceans and shallow inland seas hundreds of millions of years ago. **Petroleum** is another name for oil, from the Latin words *petra* (rock) and *oleum* (oil). Most oil deposits are located underground in tiny holes in sandstone or limestone. The oil fills the holes somewhat like water trapped in the holes of a sponge.

Petroleum accounts for more than one third of the energy produced in the world. Fuel for most cars, airplanes, trains, and ships comes from petroleum. Many homes are heated by oil.

The United States consumes about one third of all the oil produced in the world. But only three percent of the world's supply is located in this country. The difference must be purchased from countries with large oil supplies.

Locating Oil Deposits Because it is usually located deep below the surface, finding oil is difficult. Scientists

INTEGRATING TECHNOLOGY

can use sound waves to test an area for oil without drilling. This technique relies on the fact that sound waves bounce off objects and return as echoes. Scientists send pulses of sound down into the rocks below ground. Then they measure how long it takes the echoes to return. The amount of time depends on whether the sound waves must travel through solid rock or liquid oils. This information can indicate the most likely places to find oil. However, only about one out of every six wells drilled produces a usable amount of oil.

Figure 6 An oil rig bobs up and down as it pumps oil from a Texas oil field.

Refining Oil When oil is first pumped out of the ground, it is called crude oil. Crude oil can be a runny or a thick liquid. In order to be made into useful products, crude oil must undergo a process called refining. A factory where crude oil is separated into fuels and other products by heating is called a **refinery.**

In addition to gasoline and heating oil, many products you use every day are made from crude oil. **Petrochemicals** are compounds that are made from oil. Petrochemicals are used in plastics, paints, medicines, and cosmetics.

☑ *Checkpoint* *How is petroleum used?*

Natural Gas

The third major fossil fuel is natural gas, a mixture of methane and other gases. Natural gas forms from the same organisms as petroleum. Because it is less dense than oil, natural gas often rises above an oil deposit, forming a pocket of gas in the rock.

Pipelines transport the gas from its source to the places where it is used. If all the gas pipelines in the United States were connected, they would reach to the moon and back—twice! Natural gas can also be compressed into a liquid and stored in tanks as fuel for trucks and buses.

Natural gas has several advantages. It produces large amounts of energy, but lower levels of many air pollutants than coal or oil. It is also easy to transport once the network of pipelines is built. One disadvantage of natural gas is that it is highly flammable. A gas leak can cause a violent explosion and fire.

Gas companies help to prevent dangerous explosions from leaks. If you use natural gas in your home, you probably are familiar with the "gas" smell that alerts you whenever there is unburned gas in the air. You may be surprised to learn that natural gas actually has no odor at all. What causes the strong smell? The gas companies add a chemical with a distinct smell to the gas before it is piped to homes and businesses so that any leaks will be noticed.

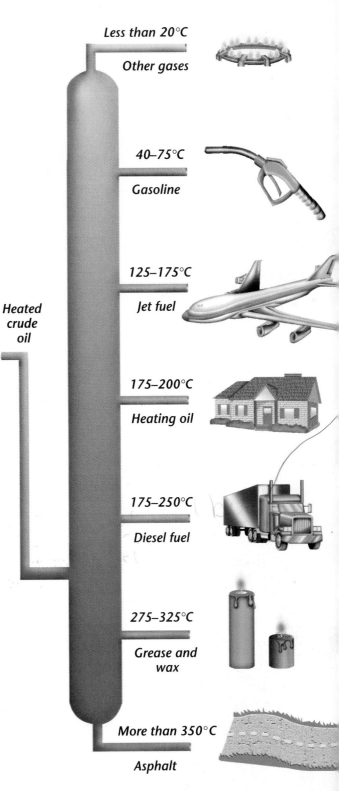

Less than 20°C

Other gases

40–75°C

Gasoline

125–175°C

Jet fuel

Heated crude oil

175–200°C

Heating oil

175–250°C

Diesel fuel

275–325°C

Grease and wax

More than 350°C

Asphalt

Figure 7 Crude oil is refined to make many different products. In the refining process, heat causes the different molecules in crude oil to separate. Different substances vaporize at specific temperatures.

Figure 8 During the gasoline crisis, people frequently had to wait in long lines to buy gas. *Relating Cause and Effect What caused the gasoline shortage?*

Fuel Supply and Demand

The many advantages of using fossil fuels as an energy source have made them essential to modern life. **But remember that fossil fuels take hundreds of millions of years to form. For this reason, fossil fuels are considered a nonrenewable resource.** For example, Earth's known oil reserves took 500 million years to form. One fourth of this oil has already been used. If fossil fuels continue to be used more rapidly than they are formed, the reserves will eventually be used up.

Many of the nations that consume large amounts of fuel have very limited reserves of their own. They have to buy oil, natural gas, and coal from the regions that have large supplies. The uneven distribution of fossil fuel reserves has often been a cause of political problems in the world. For example, in the 1970s, a group of oil-exporting nations decided to reduce their oil exports to the United States. As the supply of gasoline fell, prices rose very rapidly. People sometimes waited in line for hours to buy gasoline. This shortage reminded Americans of their dependence on oil imported from other nations.

New sources of energy are needed to replace the decreasing fossil fuel reserves. The rest of this chapter will describe some other sources of energy, as well as ways to make current fuel resources last longer.

Section 1 Review

1. Explain how fuels provide energy.
2. Name the three major fossil fuels and briefly describe each.
3. Explain why fossil fuels are classified as nonrenewable resources.
4. List two advantages and one disadvantage of natural gas as an energy source.
5. **Thinking Critically** **Applying Concepts** Why is it impossible to know exactly how large the world's oil reserves are?

Check Your Progress

CHAPTER PROJECT **6**

With your team, observe your selected area of the school. Determine which types of energy use take place in this area: heating, cooling, lighting, mechanical devices, electronic equipment, or moving vehicles. Record the specific types and amounts of energy use in a data table. To find the amounts, you will need to collect data from electric meters or fuel gauges. (*Hint:* Observe your area at several different times of the day, since the pattern of energy use may vary.)

SECTION
② Renewable Sources of Energy

DISCOVER ·······················ACTIVITY····

Can You Capture Solar Energy?

1. Pour 250 milliliters of water into each of two sealable, clear plastic bags.

2. Measure and record the water temperature in each bag. Seal the bags.

3. Put one bag in a dark or shady place. Put the other bag in a place where it will receive direct sunlight.

4. Predict what the temperature of the water in each bag will be after 30 minutes.

5. Measure and record the ending temperatures.

Think It Over

Developing Hypotheses How did the water temperature in each bag change? What could account for these results?

As the sun rises over the rim of the canyon where your family is camping, you feel its warmth on your face. The night's chill disappears quickly. A breeze stirs, carrying with it the smell of the campfire. Maybe you'll take a morning dip in the warm water of a nearby hot spring.

This relaxing scene is far from the city, with its bustling cars and trucks, factories and power plants. But there are energy resources all around you here, too. The sun warms the air, the wind blows, and heat from inside Earth warms the waters of the spring. These sources of energy are all renewable—that is, they are constantly being supplied. You can see why people are trying to find ways to use these renewable resources instead of fossil fuels. As you read about each source of renewable energy, think about how it could help meet people's energy needs.

Energy From the Sun

The warmth you feel on a sunny day is **solar energy,** energy from the sun. **The sun constantly gives off energy in the form of light and heat.** Solar energy is the source, directly or indirectly, of most other renewable energy resources. In one day, Earth receives enough solar energy to meet the energy needs of the entire world for 40 years. Solar energy does not cause pollution, and it will not run out for billions of years.

So why hasn't solar energy replaced fossil fuels? One reason is that solar energy is only available when the sun is shining. A backup energy source must be available on cloudy days and at night. Another problem is that

GUIDE FOR READING

◆ How does the sun provide energy?

◆ What are some renewable sources of energy?

Reading Tip Before you read, preview the headings in this section. Predict some sources of energy that are renewable.

Figure 9 Aimed at the sun, these mirrors provide power to an electric plant in New South Wales, Australia. *Inferring How does the shape of these mirrors make them more effective?*

although Earth receives a lot of energy from the sun every day, this energy is very spread out. To obtain enough power, it is necessary to collect this energy from a huge area.

Solar Technologies

INTEGRATING TECHNOLOGY Improving technologies to capture and use solar energy will help meet future energy needs. Some current solar technologies are described below.

Solar Plants One way to capture the sun's energy involves using giant mirrors. In a solar plant, rows of mirrors focus the sun's rays to heat a tank of water. The water boils, making steam that can be used to generate electricity.

Solar Cells Solar energy can be converted directly into electricity in a solar cell. A solar cell consists of a "sandwich" of very thin layers of the element silicon and other materials. The upper and lower parts of the sandwich have a negative and a positive terminal, like a battery. When light hits the cell, electrons move across the layers, producing an electric current.

The amount of electricity produced by solar cells depends on the area of the cell and the amount of light available. Solar cells are used to power calculators, lights, telephones, and other small devices. However, it would take more than 5,000 solar cells the size of your palm to produce enough electricity for a typical American home. Building solar cells on a large scale is very expensive. As a result, solar cells are used mostly in areas where fossil fuels are difficult to transport.

✓ *Checkpoint* *What are solar cells made of and how do they work?*

Solar Heating Systems Solar energy can be used to heat buildings. As shown in *Exploring a Solar House,* there are two types of solar heating systems: passive and active.

A **passive solar system** converts sunlight into thermal energy without using pumps or fans. If you have ever stepped into a car on a sunny day, you have experienced passive solar heating. Solar energy passes through the car's windows as light. The sun's rays heat the seats and other parts of the car, which then transfer heat to the air. The heated air is trapped inside, so the car gets warmer. The same principle can be used to heat a home.

An **active solar system** captures the sun's energy, then uses fans and pumps to distribute the heat. Light strikes the black metal surface of a solar collector. There, it is converted to thermal energy. Water is pumped through pipes in the solar collector to absorb the thermal energy. The heated water flows to a storage tank. Pumps and fans distribute the heat throughout the building.

EXPLORING *a Solar House*

This solar house uses passive and active heating systems and solar cells to convert solar energy into heat and electricity.

Passive Interior Heating
Sunlight that passes through the windows is absorbed by the walls and floors and converted to heat. At night shades covering the windows prevent the heat from flowing back outside.

Solar Cells
Active solar cells on the roof generate an electric current. A battery stores energy for night use.

Solar Water Heater
Cool water is pumped from a storage tank to an active solar collector on the roof. Sunlight heats the water in the collector panels. Then the water is returned to the tank. From there it is piped to the different rooms. Air moves over the pipes and is heated.

Window Design
Large windows on the south and west sides act as passive solar collectors. They let sunlight enter during the winter. Overhangs shade the windows during the summer.

Backup Heat Source
The house has a wood stove to provide backup heat, especially on cloudy days.

Figure 10 This wind farm in the Mojave Desert is one of many in the state of California. *Making Generalizations What are some advantages of wind power?*

Capturing the Wind

The sun is one source of renewable energy. **Other renewable sources of energy include wind, water, tides, biomass material, Earth's interior, and hydrogen.**

Wind energy is actually an indirect form of solar energy. The sun heats Earth's surface unevenly. As a result of this uneven heating, different areas of the atmosphere have different temperatures and air pressure. The differences in pressure cause winds as air moves from one area to another.

Wind can be used to turn a turbine and generate electricity. Wind power plants or "wind farms" consist of many windmills. Together, the windmills generate large amounts of power.

Although wind now provides less than one percent of the world's electricity, it is the fastest-growing energy source. Wind energy is free and does not cause pollution. In places where fuels are difficult to transport, such as Antarctica, wind energy is the major source of power. In the remote grasslands of Mongolia, electricity is obtained from more than 70,000 wind turbines.

Wind energy is not ideal for all locations. Few places have winds that blow steadily enough to be a worthwhile energy source. Wind generators are noisy and can be destroyed by very strong winds. But as fossil fuels become more scarce and expensive, wind generators will become more important.

Checkpoint *How can wind be used to generate electricity?*

The Power of Flowing Water

Solar energy is also the indirect source of water power. Recall that in the water cycle, energy from the sun heats water on Earth's surface, forming water vapor. The water vapor condenses and falls back to Earth as rain and snow. As the water flows over the land into lakes and oceans, it provides another source of energy.

Flowing water can turn a turbine and generate electricity in the same way as steam or wind. A dam across a river blocks the flow of water, creating an artificial lake called a reservoir. Water flows through tunnels at the bottom of the dam. As the water moves through the tunnels, it turns turbines connected to a generator.

Hydroelectric power is electricity produced by flowing water. This type of power is the most widely used source of renewable energy in the world today. Once a dam and power plant are built, producing the electricity is inexpensive. Another benefit is that hydroelectric power does not create air pollution. Unlike wind or solar energy, flowing water provides a steady supply of energy.

But hydroelectric power does have limitations. In the United States, for example, most of the suitable rivers have already been dammed. And dams can have negative effects on the environment. You can read more about the pros and cons of hydroelectric dams in *Science and Society* on page 180.

Figure 11 Flowing water provides the power to turn the water wheel of this historic mill in Tennessee.

Tidal Energy

Another source of moving water is the tides. The gravity of the moon and sun causes the water on Earth's surface to regularly rise and fall on its shores. Along some coastlines, enormous amounts of water move into bays at the high tide. The water flows out to sea again when the tide goes out.

A few tidal power plants have been built to take advantage of this regular motion. A low dam across the entrance to a shallow bay holds water in the bay at high tide. As the tide goes out, water flowing past turbines in the dam generate electricity, as in a hydroelectric power plant.

Only a few coastal areas in the world are suitable for building tidal power plants. A dam across a bay also blocks boats and fish from traveling up the river. For these reasons, tidal power will probably never become a major source of energy.

☑ *Checkpoint* *How are tidal power plants similar to hydroelectric power plants? How are they different?*

Social Studies
CONNECTION

Early settlers in the eastern United States often built mills along streams. The mills captured the power of flowing water at dams or waterfalls, where the water turned water wheels connected to machines. Saw mills sawed logs into boards, and grist mills ground wheat into flour. A mill site often formed the center of a new town.

In Your Journal

Suppose you are writing a news story about an old mill. Describe the mill's early importance to the settlers, how a town grew up around it, and how it is used today.

Biomass Fuels

The oldest fuel used for heat and light is wood. As trees carry out photosynthesis, they use the sun's energy to convert carbon dioxide and water into more complicated molecules. Burning wood breaks down these molecules again and releases energy.

Wood is one of a group of fuels, called **biomass fuels,** made from living things. Other biomass fuels include leaves, food wastes, and even manure. As fossil fuel supplies shrink, people are taking a closer look at biomass fuels. For instance, when oil prices rose in the early 1970s, Hawaiian sugar-cane farmers thought of a way to use sugar-cane wastes. They began burning the wastes to generate electricity instead of discarding the wastes in landfills. Now almost one fourth of the electricity used on the island of Kauai comes from biomass material.

Biomass materials can be also converted into other fuels. For example, corn, sugar cane, and other crops can be used to make alcohol. Adding the alcohol to gasoline forms a mixture called **gasohol.** Gasohol can be used as fuel for cars. When bacteria decompose wastes, they convert the wastes into methane gas. The methane produced in some landfills is used to heat buildings.

Alcohol and methane are renewable resources. But producing them in large quantities is more expensive than using fossil fuels. And though wood is renewable, it takes time for new trees to grow and replace those that have been cut down. As a result, biomass fuels are not widely used today in the United States. But as fossil fuels become scarcer, biomass fuels may play a larger role in meeting energy needs.

Figure 12 This corn field is a rich source of biomass fuel. After the corn is harvested, the stalks and leaves can be burned to provide energy. *Comparing and Contrasting How are biomass fuels similar to energy sources such as wind and water? How are these fuels different?*

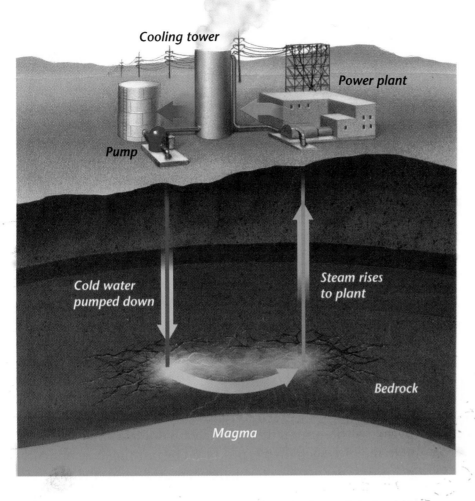

Cooling tower

Power plant

Pump

Cold water pumped down

Steam rises to plant

Bedrock

Magma

Figure 13 A geothermal power plant uses heat from Earth's interior as an energy source. Cold water is piped deep into the ground, where it is heated by magma. The resulting steam can be used for heat or to generate electricity.

Tapping Earth's Energy

Below Earth's surface is a thick layer of very hot, liquid rock called magma. In some places, magma is found very close to the surface. It may even erupt out of the ground as volcanic lava. The intense heat from Earth's interior that warms the magma is called **geothermal energy.**

In certain regions, such as Iceland and New Zealand, the magma heats underground water to the boiling point. The hot water and steam are valuable sources of energy. In Reykjavik, Iceland, 90 percent of homes are heated by water warmed underground in this way. Geothermal energy can also be used to generate electricity, as shown in Figure 13.

Geothermal energy is an unlimited source of cheap energy. But it has disadvantages, just like every other energy source. There are only a few places where magma comes close to Earth's surface. Elsewhere, a very deep well is required to tap this energy. Drilling deep wells is very expensive. Even so, geothermal energy is likely to play a part in meeting energy needs in the future.

☑ *Checkpoint* *How can geothermal energy be used to generate electricity?*

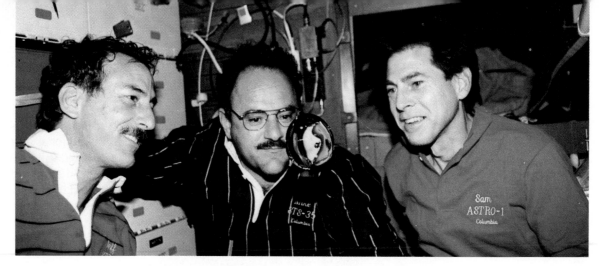

Figure 14 The object fascinating these three astronauts is a bubble of water—the harmless by-product of the hydrogen fuel cells used on the space shuttle.

Hydrogen Power

Now that you have read about so many energy sources, consider a fuel with this description: It burns cleanly, forming only water as a by-product. It creates no smoke, smog, or acid rain. It can be handled and transported through pipelines, much like natural gas. This fuel exists on Earth in large supply.

This ideal-sounding fuel is real—it's hydrogen. However, there is an obstacle. Almost all the hydrogen on Earth is combined with oxygen in the form of water. Pure hydrogen can be obtained by passing an electric current through water. But it takes more energy to obtain the hydrogen than is produced by burning it again.

Scientists aren't ruling out hydrogen as a good fuel for the future. At present, hydroelectric plants decrease their activity when the demand for electricity is low. Instead, they could run at full power all the time, using the excess electricity to produce hydrogen. Similarly, solar power plants often generate more electricity than is needed during the day. This extra electricity could be used to produce hydrogen. If a way can be found to produce hydrogen cheaply, it could someday be an important source of energy.

Section 2 Review

1. What is solar energy?
2. How are the energy of wind and flowing water each related to solar energy?
3. How are active and passive solar heating systems different?
4. List three examples of biomass fuels.
5. What limits the use of geothermal energy?
6. **Thinking Critically** **Predicting** Which of the renewable sources of energy do you think is most likely to be used in your community in 100 years? Give reasons to support your answer.

Check Your Progress
Continue to collect data on how much energy is used in your group's area of the school. Begin to brainstorm ideas for reducing energy usage in this area. For example, is there a way to use some electrical devices for shorter periods of time? (*Hint:* Interviewing some adults who are responsible for the operation of the school building may give you some good ideas. Be sure to check with your teacher before interviewing anyone.)

CHAPTER PROJECT 6

Cooking With Sunshine

In the future, will you cook your meals with sunshine instead of electricity? That's certainly a possibility. In this lab, you'll investigate how solar energy can be used to cook food.

Problem

What is the best shape for a solar cooker?

Skills Focus

predicting, designing experiments, forming operational definitions

Suggested Materials

scissors   glue   3 thermometers
3 dowels   tape   marshmallows
3 sheets of aluminum foil   clock or watch
3 sheets of oaktag paper

Procedure

Part 1 Capturing Solar Energy

1. Read over the entire lab. Then predict which shape will produce the largest temperature increase when placed in the sun.
2. Glue a sheet of aluminum foil, shiny side up, to each sheet of oaktag paper. Before the glue dries, gently smooth out any wrinkles in the foil.
3. Bend one sheet into a V shape. Bend another sheet into a U shape. Leave the last sheet flat.
4. Place the aluminum sheets in direct sunlight, using wood blocks or books to hold the U- and V-shapes in position.
5. Tape a dowel to each thermometer. Record the starting temperature on each thermometer.
6. Use the dowels to hold the thermometer bulbs in the center of the aluminum shapes. After 15 minutes, record the final temperature on each thermometer.

Part 2 Designing a Solar Cooker

7. Use the results from Step 6 to design a solar cooker that can toast a marshmallow. Prepare a written description of your plan for your teacher's approval. Include an operational definition of a "well-toasted" marshmallow.
8. After your teacher has approved your plan, test your design by placing a marshmallow on a wooden dowel. Record the time it takes to toast the marshmallow.

Analyze and Conclude

1. What was the role of the aluminum foil in this investigation? What other materials could you have used instead? Explain.
2. Which of the three shapes—V, U, or flat— produced the largest increase in temperature? Propose an explanation for this result.
3. What other variables might have affected your results? Explain.
4. **Apply** What are some possible advantages of a solar cooker based on this design? What are some possible disadvantages?

More to Explore

Try adapting your design to heat water. Show your new design to your teacher before trying it.

Hydroelectric Dams: Are They All Here to Stay?

There are hundreds of hydroelectric dams on United States rivers. These dams provide electricity for millions of people. Hydroelectric dams provide clean, inexpensive, and renewable energy. They are a good source of power.

Recently, however, people have learned that dams can have negative effects on river ecosystems. Some people have even suggested removing certain dams. But is this wise? When do the benefits of dams outweigh the problems?

The Issues

How Do Dams Affect the Environment?
Because dams change water depth and flow, they can alter the temperature of a river. The water may become too cold or too warm for fish that normally live there. A change in temperature can also reduce the number of algae in a river. This affects other organisms in the river food web.

Some species of fish, such as salmon, herring, and menhaden, hatch in rivers but then travel to the ocean. To breed, they must return to the river. Dams can block the movement of these fish populations. For example, the Columbia River Basin, which has more than 50 dams, once contained more than 10 million salmon. Today it is home to only 2 million salmon.

What Are the Effects of Removing Dams?
Some people say that the only way to restore ecosystems is to remove dams. However, these dams supply a small but important part of the nation's electricity. Removing them could force the United States to use more nonrenewable fossil fuels. Fossil fuels also produce more pollution than hydroelectric plants.

The reservoirs behind hydroelectric dams supply water for irrigation and drinking. These supplies would be difficult to replace. In addition, a series of dams on a river can reduce flooding downstream during heavy rains.

What Can People Do?
Removing dams might restore some river ecosystems. For example, Edwards Dam on the Kennebec River in Maine is scheduled to be removed to allow several threatened fish species to spawn. But Edwards Dam provides only a small percent of Maine's electric power. This small amount is easier to replace than the power provided by a much larger dam.

There are other ways to protect migrating fish. Fish ladders, for example, are step-like waterways that help fish pass over dams. Fish can even be carried around dams in trucks. Still, these methods are costly and not always successful.

The government issues licenses for hydroelectric dams. In considering license renewals, officials examine environmental impact as well as energy production.

You Decide

1. Identify the Problem
In your own words, explain some of the major issues surrounding hydroelectric dams.

2. Analyze the Options
Examine the pros and cons of removing dams. What are the benefits? What are the costs? Who will be affected by the change?

3. Find a Solution
The license of a nearby dam is up for review. The dam provides electricity, but also blocks the migration of fish. What do you recommend? Explain.

SECTION 3 Nuclear Energy

DISCOVER  .... ACTIVITY

Why Do They Fall?

1. Line up 15 dominoes to form a triangle, as shown.

2. Knock over the first domino so that it falls against the second row of dominoes. Observe the results.

3. Set up the dominoes again, but then remove the dominoes in the third row from the lineup.

4. Knock over the first domino again. Observe what happens.

Think It Over

Inferring Suppose each domino produced a large amount of energy when it fell over. Why might it be helpful to remove the dominoes as you did in Step 3?

Wouldn't it be great if people could use the same method as the sun to produce energy? In a way, they can! The kind of reactions that power the sun involve the central cores of atoms. The central core of an atom that contains the protons and neutrons is called the **nucleus** (plural nuclei). The reactions that involve nuclei, called nuclear reactions, involve tremendous amounts of energy. Two types of nuclear reactions are fission and fusion.

Fission Reactions and Energy

Nuclear reactions convert matter into energy. In 1905, Albert Einstein developed a formula that described the relationship between energy and matter. You have probably seen this famous equation, $E = mc^2$. In the equation, the E represents energy and the m represents mass. The c, which represents the speed of light, is a very large number. This equation states that when matter is changed into energy, an enormous amount of energy is released.

Nuclear fission is the splitting of an atom's nucleus into two smaller nuclei. The fuel for the reaction is a large atom that has an unstable nucleus, such as uranium-235 (U-235). A neutron is shot at the U-235 atom at high speed. **When the neutron hits the U-235 nucleus, the nucleus splits apart into two smaller nuclei and two or more neutrons.** The total mass of all these particles is a bit less than the mass of the original nucleus. The small amount of mass that makes up the difference has been converted into energy—a lot of energy, as described by Einstein's equation.

GUIDE FOR READING

◆ What happens during fission and fusion reactions?

◆ How does a nuclear power plant produce electricity?

Reading Tip As you read, create a Venn diagram to compare and contrast nuclear fission and nuclear fusion.

Figure 15 Albert Einstein, shown here in 1930, described the relationship between energy and matter.

Figure 16 In a nuclear fission reaction, a neutron "bullet" strikes a U-235 nucleus. As a result, the nucleus splits into two smaller nuclei. More neutrons are released, along with a great deal of energy.

Krypton-92 nucleus

Neutron

Neutron

Neutron

Neutron

Uranium-235 nucleus

Barium-141 nucleus

Meanwhile, the fission reaction has produced three more neutrons. If any of these neutrons strikes another nucleus, the fission reaction is repeated. More neutrons and more energy are released. If there are enough nuclei nearby, the process continues over and over in a chain reaction, just like a row of dominoes falling. In a nuclear chain reaction, the amount of energy released increases rapidly with each step in the chain.

What happens to all the energy released by these fission reactions? If a nuclear chain reaction is not controlled, the released energy causes a huge explosion. The explosion of an atomic bomb is an uncontrolled nuclear reaction. A few kilograms of matter explode with more force than several thousand tons of a nonnuclear explosive such as dynamite. However, if the chain reaction is controlled, the energy is released as heat, which can be used to generate electricity.

Nuclear Power Plants

Controlled nuclear fission reactions take place inside nuclear power plants. **In a nuclear power plant, the heat released from the reactions is used to change water into steam. As in other types of power plants, the steam then turns the blades of a turbine to generate electricity.** Look at the diagram of a nuclear power plant in Figure 17. In addition to the generator, it has two main parts: the reactor vessel and the heat exchanger.

Reactor Vessel The **reactor vessel** is the section of a nuclear reactor where nuclear fission occurs. The reactor contains rods of U-235, called **fuel rods.** When several fuel rods are placed close together, a series of fission reactions occurs. The reactions are controlled by placing **control rods** made of the metal cadmium between the fuel rods. The cadmium absorbs the neutrons

Shoot the Nucleus

ACTIVITY

In an open area of your classroom, make a model of a nuclear fission reaction. Place a handful of marbles on the floor in a tight cluster, so that they touch one another. Step back about a half-meter from the marbles. Shoot another marble at the cluster.

Making Models What does the marble you shot at the cluster represent? What effect did the marble have on the cluster? How is this similar to a nuclear fission reaction?

released during the fission reactions. As the cadmium control rods are removed, the fission reactions speed up. If the reactor vessel starts to get too hot, the control rods are moved back in place to slow the chain reaction.

Heat Exchanger   Heat is removed from the reactor vessel by water or another fluid that is pumped through the reactor. This fluid passes through a heat exchanger. There, the fluid boils water to produce steam, which runs the electrical generator. The steam is condensed again and pumped back to the heat exchanger.

✓ *Checkpoint* *How are fission reactions controlled?*

The Risks of Nuclear Fission

When it was first demonstrated, people thought that nuclear fission would provide an almost unlimited source of clean, safe energy. Today nuclear power plants generate much of the world's electricity—about 20 percent in the United States and more than 70 percent in France. But these plants have some problems.

In 1986, in Chernobyl, Ukraine, the reactor vessel in a nuclear power plant overheated. The fuel rods generated so much heat that they started to melt, a condition called a **meltdown.** The excess heat increased the steam pressure in the generator. A series of explosions blew parts of the roof off and injured or killed dozens of plant workers and firefighters. Radioactive materials escaped into the environment. Today, the soil in an area the size of Florida remains contaminated with radioactive waste.

Sharpen your Skills

Calculating

A single pellet of U-235 the size of a breath mint can produce as much energy as 615 liters of fuel oil. An average home uses 5,000 liters of oil a year. How many U-235 pellets would be needed to supply the same amount of energy?

Figure 17 In a nuclear plant, uranium fuel undergoes fission, producing heat. The heat boils water, and the resulting steam drives the turbines that generate electricity. *Interpreting Diagrams From which part of the power plant is heat released to the environment?*

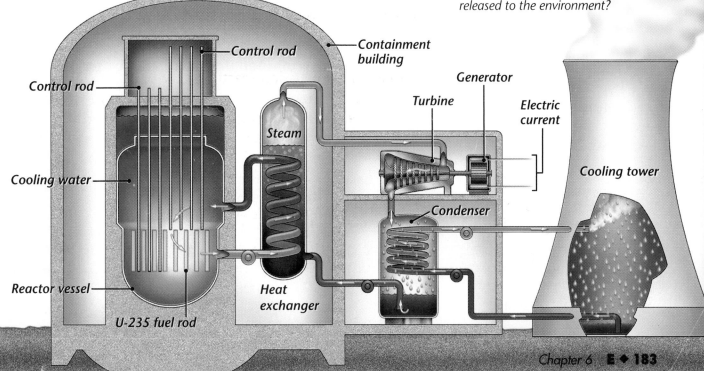

Control rod

Containment building

Generator

Turbine

Electric current

Control rod

Steam

Cooling water

Condenser

Cooling tower

Reactor vessel

Heat exchanger

U-235 fuel rod

Figure 18 One problem with nuclear power is disposal of the used radioactive fuel rods. In this plant in France, the fuel rods are stored in a deep pool of water.

Chernobyl and less-serious accidents at other nuclear power plants have led to public concerns about nuclear plant safety.

The danger of a meltdown is a serious concern. However, a meltdown can be avoided by careful planning. A more difficult problem is the disposal of radioactive wastes produced by power plants. Radioactive wastes remain dangerous for many thousands of years. Scientists must find a way to safely store these wastes for a long period of time. Finally, nuclear power has turned out to be a much more costly source of power than was originally expected. The safety features required for nuclear plants make the plants very expensive.

Checkpoint *What are three problems with using nuclear fission as an energy source?*

The Quest to Control Fusion

A second type of nuclear reaction is fusion. **Nuclear fusion** is the combining of two atomic nuclei to produce a single larger nucleus. **As shown in Figure 19, two kinds of hydrogen nuclei are forced together in a fusion reaction.** One kind (hydrogen-2) has one proton and one neutron, and the other kind (hydrogen-3) has one proton and two neutrons. The tremendous heat and pressure

Figure 19 In a nuclear fusion reaction, two nuclei combine to form a single larger nucleus. *Interpreting Diagrams What is released during a fusion reaction?*

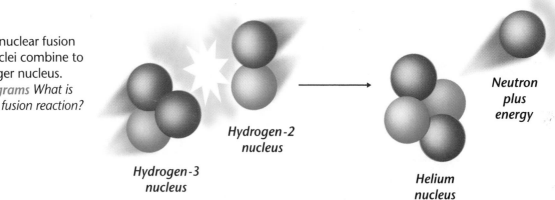

Hydrogen-2
nucleus

Hydrogen-3
nucleus

Neutron
plus
energy

Helium
nucleus

cause them to combine and create a helium nucleus with two protons and two neutrons. This helium nucleus has slightly less mass than the total mass of the two hydrogen nuclei. The difference is converted to energy.

Nuclear fusion would have many advantages as an energy source. Fusion can produce much more energy per atom than nuclear fission. The fuel for a nuclear fusion reactor is also readily available. Water, which is plentiful in Earth's oceans, contains one of the kinds of hydrogen needed for fusion. Fusion should be safer and less polluting than nuclear fission. You can see why scientists are eager to find a way to build a nuclear fusion reactor!

Although some fusion bombs have been exploded, scientists have not yet been able to control a large-scale fusion reaction. The biggest problem is temperature. In the sun, nuclear fusion occurs at 15 million degrees Celsius. Such conditions are almost impossible to create on Earth. Very great pressure would also work to contain a fusion reaction. But no material has been found that could serve as a reactor vessel under such high pressure. Extremely powerful magnetic fields can contain a fusion reaction. However, it takes more energy to generate these fields than the fusion reaction produces.

Although many more years of research are expected, some scientists believe that they will eventually be able to control fusion reactions. If they succeed, the quest for a clean, cheap energy source may be over at last.

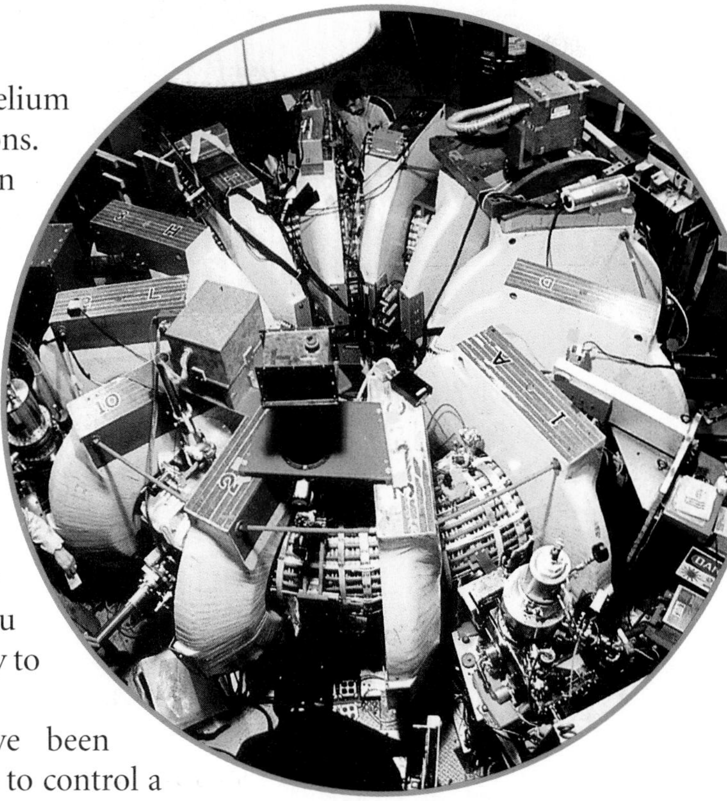

Figure 20 Researchers at Los Alamos National Laboratory in New Mexico are studying fusion as an energy source. This machine creates strong magnetic fields that allow fusion to occur for short periods of time.

Section 3 Review

1. Draw and label a simple diagram of a nuclear fission reaction. Include the following labels: U-235 nucleus, neutrons, smaller nuclei, and energy.
2. How can the energy released in a fission reaction be used to produce electricity?
3. Explain the purpose of control rods.
4. Give two reasons that people have not been able to use nuclear fusion as an energy source.
5. **Thinking Critically Classifying** Is nuclear fission a renewable or nonrenewable energy source? Is nuclear fusion renewable or nonrenewable? Explain.

Check Your Progress

CHAPTER PROJECT 6

By now you should begin preparing the written report of your findings about energy use in your group's area of the school. Your report should include the major ways energy is used in your chosen area. You should also include recommendations on how energy use might be reduced.

Keeping Comfortable

Two ways to use less energy are to keep heat out of your home when the weather is hot, and to keep heat in when the weather is cold. In this lab, you will design an experiment to compare how well different materials do this.

Problem

How well do different materials stop heat transfer?

Suggested Materials

thermometers   ice water   hot water
watch or clock   beakers
containers and lids made of paper, plastic foam, plastic, glass, and metal

Design a Plan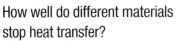

Part 1 Measuring Temperature Changes

1. Use a pencil to poke a hole in the lid of a paper cup. Fill the cup about halfway with cold water.

2. Put the lid on the cup. Insert a thermometer into the water through the hole. When the temperature stops dropping, place the cup in a beaker. Add hot water to the beaker until the water level is about 1 cm below the lid.

3. Record the water temperature once every minute until it has increased by 5°C. Use the time it takes for the temperature to increase 1°C as a measure of the effectiveness of the paper cup in preventing heat transfer.

Part 2 Comparing Materials

4. Use the ideas from Part 1 to design a controlled experiment to rank the effectiveness of different materials in preventing heat transfer.

5. Use these questions to help you plan your experiment:
   - What hypothesis will you test?
   - Which materials do you predict will be the best and worst at preventing heat transfer? How will you define these terms?
   - What will your manipulated variable be? What will your responding variable be?
   - What variables do you need to control? How will you control them?
   - What step-by-step procedures will you use?
   - What kind of data table will you use?

6. After your teacher has reviewed your plans, make any necessary changes in your design. Then perform your experiment.

Analyze and Conclude

1. In Part 1, what was the starting temperature of the hot water? What was the starting temperature of the cold water? In which direction did the heat flow? How do you know?

2. If the materials in Part 1 are used to represent your home in very hot weather, which material would represent the rooms in your home? Which would represent the outdoor weather? Which would represent the walls of the building?

3. Which material was most effective at preventing the transfer of heat? Which was the least effective? Explain.

4. **Think About It** Would experiments similar to this one provide you with enough information to choose materials to build a home? Explain.

More to Explore

Create a plan to compare how well the materials would work if the hot water were inside the cup and the cold water were outside. With your teacher's permission, carry out your plan.

SECTION
4 Energy Conservation

Imagine what would happen if the world ran out of fossil fuels today. Eighty percent of the electric power would disappear. Most buildings would lose their heating and cooling. Forests would disappear as people began to burn wood for heat and cooking. Almost all transportation would stop. Cars, buses, trains, airplanes, and ships would be stranded wherever they ran out of fuel. Since radios, televisions, computers, and telephones depend on electricity, communication would be greatly reduced.

Although fossil fuels won't run out immediately, they also won't last forever. Most people think that it makes sense to start planning now to avoid a fuel shortage in the future. **One approach to the problem is to find new sources of energy. The second way is to make the fuels that are available now last as long as possible while other solutions are being developed.**

Conservation and Efficiency

Reducing energy use is called **energy conservation.** For example, if you walk to the store instead of getting a ride, you are conserving the gasoline needed to drive to the store. Reducing energy use is a solution to energy problems that will help no matter what form of energy is used in the future.

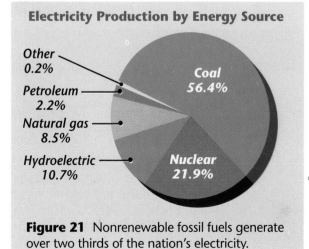

Electricity Production by Energy Source

Other 0.2%
Petroleum 2.2%
Natural gas 8.5%
Hydroelectric 10.7%
Coal 56.4%
Nuclear 21.9%

Figure 21 Nonrenewable fossil fuels generate over two thirds of the nation's electricity.

A way to get as much work as possible out of fuels is to use them efficiently. **Efficiency** is the percentage of energy that is actually used to perform work. The rest of the energy is "lost" to the surroundings, usually as heat. People have developed many ways to increase energy efficiency.

Lighting Lights can use as much as 10 percent of the electricity in your home, but much of that electricity is wasted. An incandescent light bulb converts less than 10 percent of the electricity it uses into light. The rest is given off as heat. You can prove this to yourself by holding your hand close to an incandescent light bulb. But don't touch it! Compact fluorescent bulbs, on the other hand, use only about one fourth as much energy to provide the same amount of light.

✓ *Checkpoint* *Which type of light bulb is more energy-efficient?*

SCIENCE & History

Energy-Efficient Devices

Scientists and engineers have developed many technologies that improve energy efficiency and reduce energy use.

1932
Fiberglass Insulation

Long strands of glass fibers trap air and keep buildings from losing heat. Less fuel is used for heating.

1958
Solar Cells

More than 150 years ago, scientists discovered that silicon can convert light into electricity. The first useful application of solar cells was to power the radio on a satellite. Now solar cells are even used on experimental cars like the one below.

1930   **1940**   **1950**

1936
Fluorescent Lighting

Fluorescent bulbs were introduced to the public at the 100th anniversary celebration of the United States Patent Office. Because these bulbs use less energy than incandescent bulbs, most offices and schools use fluorescent lights.

Heating and Cooling One method of increasing the efficiency of heating and cooling systems is insulation. **Insulation** is a layer of material that helps block the transfer of heat between the air inside and outside a building. You have probably seen insulation made of fiberglass, which looks like fluffy pink cotton candy. The mat of thin glass fibers trap air. **This layer of trapped air helps keep the building from losing or gaining heat from the outside.** A layer of fiberglass 15 centimeters thick insulates a room as well as a brick wall 2 meters thick or a stone wall almost 6 meters thick!

Buildings lose a lot of heat around the windows. Look at the windows in your school or home. Was the building built after 1980? Have the windows been replaced recently? If so, you will most likely see two panes of glass with space between them. The air between the panes of glass acts as insulation.

In Your Journal

Design an advertisement for one of the energy-saving inventions described in this time line. The advertisement may be a print, radio, or television ad. Be sure that your advertisement clearly explains the benefits of the invention.

1967
Microwave Ovens

The first countertop microwave oven for the home was introduced. Microwaves cook food by heating the water the food contains. The microwave oven heats only the food, not the air, racks, and oven walls as in a conventional oven. Preheating is also not required, saving even more energy.

1997
Smart Roads

The Department of Transportation demonstrated that cars can be controlled by computers. Sensors built into the road control all the cars, making traffic flow more smoothly. This uses less energy.

1970   **1980**   **1990**   **2000**

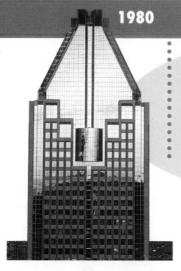

1981
High-Efficiency Window Coatings

Materials that reflect sunlight were first used to coat windows in the early 1980s. This coating reduces the air conditioning needed to keep the inside of the building cool.

Figure 22 A single city bus can transport dozens of people, reducing the number of cars on the roads and saving energy.
Applying Concepts How does riding a bus conserve energy?

Transportation Engineers have improved the energy efficiency of cars by designing better engines and tires. Another way to save energy is to reduce the number of cars on the road. In many communities, public transit systems provide an alternative to driving. Other cities encourage carpooling. If four people travel together in one car, they use much less energy than they would by driving separately. Many cities now set aside lanes for cars containing two or more people.

In the future, cars that run on electricity may provide the most energy savings of all. Electric power plants can convert fuel into electricity more efficiently than a car engine converts gasoline into motion. Therefore, a car that runs on electricity is more energy-efficient than one that runs directly on fuel.

What You Can Do

You can reduce your personal energy use by changing your behavior in some simple ways.

- Keep your home cooler in winter and warmer in summer. Instead of turning up the heat, put on a sweater. Use fans instead of air conditioners.
- Use natural lighting instead of electric lights when possible.
- Turn off the lights or television when you leave a room.
- Walk or ride a bike for short trips. Ride buses and trains.
- Recycle, especially metal products. Recycling an aluminum can uses only 5 percent of the energy making a new can uses!

The items in this list are small things, but multiplied by millions of people they add up to a lot of energy saved for the future.

Section 4 Review

1. What are two ways to make energy resources last longer?
2. Explain how putting insulation in a building conserves energy.
3. How does carpooling conserve energy?
4. **Thinking Critically Predicting** An office building contains only incandescent lights. The building next door contains fluorescent lights. Predict which building has higher energy bills. Explain your answer.

Science at Home

With an adult family member, conduct an energy audit of your home. Look for places where energy is being lost, such as cracks around windows and doors. Also look for ways to reduce energy use, such as running the dishwasher only when it is full. Together, create a list of energy-saving suggestions for your family. Post the list where everyone can see it.

SECTION 1 Fossil Fuels

Key Ideas

◆ A fuel is a substance that provides a form of energy as a result of a chemical change.

◆ Energy can be converted from one form to another.

◆ The three major fossil fuels are coal, oil, and natural gas. These fuels release more energy when they are burned than most other substances do.

◆ Because fossil fuels take hundreds of millions of years to form, they are considered nonrenewable resources.

Key Terms

combustion   petroleum
fossil fuels   refinery
hydrocarbons   petrochemicals
reserves

SECTION 2 Renewable Sources of Energy

Key Ideas

◆ Solar energy is plentiful and renewable, and does not cause pollution. However, a backup energy source is needed.

◆ Because the sun causes winds and drives the water cycle, wind power and water power are considered indirect forms of solar energy.

◆ Biomass fuels, geothermal energy, and hydrogen power are other renewable energy sources that are currently in limited use.

Key Terms

solar energy   biomass fuels
passive solar system gasohol
active solar system   geothermal energy
hydroelectric power

SECTION 3 Nuclear Energy

INTEGRATING CHEMISTRY

Key Ideas

◆ Nuclear reactions include fission reactions and fusion reactions.

◆ In a fission reaction, the impact of a neutron splits an atom's nucleus into two smaller nuclei and two or more neutrons. A large amount of energy is released in the process.

◆ In a nuclear power plant, the thermal energy released from controlled fission reactions is used to generate electricity.

◆ Disadvantages of nuclear power include the risk of a meltdown and radioactive waste.

◆ Scientists have not yet been able to control a major nuclear fusion reaction.

Key Terms

nucleus   control rods
nuclear fission   meltdown
reactor vessel   nuclear fusion
fuel rods

SECTION 4 Energy Conservation

Key Ideas

◆ To avoid an energy shortage in the future, people must find new sources of energy and conserve the fuels that are available now.

◆ Insulation keeps a building from losing heat to, or gaining heat from, the outside.

◆ Ways to conserve energy use in transportation include making more efficient vehicles, carpooling, and using public transit.

Key Terms

energy conservation   insulation
efficiency

USING THE INTERNET

ACTIVITY

www.science-explorer.phschool.com

Reviewing Content

For more review of key concepts, see the Interactive Student Tutorial CD-ROM.

Multiple Choice
Choose the letter of the best answer.

1. Which of the following is *not* a fossil fuel?
   a. coal   b. wood
   c. oil   d. natural gas
2. Wind and water energy are both indirect forms of
   a. nuclear energy.
   b. electrical energy.
   c. solar energy.
   d. geothermal energy.
3. Which of the following is *not* a biomass fuel?
   a. methane
   b. gasohol
   c. hydrogen
   d. sugar-cane wastes
4. The particle used to start a nuclear fission reaction is a(n)
   a. neutron.
   b. nucleus.
   c. proton.
   d. atom.
5. A part of a nuclear power plant that undergoes a fission reaction is called a
   a. turbine.
   b. control rod.
   c. heat exchanger.
   d. fuel rod.

True or False
If the statement is true, write true. If it is false, change the underlined word or words to make the statement true.

6. Products made from petroleum are called <u>hydrocarbons</u>.
7. The process of burning a fuel for energy is <u>combustion</u>.
8. Geothermal energy is an example of a <u>nonrenewable</u> energy source.
9. Solar energy is harnessed to run calculators using <u>solar satellites</u>.
10. Most of the energy used in the United States today comes from <u>fossil fuels</u>.

Checking Concepts

11. Explain why coal mining is a difficult task.
12. Describe how coal forms.
13. Describe three features of a solar home. (Your answer may include passive or active solar systems.)
14. Explain how wind can be used to generate electricity.
15. What factors limit the use of tides as an energy source?
16. How is a nuclear fission reaction controlled in a nuclear power plant?
17. Define *energy efficiency*. Give three examples of inventions that increase energy efficiency.
18. **Writing to Learn** Suppose you had no electricity. Write a journal entry describing a typical weekday, including your meals, classes, and after-school activities. Explain how you might get things done without electricity.

Thinking Visually

19. **Compare/Contrast Table** Copy the table about types of energy onto a separate sheet of paper. Then complete the table and add a title. The first line is filled in as an example. (For more on compare/contrast tables see the Skills Handbook.)

Energy Type	Advantages	Disadvantages
Coal	Produces large amount of energy; easy to transport	Causes air pollution when burned; difficult to mine
Petroleum		
Solar		
Wind		
Water		
Geothermal		
Nuclear		

Applying Skills

The table below shows how the world's energy production changed between 1973 and 1995. Use the information in the table to answer Questions 20–23.

Source of Energy	Energy Units Produced 1973	Energy Units Produced 1995
Coal	1,498	2,179
Gas	964	1,775
Hydroelectric	107	242
Nuclear	54	646
Oil	2,730	3,228
TOTAL Energy Units	5,353	8,070

20. Interpreting Data How did the total energy production change between 1973 and 1995?

21. Calculating What percentage of the total world energy production did nuclear power provide in 1973? In 1995?

22. Classifying Classify the different types of energy according to whether they are renewable or nonrenewable. How important was renewable energy to the world's energy production in 1995?

23. Drawing Conclusions Which energy source was the most important in the world in 1995?

Critical Thinking

24. Comparing and Contrasting Discuss how the three major fossil fuels are alike and how they are different.

25. Classifying State whether each of the following energy sources is renewable or nonrenewable: coal, solar power, methane, hydrogen. Give a reason for each answer.

26. Making Judgments Write a short paragraph explaining why you agree or disagree with the following statement: "The United States should build more nuclear power plants to prepare for the future shortage of fossil fuels."

Performance Assessment

CHAPTER PROJECT 6 Wrap Up

Present Your Project Share your report with another group. The group should review the report for clarity, organization, and detail. Make revisions based on feedback from the other group. As a class, discuss each group's findings. Prepare a class proposal with the best suggestions for conserving energy in your school.

Reflect and Record In your project notebook, explain what types of energy use were the hardest to measure. What other information would you have liked to have when making your recommendations? Record your overall opinion of energy efficiency in your school.

Getting Involved

In Your Community Find out what major sources of energy provide electricity to your area. Create a public-service announcement or poster informing people about these energy sources and explaining the importance of energy conservation. Be sure to include some practical suggestions of what families can do to conserve.

African Rain Forests
Preserving Diversity

What forest—

is home to a beetle with wings larger than a sparrow's?

contains a frog that's 30 cm long?

is home to gorillas, chimpanzees, and pygmy hippos?

▲ Ball python

▲ Comet moth

I t's an African rain forest. Thousands of plants and animals live here, from colorful orchids to fruit bats, tree frogs, and elephants.

The rain forests of Africa grow in a band near the equator. About 80 percent of the rain-forested area is in central Africa, in the vast basin of the great Congo River. Some parts of the central African rain forest are so dense and hard to reach that explorers have never visited them. East Africa, which is drier and more heavily populated, has only scattered areas of rain forest.

The rain forest regions of the world have similar life forms and niches. But the rain forests of different continents have very different species.

African Rain Forests

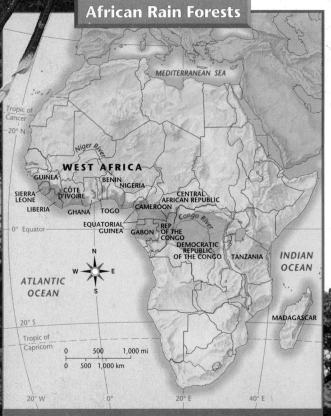

MEDITERRANEAN SEA

Tropic of Cancer

20° N

Niger River

WEST AFRICA

GUINEA

BENIN

SIERRA LEONE

CÔTE D'IVOIRE

NIGERIA

CENTRAL AFRICAN REPUBLIC

LIBERIA

GHANA

TOGO

CAMEROON

EQUATORIAL GUINEA

GABON

REP. OF THE CONGO

Congo River

0° Equator

DEMOCRATIC REPUBLIC OF THE CONGO

TANZANIA

INDIAN OCEAN

ATLANTIC OCEAN

N W E S

20° S

MADAGASCAR

Tropic of Capricorn

0   500   1,000 mi

0   500   1,000 km

20° W   0°   20° E   40° E

Major areas of tropical rain forest, shown in green on the map, cover only 7 percent of Africa.

Bonobo chimpanzee ▶

Layers of the Rain Forest

From above, the rain forest may look like a mass of broccoli. But it's really many forests in one—like different levels in an apartment building.

Each layer from the forest floor to the emergent, or top, layer varies in climate and is home to different plants and animals. The emergent layer captures the most rain, sunlight, heat, and wind. Colobus monkeys swing from vines and branches. Vast numbers of birds live in the trees.

Over time, African rain forest plants and animals have developed unusual adaptations to life at different layers of the forest. Some monkeys living in the canopy have long, muscular legs. They can run and leap through the branches. Guenons and baboons have strong teeth and jaws that allow them to crunch fruits, nuts, and seeds. Other monkeys have shorter tails but longer front legs. They live mainly on the forest floor.

In the understory, small animals such as frogs and squirrels "fly." They have tough membranes that stretch between their front and hind legs and allow them to glide from branch to branch.

The forest floor is dark, humid, and still. Termites feed on dead leaves and brush. Many plants have large leaves that allow them to catch the dim light. Some animals, such as frogs and insects, grow to gigantic sizes. Others are little, like the pygmy hippo that runs through the forest.

Science Activity

Design a rain forest animal that is adapted to life at a certain level of the rain forest. Consider how your animal lives, how it travels, and what food it eats. Outline its characteristics and explain how each adaptation helps the animal survive. Draw a sketch.

The emergent layer is formed by a few taller trees that poke through the canopy. Some of these trees are as much as 70 meters high—about as tall as a 17-story building. Colobus monkeys (above) live at this level.

The canopy, from 10 to 40 meters high, is the dense "roof" of the rain forest. The crowns of trees capture sunlight to use in photosynthesis. Rainwater and sunlight filter through thick vegetation. Epiphytic orchids grow to the top of the canopy (below).

The understory has trees and plants that need little light. Pythons lurk in the vegetation. On the forest floor live other animals like the pygmy hippo and the gorilla.

70 meters
60 meters
50 meters
40 meters
30 meters
20 meters
10 meters
0 meters

Reaching for Sunlight

Most rain forest trees are evergreens with broad leathery leaves. Some, like the African yellowwood, are conifers. Because the forest is so dense, trees must grow tall and straight to reach sunlight at the top of the canopy.

Along rivers, the floor and understory of the rain forest are a tangle of plants. Early explorers traveling the rivers assumed that the entire rain forest had similar thick vegetation, or jungle. In fact, the rain forest floor is surprisingly bare.

The canopy trees block the sunlight from plants below. Shaded by the dense canopy, the understory and forest floor are humid and dark. Water drips from the leaves of the canopy high overhead. Young trees have the best chance to grow when trees fall, opening up sunny clearings.

West Africa's tropical forests contain many valuable trees. African mahogany and teak are used to make furniture, tools, and boats. Oil from the oil palm is used in soaps, candles, and some foods. Trees such as ebony that can tolerate shade, grow slowly and develop dark, hard, long-lasting wood.

Trees of the Rain Forest	
Tree	**Maximum Height**
African oil palm	18 m
African yellowwood	20 m
Cape fig	7 m
Ebony	30 m
Kapok	70 m
Raffia palm	12 m
Teak	46 m

African oil palms ▲ grow in Nigeria.

Math Activity

The table on this page gives the height of some of the trees in the rain forest. Use the information in the table to make a bar graph. On the horizontal axis, label the trees. Use the vertical axis to show the height of the trees.

◆ Which tree has the greatest maximum height? The least maximum height?

◆ What is the height difference between the tallest and the shortest trees?

◆ What is the average height of all the trees shown in the graph?

◀ This African sculpture is made of wood from the African rain forest.

The Mbuti (above) hunt and fish along the Congo River. Their clothing is made of bark cloth (left).

Ituri Forest People

The native peoples of the African rain forest live as they have for thousands of years—by hunting and gathering. The forest supplies them with everything they need—food, water, firewood, building materials, and medicines.

One group of rain forest dwellers is the Mbuti people. The Mbuti live in the Ituri forest of the Democratic Republic of the Congo. Many of the Mbuti are quite small. The men hunt game, such as gazelle and antelope. The women gather wild fruits, nuts, and greens. Their traditional Mbuti clothing is made of tree bark and is wrapped around the waist. The bark is beaten to make it soft. Then it's decorated with geometric designs.

Most Mbuti live as nomads, with no single settled home. Every few months they set up new hunting grounds. They build temporary dome-shaped huts of branches and leaves. Hunting groups of about 10 to 25 families live together. They divide the hunting area among the family groups. On occasion, larger groups gather for ceremonies with dances and ritual music.

Modern Africa has brought changes to the forest people, especially for those who live near the edges of the rain forest. For a few months of the year, some Mbuti work as laborers for farmers who live in villages at the edge of the forest. When their work is finished, the Mbuti return to the Ituri forest. Most forest people prefer not to cultivate their own land. Since the farmers don't hunt, they trade their goods for meat. In exchange for meat, the Mbuti receive goods such as iron tools, cooking pots, clothes, bananas, and other farm produce.

Social Studies Activity

List the goods that forest people and farmers might have to trade. Assume that no modern conveniences, such as tractors and stoves, are available. Write a paragraph or two explaining how goods might be exchanged. Assign a value to the farmers' goods and the Mbuti goods, depending upon each group's needs. For example, decide how much meat a farmer should pay for medicines from the rain forest. How would the trading process change if money were exchanged?

Climbing the Canopy

Much of the rain forest is still a mystery because it's so difficult for scientists to study the canopy. Native forest people sometimes climb these tall trees using strong, thick vines called lianas as support. But rain forest scientists have had to find different methods. Naturalist Gerald Durrell, working in the African rain forest, was lucky enough to find another way to observe the canopy. He describes it here:

*W*hile the canopy is one of the most richly inhabited regions of the forest it is also the one that causes the naturalist the greatest frustration. There he is, down in the gloom among the giant tree trunks, hearing the noises of animal life high above him and having half-eaten fruit, flowers, or seeds rained on him by legions of animals high in their sunlit domain—all of which he cannot see. Under these circumstances the naturalist develops a very bad temper and a permanent crick in the neck.

However, there was one occasion when I managed to transport myself into the forest canopy, and it was a magical experience. It happened in West Africa when I was camped on the thickly forested lower slopes of a mountain called N'da Ali. Walking through the forest one day I found I was walking along the edge of a great step cut out of the mountain. The cliff face, covered with creepers, dropped away for about 50 yards, so that although I was walking through forest, just next to me and slightly below was the canopy of the forest growing up from the base of the cliff. This cliff was over half a mile in length and provided me with a natural balcony from which I could observe the treetop life simply by lying on the cliff edge, concealed in the low undergrowth.

Over a period of about a week I spent hours up there and a whole pageant of wildlife passed by. The numbers of birds were incredible, ranging from minute glittering sunbirds in rainbow coloring, zooming like helicopters from blossom to blossom as they fed on the nectar, to the flocks of huge black hornbills with their monstrous yellow beaks who flew in such an ungainly manner and made such a noise over their choice of forest fruits.

From early morning to evening when it grew too dark to see, I watched this parade of creatures. Troops of monkeys swept past, followed by attendant flocks of birds who fed eagerly on the insects that the monkeys disturbed during their noisy crashing through the trees. Squirrels chased each other, or hotly pursued lizards, or simply lay spread-eagled on branches high up in the trees, enjoying the sun.

Language Arts Activity

◆ Besides being an experienced naturalist and writer, Gerald Durrell is also a careful observer. In this selection, he describes in detail the "magical experience" of being in the canopy. Reread Durrell's description. Now work with a partner to write and design a pamphlet that will persuade visitors to come to an African rain forest. For your pamphlet, write strong, lively descriptions of what you might see, hear, and experience. Be persuasive.

Tie It Together

Celebrate Diversity

Rain forests have the greatest biodiversity—variety of plant and animal life—of any ecosystem on Earth. Many species have yet to be discovered! Plan a display for your school to celebrate biodiversity in the rain forests. Include drawings, photos, and detailed captions.

◆ On a large map, locate and label Earth's tropical rain forests. Divide into groups to choose one rain forest region to research, such as Africa, Brazil, Costa Rica, Hawaii, Indonesia, or Borneo.

◆ Have your group study several animal and plant species in its chosen rain forest. You might choose monkeys, butterflies, birds, orchids, or medicinal plants.

◆ For each species, describe its appearance, where it occurs in the rain forest, its role in the ecosystem, and how it is useful to humans.

British conservationist Gerald Durrell wrote about his adventures with wildlife around the world. He established a zoo on the British island of Jersey and worked to preserve threatened species. In the photo, Durrell holds an anteater.

Think Like a Scientist

Although you may not know it, you think like a scientist
every day. Whenever you ask a question and explore
possible answers, you use many of the same skills that
scientists do. Some of these skills are described on this page.

Observing

When you use one or more of your five senses
to gather information about the world, you are
observing. Hearing a dog bark, counting
twelve green seeds, and smelling smoke are all
observations. To increase the power of their
senses, scientists sometimes use microscopes,
telescopes, or other instruments that help
them make more detailed observations.

An observation must be factual and
accurate—an exact report of what your senses
detect. It is important to keep careful records
of your observations in science class by
writing or drawing in a notebook. The
information collected through observations
is called evidence, or data.

Inferring

When you explain or interpret an observation, you are **inferring,** or making an
inference. For example, if you hear your dog
barking, you may infer that someone is at
your front door. To make this inference, you
combine the evidence—the barking dog—
and your experience or knowledge—you
know that your dog barks when strangers
approach—to reach a logical conclusion.

Notice that an inference is not a fact;
it is only one of many possible
explanations for an observation. For
example, your dog may be barking
because it wants to go for a walk. An
inference may turn out to be incorrect
even if it is based on accurate observations and logical reasoning. The only
way to find out if an inference is correct
is to investigate further.

Predicting

When you listen to the weather forecast, you
hear many predictions about the next day's
weather—what the temperature will be,
whether it will rain, and how windy it will be.
Weather forecasters use observations and
knowledge of weather patterns to predict the
weather. The skill of **predicting** involves
making an inference about a future event
based on current evidence or past experience.

Because a prediction is an inference, it
may prove to be false. In science class, you can
test some of your predictions by
doing experiments. For
example, suppose you predict
that larger paper airplanes can
fly farther than smaller
airplanes. How could you
test your prediction?

 Use the photograph to answer the
questions below.

Observing Look closely at the photograph. List at
least three observations.

Inferring Use your observations to make an inference
about what has happened. What experience or
knowledge did you use to make the inference?

Predicting Predict what will happen next. On what
evidence or experience do you base your prediction?

Classifying

Could you imagine searching for a book in the library if the books were shelved in no particular order? Your trip to the library would be an all-day event! Luckily, librarians group together books on similar topics or by the same author. Grouping together items that are alike in some way is called **classifying.** You can classify items in many ways: by size, by shape, by use, and by other important characteristics.

Like librarians, scientists use the skill of classifying to organize information and objects. When things are sorted into groups, the relationships among them become easier to understand.

ACTIVITY

Classify the objects in the photograph into two groups based on any characteristic you choose. Then use another characteristic to classify the objects into three groups.

Making Models

Have you ever drawn a picture to help someone understand what you were saying? Such a drawing is one type of model. A model is a picture, diagram, computer image, or other representation of a complex object or process. **Making models** helps people understand things that they cannot observe directly.

Scientists often use models to represent things that are either very large or very small, such as the planets in the solar system, or the parts of a cell. Such models are physical models—drawings or three-dimensional structures that look like the real thing. Other models are mental models—mathematical equations or words that describe how something works.

ACTIVITY

This student is using a model to demonstrate what causes day and night on Earth. What do the flashlight and the tennis ball in the model represent?

Communicating

Whenever you talk on the phone, write a letter, or listen to your teacher at school, you are communicating. **Communicating** is the process of sharing ideas and information with other people. Communicating effectively requires many skills, including writing, reading, speaking, listening, and making models.

Scientists communicate to share results, information, and opinions. Scientists often communicate about their work in journals, over the telephone, in letters, and on the Internet. They also attend scientific meetings where they share their ideas with one another in person.

ACTIVITY

On a sheet of paper, write out clear, detailed directions for tying your shoe. Then exchange directions with a partner. Follow your partner's directions exactly. How successful were you at tying your shoe? How could your partner have communicated more clearly?

Making Measurements

When scientists make observations, it is not sufficient to say that something is "big" or "heavy." Instead, scientists use instruments to measure just how big or heavy an object is. By measuring, scientists can express their observations more precisely and communicate more information about what they observe.

Measuring in SI

The standard system of measurement used by scientists around the world is known as the International System of Units, which is abbreviated as SI (in French, *Système International d'Unités*). SI units are easy to use because they are based on multiples of 10. Each unit is ten times larger than the next smallest unit and one tenth the size of the next largest unit. The table lists the prefixes used to name the most common SI units.

Common SI Prefixes		
Prefix	**Symbol**	**Meaning**
kilo-	k	1,000
hecto-	h	100
deka-	da	10
deci-	d	0.1 (one tenth)
centi-	c	0.01 (one hundredth)
milli-	m	0.001 (one thousandth)

Length To measure length, or the distance between two points, the unit of measure is the **meter (m).** One meter is the approximate distance from the floor to a doorknob. Long distances, such as the distance between two cities, are measured in kilometers (km). Small lengths are measured in centimeters (cm) or millimeters (mm). Scientists use metric rulers and meter sticks to measure length.

Common Conversions
1 km = 1,000 m
1 m = 100 cm
1 m = 1,000 mm
1 cm = 10 mm

ACTIVITY

The larger lines on the metric ruler in the picture show centimeter divisions, while the smaller, unnumbered lines show millimeter divisions. How many centimeters long is the shell? How many millimeters long is it?

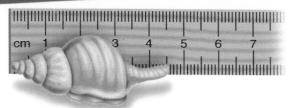

Liquid Volume To measure the volume of a liquid, or the amount of space it takes up, you will use a unit of measure known as the **liter (L).** One liter is the approximate volume of a medium-sized carton of milk. Smaller volumes are measured in milliliters (mL). Scientists use graduated cylinders to measure liquid volume.

Common Conversion
1 L = 1,000 mL

ACTIVITY

The graduated cylinder in the picture is marked in milliliter divisions. Notice that the water in the cylinder has a curved surface. This curved surface is called the *meniscus.* To measure the volume, you must read the level at the lowest point of the meniscus. What is the volume of water in this graduated cylinder?

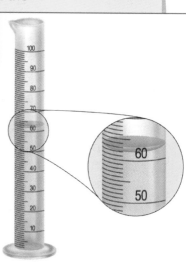

Mass To measure mass, or the amount of matter in an object, you will use a unit of measure known as the **gram (g)**. One gram is approximately the mass of a paper clip. Larger masses are measured in kilograms (kg). Scientists use a balance to find the mass of an object.

Common Conversion

1 kg = 1,000 g

The electronic balance displays the mass of an apple in kilograms. **ACTIVITY** What is the mass of the apple? Suppose a recipe for applesauce called for one kilogram of apples. About how many apples would you need?

Temperature
To measure the temperature of a substance, you will use the **Celsius scale**. Temperature is measured in degrees Celsius (°C) using a Celsius thermometer. Water freezes at 0°C and boils at 100°C.

ACTIVITY What is the temperature of the liquid in degrees Celsius?

Converting SI Units

To use the SI system, you must know how to convert between units. Converting from one unit to another involves the skill of **calculating**, or using mathematical operations. Converting between SI units is similar to converting between dollars and dimes because both systems are based on multiples of ten.

Suppose you want to convert a length of 80 centimeters to meters. Follow these steps to convert between units.

1. Begin by writing down the measurement you want to convert—in this example, 80 centimeters.

2. Write a conversion factor that represents the relationship between the two units you are converting. In this example, the relationship is *1 meter = 100 centimeters*. Write this conversion factor as a fraction, making sure to place the units you are converting from (centimeters, in this example) in the denominator.

3. Multiply the measurement you want to convert by the fraction. When you do this, the units in the first measurement will cancel out with the units in the denominator. Your answer will be in the units you are converting to (meters, in this example).

Example

80 centimeters = ____?____ meters

$$80 \text{ centimeters} \times \frac{1 \text{ meter}}{100 \text{ centimeters}} = \frac{80 \text{ meters}}{100}$$

$$= 0.8 \text{ meters}$$

Convert between the following units. **ACTIVITY**
1. 600 millimeters = __?__ meters
2. 0.35 liters = __?__ milliliters
3. 1,050 grams = __?__ kilograms

Conducting a Scientific Investigation

In some ways, scientists are like detectives, piecing together clues to learn about a process or event. One way that scientists gather clues is by carrying out experiments. An experiment tests an idea in a careful, orderly manner. Although all experiments do not follow the same steps in the same order, many follow a pattern similar to the one described here.

Posing Questions

Experiments begin by asking a scientific question. A scientific question is one that can be answered by gathering evidence. For example, the question "Which freezes faster— fresh water or salt water?" is a scientific question because you can carry out an investigation and gather information to answer the question.

Developing a Hypothesis

The next step is to form a hypothesis. A **hypothesis** is a prediction about the outcome of the experiment. Like all predictions, hypotheses are based on your observations and previous knowledge or experience. But, unlike many predictions, a hypothesis must be something that can be tested. A properly worded hypothesis should take the form of an *If . . . then . . .* statement. For example, a hypothesis might be *"If I add salt to fresh water, then the water will take longer to freeze."* A hypothesis worded this way serves as a rough outline of the experiment you should perform.

Designing an Experiment

Next you need to plan a way to test your hypothesis. Your plan should be written out as a step-by-step procedure and should describe the observations or measurements you will make.

Two important steps involved in designing an experiment are controlling variables and forming operational definitions.

Controlling Variables In a well-designed experiment, you need to keep all variables the same except for one. A **variable** is any factor that can change in an experiment. The factor that you change is called the **manipulated variable.** In this experiment, the manipulated variable is the amount of salt added to the water. Other factors, such as the amount of water or the starting temperature, are kept constant.

The factor that changes as a result of the manipulated variable is called the responding variable. The **responding variable** is what you measure or observe to obtain your results. In this experiment, the responding variable is how long the water takes to freeze.

An experiment in which all factors except one are kept constant is a **controlled experiment.** Most controlled experiments include a test called the control. In this experiment, Container 3 is the control. Because no salt is added to Container 3, you can compare the results from the other containers to it. Any difference in results must be due to the addition of salt alone.

Forming Operational Definitions
Another important aspect of a well-designed experiment is having clear operational definitions. An **operational definition** is a statement that describes how a particular variable is to be measured or how a term is to be defined. For example, in this experiment, how will you determine if the water has frozen? You might decide to insert a stick in each container at the start of the experiment. Your operational definition of "frozen" would be the time at which the stick can no longer move.

EXPERIMENTAL PROCEDURE

1. Fill 3 containers with 300 milliliters of cold tap water.

2. Add 10 grams of salt to Container 1; stir. Add 20 grams of salt to Container 2; stir. Add no salt to Container 3.

3. Place the 3 containers in a freezer.

4. Check the containers every 15 minutes. Record your observations.

Interpreting Data

The observations and measurements you make in an experiment are called data. At the end of an experiment, you need to analyze the data to look for any patterns or trends. Patterns often become clear if you organize your data in a data table or graph. Then think through what the data reveal. Do they support your hypothesis? Do they point out a flaw in your experiment? Do you need to collect more data?

Drawing Conclusions

A conclusion is a statement that sums up what you have learned from an experiment. When you draw a conclusion, you need to decide whether the data you collected support your hypothesis or not. You may need to repeat an experiment several times before you can draw any conclusions from it. Conclusions often lead you to pose new questions and plan new experiments to answer them.

Is a ball's bounce affected by the height from which it is dropped? Using the steps just described, plan a controlled experiment to investigate this problem. **ACTIVITY**

Thinking Critically

Has a friend ever asked for your advice about a problem? If so, you may have helped your friend think through the problem in a logical way. Without knowing it, you used critical-thinking skills to help your friend. Critical thinking involves the use of reasoning and logic to solve problems or make decisions. Some critical-thinking skills are described below.

Comparing and Contrasting

When you examine two objects for similarities and differences, you are using the skill of **comparing and contrasting.** Comparing involves identifying similarities, or common characteristics. Contrasting involves identifying differences. Analyzing objects in this way can help you discover details that you might otherwise overlook.

ACTIVITY

Compare and contrast the two animals in the photo. First list all the similarities that you see. Then list all the differences.

Applying Concepts

When you use your knowledge about one situation to make sense of a similar situation, you are using the skill of **applying concepts.** Being able to transfer your knowledge from one situation to another shows that you truly understand a concept. You may use this skill in answering test questions that present different problems from the ones you've reviewed in class.

ACTIVITY

You have just learned that water takes longer to freeze when other substances are mixed into it. Use this knowledge to explain why people need a substance called antifreeze in their car's radiator in the winter.

Interpreting Illustrations

Diagrams, photographs, and maps are included in textbooks to help clarify what you read. These illustrations show processes, places, and ideas in a visual manner. The skill called **interpreting illustrations** can help you learn from these visual elements. To understand an illustration, take the time to study the illustration along with all the written information that accompanies it. Captions identify the key concepts shown in the illustration. Labels point out the important parts of a diagram or map, while keys identify the symbols used in a map.

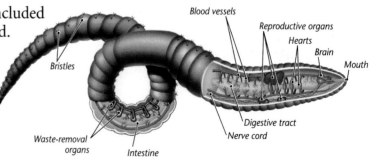

Blood vessels

Reproductive organs

Hearts

Brain

Mouth

Bristles

Digestive tract

Nerve cord

Waste-removal organs

Intestine

▲ Internal anatomy of an earthworm

ACTIVITY

Study the diagram above. Then write a short paragraph explaining what you have learned.

Relating Cause and Effect

If one event causes another event to occur, the two events are said to have a cause-and-effect relationship. When you determine that such a relationship exists between two events, you use a skill called **relating cause and effect.** For example, if you notice an itchy, red bump on your skin, you might infer that a mosquito bit you. The mosquito bite is the cause, and the bump is the effect.

It is important to note that two events do not necessarily have a cause-and-effect relationship just because they occur together. Scientists carry out experiments or use past experience to determine whether a cause-and-effect relationship exists.

You are on a camping trip and your flashlight has stopped working. List some possible causes for the flashlight malfunction. How could you determine which cause-and-effect relationship has left you in the dark?

Making Generalizations

When you draw a conclusion about an entire group based on information about only some of the group's members, you are using a skill called **making generalizations.** For a generalization to be valid, the sample you choose must be large enough and representative of the entire group. You might, for example, put this skill to work at a farm stand if you see a sign that says, "Sample some grapes before you buy." If you sample a few sweet grapes, you may conclude that all the grapes are sweet—and purchase a large bunch.

A team of scientists needs to determine whether the water in a large reservoir is safe to drink. How could they use the skill of making generalizations to help them? What should they do?

Making Judgments

When you evaluate something to decide whether it is good or bad, or right or wrong, you are using a skill called **making judgments.** For example, you make judgments when you decide to eat healthful foods or to pick up litter in a park. Before you make a judgment, you need to think through the pros and cons of a situation, and identify the values or standards that you hold.

Should children and teens be required to wear helmets when bicycling? Explain why you feel the way you do.

Problem Solving

When you use critical-thinking skills to resolve an issue or decide on a course of action, you are using a skill called **problem solving.** Some problems, such as how to convert a fraction into a decimal, are straightforward. Other problems, such as figuring out why your computer has stopped working, are complex. Some complex problems can be solved using the trial and error method—try out one solution first, and if that doesn't work, try another. Other useful problem-solving strategies include making models and brainstorming possible solutions with a partner.

Organizing Information

As you read this textbook, how can you make sense of all the information it contains? Some useful tools to help you organize information are shown on this page. These tools are called *graphic organizers* because they give you a visual picture of a topic, showing at a glance how key concepts are related.

Concept Maps

Concept maps are useful tools for organizing information on broad topics. A concept map begins with a general concept and shows how it can be broken down into more specific concepts. In that way, relationships between concepts become easier to understand.

A concept map is constructed by placing concept words (usually nouns) in ovals and connecting them with linking words. Often, the most general concept word is placed at the top, and the words become more specific as you move downward. Often the linking words, which are written on a line extending between two ovals, describe the relationship between the two concepts they connect. If you follow any string of concepts and linking words down the map, it should read like a sentence.

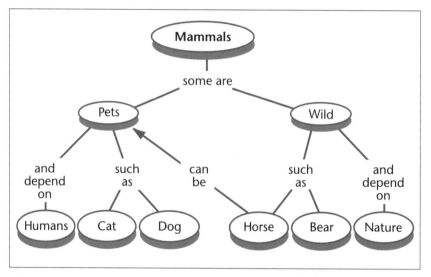

Some concept maps include linking words that connect a concept on one branch of the map to a concept on another branch. These linking words, called cross-linkages, show more complex interrelationships among concepts.

Compare/Contrast Tables

Compare/contrast tables are useful tools for sorting out the similarities and differences ~~be~~tween two or more items. A table provides ~~an or~~ganized framework in which to compare ~~base~~d on specific characteristics that

Characteristic	Baseball	Basketball
Number of Players	9	5
Playing Field	Baseball diamond	Basketball court
Equipment	Bat, baseball, mitts	Basket, basketball

~~To create a co~~mpare/contrast table, list the ~~items to be compared~~ across the top of a table. ~~Then list the charac~~teristics that will form the ~~basis of your com~~parison in the left-hand

column. Complete the table by filling in information about each characteristic, first for one item and then for the other.

Venn Diagrams

Another way to show similarities and differences between items is with a Venn diagram. A Venn diagram consists of two or more circles that partially overlap. Each circle represents a particular concept or idea. Common characteristics, or similarities, are written within the area of overlap between the two circles. Unique characteristics, or differences, are written in the parts of the circles outside the area of overlap.

To create a Venn diagram, draw two over-lapping circles. Label the circles with the names of the items being compared. Write the

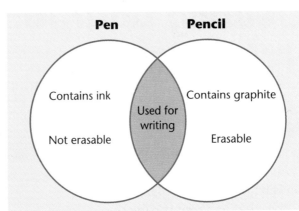

unique characteristics in each circle outside the area of overlap. Then write the shared characteristics within the area of overlap.

Flowcharts

A flowchart can help you understand the order in which certain events have occurred or should occur. Flowcharts are useful for outlining the stages in a process or the steps in a procedure.

To make a flowchart, write a brief description of each event in a box. Place the first event at the top of the page, followed by the second event, the third event, and so on. Then draw an arrow to connect each event to the one that occurs next.

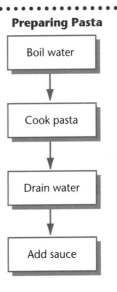

Cycle Diagrams

A cycle diagram can be used to show a sequence of events that is continuous, or cyclical. A continuous sequence does not have an end because, when the final event is over, the first event begins again. Like a flowchart, a cycle diagram can help you understand the order of events.

To create a cycle diagram, write a brief description of each event in a box. Place one event at the top of the page in the center. Then, moving in a clockwise direction around an imaginary circle, write each event in its proper sequence. Draw arrows that connect each event to the one that occurs next, forming a continuous circle.

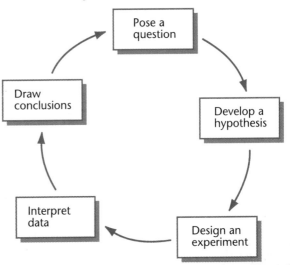

Creating Data Tables and Graphs

How can you make sense of the data in a science experiment? The first step is to organize the data to help you understand them. Data tables and graphs are helpful tools for organizing data.

Data Tables

You have gathered your materials and set up your experiment. But before you start, you need to plan a way to record what happens during the experiment. By creating a data table, you can record your observations and measurements in an orderly way.

Suppose, for example, that a scientist conducted an experiment to find out how many Calories people of different body masses burn while doing various activities. The data table shows the results.

Notice in this data table that the manipulated variable (body mass) is the heading of one column. The responding variable (for Experiment 1, the number of Calories burned while bicycling) is the heading of the next column. Additional columns were added for related experiments.

CALORIES BURNED IN 30 MINUTES OF ACTIVITY			
Body Mass	Experiment 1 Bicycling	Experiment 2 Playing Basketball	Experiment 3 Watching Television
30 kg	60 Calories	120 Calories	21 Calories
40 kg	77 Calories	164 Calories	27 Calories
50 kg	95 Calories	206 Calories	33 Calories
60 kg	114 Calories	248 Calories	38 Calories

Bar Graphs

To compare how many Calories a person burns doing various activities, you could create a bar graph. A bar graph is used to display data in a number of separate, or distinct, categories. In this example, bicycling, playing basketball, and watching television are three separate categories.

To create a bar graph, follow these steps.
1. On graph paper, draw a horizontal, or *x*-, axis and a vertical, or *y*-, axis.
2. Write the names of the categories to be graphed along the horizontal axis. Include an overall label for the axis as well.
3. Label the vertical axis with the name of the responding variable. Include units of measurement. Then create a scale along the axis by marking off equally spaced numbers that cover the range of the data collected.
4. For each category, draw a solid bar using the scale on the vertical axis to determine the

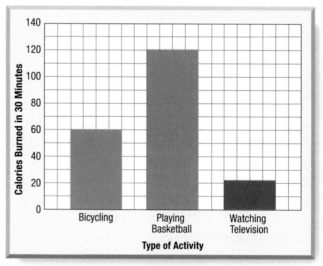

Calories Burned by a 30-kilogram Person in Various Activities

appropriate height. For example, for bicycling, draw the bar as high as the 60 mark on the vertical axis. Make all the bars the same width and leave equal spaces between them.
5. Add a title that describes the graph.

Line Graphs

To see whether a relationship exists between body mass and the number of Calories burned while bicycling, you could create a line graph. A line graph is used to display data that show how one variable (the responding variable) changes in response to another variable (the manipulated variable). You can use a line graph when your manipulated variable is *continuous*, that is, when there are other points between the ones that you tested. In this example, body mass is a continuous variable because there are other body masses between 30 and 40 kilograms (for example, 31 kilograms). Time is another example of a continuous variable.

Line graphs are powerful tools because they allow you to estimate values for conditions that you did not test in the experiment. For example, you can use the line graph to estimate that a 35-kilogram person would burn 68 Calories while bicycling.

To create a line graph, follow these steps.

1. On graph paper, draw a horizontal, or *x*-, axis and a vertical, or *y*-, axis.
2. Label the horizontal axis with the name of the manipulated variable. Label the vertical axis with the name of the responding variable. Include units of measurement.
3. Create a scale on each axis by marking off equally spaced numbers that cover the range of the data collected.
4. Plot a point on the graph for each piece of data. In the line graph above, the dotted lines show how to plot the first data point (30 kilograms and 60 Calories). Draw an imaginary vertical line extending up from the horizontal axis at the 30-kilogram mark. Then draw an imaginary horizontal line extending across from the vertical axis at the 60-Calorie mark. Plot the point where the two lines intersect.

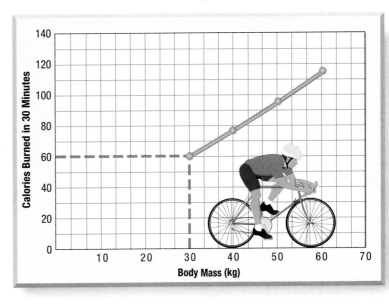

Effect of Body Mass on Calories Burned While Bicycling

5. Connect the plotted points with a solid line. (In some cases, it may be more appropriate to draw a line that shows the general trend of the plotted points. In those cases, some of the points may fall above or below the line.)
6. Add a title that identifies the variables or relationship in the graph.

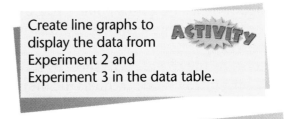

ACTIVITY

Create line graphs to display the data from Experiment 2 and Experiment 3 in the data table.

ACTIVITY

You read in the newspaper that a total of 4 centimeters of rain fell in your area in June, 2.5 centimeters fell in July, and 1.5 centimeters fell in August. What type of graph would you use to display these data? Use graph paper to create the graph.

Circle Graphs

Like bar graphs, circle graphs can be used to display data in a number of separate categories. Unlike bar graphs, however, circle graphs can only be used when you have data for *all* the categories that make up a given topic. A circle graph is sometimes called a pie chart because it resembles a pie cut into slices. The pie represents the entire topic, while the slices represent the individual categories. The size of a slice indicates what percentage of the whole a particular category makes up.

The data table below shows the results of a survey in which 24 teenagers were asked to identify their favorite sport. The data were then used to create the circle graph at the right.

Sports That Teens Prefer

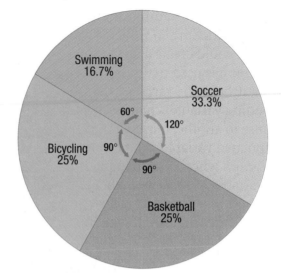

FAVORITE SPORTS	
Sport	Number of Students
Soccer	8
Basketball	6
Bicycling	6
Swimming	4

To create a circle graph, follow these steps.

1. Use a compass to draw a circle. Mark the center of the circle with a point. Then draw a line from the center point to the top of the circle.

2. Determine the size of each "slice" by setting up a proportion where *x* equals the number of degrees in a slice. (NOTE: A circle contains 360 degrees.) For example, to find the number of degrees in the "soccer" slice, set up the following proportion:

$$\frac{\text{students who prefer soccer}}{\text{total number of students}} = \frac{x}{\text{total number of degrees in a circle}}$$

$$\frac{8}{24} = \frac{x}{360}$$

Cross-multiply and solve for *x*.

$$24x = 8 \times 360$$
$$x = 120$$

The "soccer" slice should contain 120 degrees.

3. Use a protractor to measure the angle of the first slice, using the line you drew to the top of the circle as the 0° line. Draw a line from the center of the circle to the edge for the angle you measured.

4. Continue around the circle by measuring the size of each slice with the protractor. Start measuring from the edge of the previous slice so the wedges do not overlap. When you are done, the entire circle should be filled in.

5. Determine the percentage of the whole circle that each slice represents. To do this, divide the number of degrees in a slice by the total number of degrees in a circle (360), and multiply by 100%. For the "soccer" slice, you can find the percentage as follows:

$$\frac{120}{360} \times 100\% = 33.3\%$$

6. Use a different color to shade in each slice. Label each slice with the name of the category and with the percentage of the whole it represents.

7. Add a title to the circle graph.

ACTIVITY

In a class of 28 students, 12 students take the bus to school, 10 students walk, and 6 students ride their bicycles. Create a circle graph to display these data.

Laboratory Safety

Safety Symbols

These symbols alert you to possible dangers in the laboratory and remind you to work carefully.

Safety Goggles Always wear safety goggles to protect your eyes in any activity involving chemicals, flames or heating, or the possibility of broken glassware.

Lab Apron Wear a laboratory apron to protect your skin and clothing from damage.

Breakage You are working with materials that may be breakable, such as glass containers, glass tubing, thermometers, or funnels. Handle breakable materials with care. Do not touch broken glassware.

Heat-resistant Gloves Use an oven mitt or other hand protection when handling hot materials. Hot plates, hot glassware, or hot water can cause burns. Do not touch hot objects with your bare hands.

Heating Use a clamp or tongs to pick up hot glassware. Do not touch hot objects with your bare hands.

Sharp Object Pointed-tip scissors, scalpels, knives, needles, pins, or tacks are sharp. They can cut or puncture your skin. Always direct a sharp edge or point away from yourself and others. Use sharp instruments only as instructed.

Electric Shock Avoid the possibility of electric shock. Never use electrical equipment around water, or when the equipment is wet or your hands are wet. Be sure cords are untangled and cannot trip anyone. Disconnect the equipment when it is not in use.

Corrosive Chemical You are working with an acid or another corrosive chemical. Avoid getting it on your skin or clothing, or in your eyes. Do not inhale the vapors. Wash your hands when you are finished with the activity.

Poison Do not let any poisonous chemical come in contact with your skin, and do not inhale its vapors. Wash your hands when you are finished with the activity.

Physical Safety When an experiment involves physical activity, take precautions to avoid injuring yourself or others. Follow instructions from your teacher. Alert your teacher if there is any reason you should not participate in the activity.

Animal Safety Treat live animals with care to avoid harming the animals or yourself. Working with animal parts or preserved animals also may require caution. Wash your hands when you are finished with the activity.

Plant Safety Handle plants in the laboratory or during field work only as directed by your teacher. If you are allergic to certain plants, tell your teacher before doing an activity in which those plants are used. Avoid touching harmful plants such as poison ivy, poison oak, or poison sumac, or plants with thorns. Wash your hands when you are finished with the activity.

Flames You may be working with flames from a lab burner, candle, or matches. Tie back loose hair and clothing. Follow instructions from your teacher about lighting and extinguishing flames.

No Flames Flammable materials may be present. Make sure there are no flames, sparks, or other exposed heat sources present.

Fumes When poisonous or unpleasant vapors may be involved, work in a ventilated area. Avoid inhaling vapors directly. Only test an odor when directed to do so by your teacher, and use a wafting motion to direct the vapor toward your nose.

Disposal Chemicals and other laboratory materials used in the activity must be disposed of safely. Follow the instructions from your teacher.

Hand Washing Wash your hands thoroughly when finished with the activity. Use antibacterial soap and warm water. Lather both sides of your hands and between your fingers. Rinse well.

General Safety Awareness You may see this symbol when none of the symbols described earlier appears. In this case, follow the specific instructions provided. You may also see this symbol when you are asked to develop your own procedure in a lab. Have your teacher approve your plan before you go further.

Science Safety Rules

To prepare yourself to work safely in the laboratory, read over the following safety rules. Then read them a second time. Make sure you understand and follow each rule. Ask your teacher to explain any rules you do not understand.

Dress Code

1. To protect yourself from injuring your eyes, wear safety goggles whenever you work with chemicals, burners, glassware, or any substance that might get into your eyes. If you wear contact lenses, notify your teacher.
2. Wear a lab apron or coat whenever you work with corrosive chemicals or substances that can stain.
3. Tie back long hair to keep it away from any chemicals, flames, or equipment.
4. Remove or tie back any article of clothing or jewelry that can hang down and touch chemicals, flames, or equipment. Roll up or secure long sleeves.
5. Never wear open shoes or sandals.

General Precautions

6. Read all directions for an experiment several times before beginning the activity. Carefully follow all written and oral instructions. If you are in doubt about any part of the experiment, ask your teacher for assistance.
7. Never perform activities that are not assigned or authorized by your teacher. Obtain permission before "experimenting" on your own. Never handle any equipment unless you have specific permission.
8. Never perform lab activities without direct supervision.
9. Never eat or drink in the laboratory.
10. Keep work areas clean and tidy at all times. Bring only notebooks and lab manuals or written lab procedures to the work area. All other items, such as purses and backpacks, should be left in a designated area.
11. Do not engage in horseplay.

First Aid

12. Always report all accidents or injuries to your teacher, no matter how minor. Notify your teacher immediately about any fires.
13. Learn what to do in case of specific accidents, such as getting acid in your eyes or on your skin. (Rinse acids from your body with lots of water.)
14. Be aware of the location of the first-aid kit, but do not use it unless instructed by your teacher. In case of injury, your teacher should administer first aid. Your teacher may also send you to the school nurse or call a physician.
15. Know the location of emergency equipment, such as the fire extinguisher and fire blanket, and know how to use it.
16. Know the location of the nearest telephone and whom to contact in an emergency.

Heating and Fire Safety

17. Never use a heat source, such as a candle, burner, or hot plate, without wearing safety goggles.
18. Never heat anything unless instructed to do so. A chemical that is harmless when cool may be dangerous when heated.
19. Keep all combustible materials away from flames. Never use a flame or spark near a combustible chemical.
20. Never reach across a flame.
21. Before using a laboratory burner, make sure you know proper procedures for lighting and adjusting the burner, as demonstrated by your teacher. Do not touch the burner. It may be hot. And never leave a lighted burner unattended!
22. Chemicals can splash or boil out of a heated test tube. When heating a substance in a test tube, make sure that the mouth of the tube is not pointed at you or anyone else.
23. Never heat a liquid in a closed container. The expanding gases produced may blow the container apart.
24. Before picking up a container that has been heated, hold the back of your hand near it. If you can feel heat on the back of your hand, the container is too hot to handle. Use an oven mitt to pick up a container that has been heated.

Using Chemicals Safely

25. Never mix chemicals "for the fun of it." You might produce a dangerous, possibly explosive substance.

26. Never put your face near the mouth of a container that holds chemicals. Never touch, taste, or smell a chemical unless you are instructed by your teacher to do so. Many chemicals are poisonous.

27. Use only those chemicals needed in the activity. Read and double-check labels on supply bottles before removing any chemicals. Take only as much as you need. Keep all containers closed when chemicals are not being used.

28. Dispose of all chemicals as instructed by your teacher. To avoid contamination, never return chemicals to their original containers. Never simply pour chemicals or other substances into the sink or trash containers.

29. Be extra careful when working with acids or bases. Pour all chemicals over the sink or a container, not over your work surface.

30. If you are instructed to test for odors, use a wafting motion to direct the odors to your nose. Do not inhale the fumes directly from the container.

31. When mixing an acid and water, always pour the water into the container first and then add the acid to the water. Never pour water into an acid.

32. Take extreme care not to spill any material in the laboratory. Wash chemical spills and splashes immediately with plenty of water. Immediately begin rinsing with water any acids that get on your skin or clothing, and notify your teacher of any acid spill at the same time.

Using Glassware Safely

33. Never force glass tubing or thermometers into a rubber stopper or rubber tubing. Have your teacher insert the glass tubing or thermometer if required for an activity.

34. If you are using a laboratory burner, use a wire screen to protect glassware from any flame. Never heat glassware that is not thoroughly dry on the outside.

35. Keep in mind that hot glassware looks cool. Never pick up glassware without first checking to see if it is hot. Use an oven mitt. See rule 24.

36. Never use broken or chipped glassware. If glassware breaks, notify your teacher and dispose of the glassware in the proper broken-glassware container. Never handle broken glass with your bare hands.

37. Never eat or drink from lab glassware.

38. Thoroughly clean glassware before putting it away.

Using Sharp Instruments

39. Handle scalpels or other sharp instruments with extreme care. Never cut material toward you; cut away from you.

40. Immediately notify your teacher if you cut your skin when working in the laboratory.

Animal and Plant Safety

41. Never perform experiments that cause pain, discomfort, or harm to mammals, birds, reptiles, fishes, or amphibians. This rule applies at home as well as in the classroom.

42. Animals should be handled only if absolutely necessary. Your teacher will instruct you as to how to handle each animal species brought into the classroom.

43. If you know that you are allergic to certain plants, molds, or animals, tell your teacher before doing an activity in which these are used.

44. During field work, protect your skin by wearing long pants, long sleeves, socks, and closed shoes. Know how to recognize the poisonous plants and fungi in your area, as well as plants with thorns, and avoid contact with them.

45. Never eat any part of an unidentified plant or fungus.

46. Wash your hands thoroughly after handling animals or the cage containing animals. Wash your hands when you are finished with any activity involving animal parts, plants, or soil.

End-of-Experiment Rules

47. After an experiment has been completed, clean up your work area and return all equipment to its proper place.

48. Dispose of waste materials as instructed by your teacher.

49. Wash your hands after every experiment.

50. Always turn off all burners or hot plates when they are not in use. Unplug hot plates and other electrical equipment. If you used a burner, check that the gas-line valve to the burner is off as well.

Glossary

abiotic factor A nonliving part of an ecosystem. (p. 18)

acid rain Precipitation that is more acidic than normal. (p. 142)

active solar system A method of capturing the sun's energy and distributing it using pumps and fans. (p. 173)

adaptation The behaviors and physical characteristics of species that allow them to live successfully in their environments. (p. 32)

air pollution A change to the atmosphere that has harmful effects. (p. 140)

aquaculture The practice of raising fish and other water organisms for food. (p. 95)

bedrock Rock that makes up Earth's crust. (p. 116)

biodegradable Capable of being broken down by bacteria and other natural decomposers. (p. 124)

biodiversity The number of different species in an area. (p. 97)

biogeography The study of where organisms live. (p. 56)

biomass fuel Fuel made from living things. (p. 176)

biome A group of ecosystems with similar climates and organisms. (p. 62)

biotic factor A living part of an ecosystem. (p. 17)

birth rate The number of births in a population in a certain amount of time. (p. 25)

canopy A leafy roof formed by tall trees. (p. 63)

captive breeding The mating of endangered animals in zoos or preserves. (p. 104)

carnivore Consumer that eats only animals. (p. 46)

carrying capacity The largest population that an area can support. (p. 27)

catalytic converter A device that reduces carbon monoxide emissions from vehicles. (p. 156)

chlorofluorocarbons Gases containing chlorine and fluorine (also called CFCs). (p. 145)

clear-cutting The process of cutting down all the trees in an area at once. (p. 92)

climate The typical weather pattern in an area over a long period of time. (p. 59)

combustion The burning of a fuel. (p. 165)

commensalism A relationship between two species in which one species benefits and the other is neither helped nor harmed. (p. 37)

community All the different populations that live together in an area. (p. 20)

competition The struggle between organisms for the limited resources in a habitat. (p. 33)

composting Helping the natural decomposition process to break down certain wastes. (p. 127)

condensation The process by which a gas changes to a liquid. (p. 53)

coniferous trees Trees that produce their seeds in cones and have needle-shaped leaves. (p. 67)

conservation viewpoint The belief that people should use natural resources as long as they do not destroy those resources. (p. 88)

consumer An organism that obtains energy by feeding on other organisms. (p. 46)

continental drift The very slow motion of the continents. (p. 56)

control rod Cadmium rod used in a nuclear reactor to absorb neutrons from fission. (p. 182)

controlled experiment An experiment in which all factors except one are kept constant. (p. 205)

corrosive Able to dissolve or break down many other substances, such as an acid. (p. 131)

crop rotation The planting of different crops in a field each year. (p. 118)

D

death rate The number of deaths in a population in a certain amount of time. (p. 25)

deciduous trees Trees that shed their leaves and grow new ones each year. (p. 66)

decomposer An organism that breaks down wastes and dead organisms. (p. 47)

desert An area that receives less than 25 cm of precipitation a year. (p. 64)

desertification The advance of desertlike conditions into areas that previously were fertile. (p. 118)

development The construction of buildings, roads, dams, and other structures. (p. 115)

development viewpoint The belief that humans should be able to freely use and benefit from all of Earth's resources. (p. 88)

dispersal The movement of organisms from one place to another. (p. 57)

drought A period of less rain than normal. (p. 150)

ecology The study of how living things interact with each other and their environment. (p. 20)

ecosystem All the living and nonliving things that interact in an area. (p. 16)

efficiency The percentage of energy that is used by a device to perform work. (p. 188)

emigration Leaving a population. (p. 26)

emissions Particles and gases released into the air from a smokestack or motor vehicle. (p. 141)

endangered species A species in danger of becoming extinct in the near future. (p. 100)

energy conservation The practice of reducing energy use. (p. 187)

energy pyramid A diagram that shows the amount of energy that moves from one feeding level to another in a food web. (p. 49)

erosion The process by which water, wind, or ice moves particles of rock or soil. (p. 116)

estimate An approximation of a number based on reasonable assumptions. (p. 24)

estuary A habitat in which the fresh water of a river meets the salt water of the ocean. (p. 71)

evaporation The process by which molecules of a liquid absorb energy and change to the gas state. (p. 52)

exotic species Species that are carried to a new location by people. (p. 58)

explosive Capable of reacting very quickly when exposed to air or water or of exploding when dropped. (p. 131)

extinction The disappearance of all members of a species from Earth. (p. 100)

fallow Left unplanted with crops. (p. 117)

fertilizer A chemical that provides nutrients to help crops grow better. (p. 151)

fishery An area with a large population of valuable ocean organisms. (p. 94)

flammable Capable of catching fire easily and burning at low temperatures. (p. 131)

food chain A series of events in which one organism eats another. (p. 47)

food web The pattern of overlapping food chains in an ecosystem. (p. 47)

fossil fuel An energy-rich substance (such as coal, oil, or natural gas) formed from the remains of organisms. (p. 166)

fuel rod Uranium rod that undergoes fission in a nuclear reactor. (p. 182)

gasohol A mixture of gasoline and alcohol. (p. 176)

gene A structure in an organism's cells that carries its hereditary information. (p. 100)

geothermal energy Heat from Earth's interior. (p. 177)

global warming The theory that increasing carbon dioxide in the atmosphere will raise Earth's average temperature. (p. 146)

grassland An area populated by grasses that gets 25 to 75 centimeters of rain each year. (p. 65)

greenhouse effect The trapping of heat by certain gases in the atmosphere. (p. 146)

groundwater Water stored in underground layers of soil and rock. (p. 149)

habitat The place where an organism lives and that provides the things it needs. (p. 17)

habitat destruction The loss of a natural habitat. (p. 101)

habitat fragmentation The breaking of a habitat into smaller, isolated pieces. (p. 101)

hazardous waste A material that can be harmful if it is not properly disposed of. (p. 131)

herbivore Consumer that eats only plants. (p. 46)

hibernation A low-energy state similar to sleep that some mammals enter in the winter. (p. 67)

host The organism that a parasite lives in or on in parasitism. (p. 38)

hydrocarbon A compound that contains carbon and hydrogen atoms. (p. 166)

hydroelectric power Electricity produced using the energy of flowing water. (p. 175)

hypothesis A prediction about the outcome of an experiment. (p. 204)

immigration Moving into a population. (p. 26)

incineration The burning of solid waste. (p. 123)

insulation Building material that blocks heat transfer between the air inside and outside. (p. 189)

intertidal zone The area between the highest high-tide line and lowest low-tide line. (p. 72)

keystone species A species that influences the survival of many others in an ecosystem. (p. 99)

land reclamation The process of restoring land to a more natural state. (p. 119)

leachate Water that has passed through buried wastes in a landfill. (p. 123)

limiting factor An environmental factor that prevents a population from increasing. (p. 27)

litter Layer of dead leaves and grass on top of the soil. (p. 116)

manipulated variable The one factor that a scientist changes during an experiment. (p. 205)

meltdown A dangerous condition caused by overheating inside a nuclear reactor. (p. 183)

municipal solid waste Waste produced in homes, businesses, and schools. (p. 122)

mutualism A relationship between two species in which both species benefit. (p. 37)

native species Species that have naturally evolved in an area. (p. 58)

natural selection Process by which individuals that are better adapted to the environment are more likely to survive and reproduce than others. (p. 32)

neritic zone The region of shallow ocean water over the continental shelf. (p. 72)

niche An organism's particular role in an ecosystem, or how it makes its living. (p. 32)

nitrogen fixation The process of changing free nitrogen gas into a usable form. (p. 55)

nodules Bumps on the roots of certain plants that house nitrogen-fixing bacteria. (p. 55)

nonrenewable resource A natural resource that is not replaced as it is used. (p. 85)

nuclear fission The splitting of an atom's nucleus into smaller nuclei. (p. 181)

nuclear fusion The combining of two atomic nuclei into a single larger nucleus. (p. 184)

nucleus The central core of an atom that contains the protons and neutrons. (p. 181)

nutrient depletion The situation that arises when more soil nutrients are used than the decomposers can replace. (p. 117)

omnivore A consumer that eats both plants and animals. (p. 46)

ozone A toxic form of oxygen. (p. 141)

ozone layer The layer of the atmosphere that contains a higher concentration of ozone than the rest of the atmosphere. (p. 144)

parasite The organism that benefits by living on or in a host in parasitism. (p. 38)

parasitism A relationship in which one organism lives on or inside another and harms it. (p. 38)

passive solar system A method of converting solar energy into heat without pumps or fans. (p. 173)

permafrost Soil that is frozen all year. (p. 68)

pesticide A chemical that kills crop-destroying organisms. (p. 151)

petrochemical Compound made from oil. (p. 169)

petroleum Liquid fossil fuel; oil. (p. 168)

photochemical smog A thick, brown haze formed when certain gases react in sunlight. (p. 141)

photosynthesis The process in which organisms use water along with sunlight and carbon dioxide to make food. (p. 18)

pioneer species The first species to populate an area. (p. 77)

poaching Illegal hunting of wildlife. (p. 102)

pollution A change to the environment that has a negative effect on living things. (p. 85)

population All the members of one species in a particular area. (p. 19)

population density The number of individuals in a specific area. (p. 23)

precipitation Rain, snow, sleet, or hail. (p. 53)

predation An interaction in which one organism kills and eats another. (p. 34)

predator The organism that does the killing in predation. (p. 34)

preservation viewpoint The belief that all parts of the environment are equally important, no matter how useful they are to humans. (p. 88)

prey An organism that is killed in predation. (p. 34)

primary succession The changes that occur in an area where no ecosystem had existed. (p. 77)

primary treatment The removal of solid materials from wastewater. (p. 157)

producer An organism that can make its own food. (p. 45)

radioactive Containing unstable atoms. (p. 131)

reactor vessel The part of a nuclear reactor where nuclear fission occurs. (p. 182)

recycling The process of reclaiming and reusing raw materials. (p. 124)

refinery A factory where crude oil is separated into fuels and other products. (p. 169)

renewable resource A resource that is naturally replaced in a relatively short time. (p. 85)

reserve A known deposit of fuels. (p. 167)

resin Solid material produced during oil refining that can be used to make plastics. (p. 125)

responding variable The factor that changes as a result of changes to the manipulated variable in an experiment. (p. 205)

sanitary landfill A landfill that holds nonhazardous waste such as municipal solid waste and construction debris. (p. 123)

savanna A grassland close to the equator. (p. 65)

scavenger A carnivore that feeds on the bodies of dead organisms. (p. 46)

scrubber A device that uses water droplets to clean smokestack emissions. (p. 156)

secondary succession The changes that occur after a disturbance in an ecosystem. (p. 78)

secondary treatment The use of bacteria to break down wastes in wastewater. (p. 157)

sediments Particles of rock and sand. (p. 152)

selective cutting The process of cutting down only some trees in an area. (p. 92)

sewage The water and human wastes that are washed down sinks and toilets. (p. 151)

species A group of organisms that are similar and reproduce to produce fertile offspring. (p. 19)

subsoil Layer of soil below topsoil. (p. 116)

succession The series of predictable changes that occur in a community over time. (p. 76)

sustainable yield A regular amount of a renewable resource that can be harvested without reducing the future supply. (p. 92)

symbiosis A close relationship between species that benefits at least one of the species. (p. 37)

taxol Chemical in Pacific yew tree bark that has cancer-fighting properties. (p. 107)

temperature inversion Condition in which a layer of warm air traps polluted air close to Earth's surface. (p. 142)

threatened species A species that could become endangered in the near future. (p. 100)

topsoil An upper layer of soil consisting of rock fragments, organisms, nutrients, water, air, and decaying matter. (p. 116)

toxic Damaging to the health of humans or other organisms; poisonous. (p. 131)

tundra An extremely cold, dry biome. (p. 68)

U

understory A layer of shorter plants that grow in the shade of a forest canopy. (p. 63)

V

variable Any factor that can change in an experiment. (p. 205)

W

water cycle The continuous process by which water moves from Earth's surface to the atmosphere and back. (p. 52)

water pollution A change to water that has a harmful effect. (p. 150)

Index

Acknowledgments

Illustration

John Edwards & Associates: 50, 59, 72–73, 122, 147, 156, 165, 166, 173, 177, 183, 195
GeoSystems Global Corporation: 11, 63, 64, 66, 68, 118, 133, 167, 194
Andrea Golden: 74t
Biruta Hansen: 20–21, 32
Jared Lee: 143
Martucci Design: 31, 69, 81, 85, 115, 161, 168, 187, 210, 211, 212
Matt Mayerchak: 40, 80, 110, 160, 208, 209
Karen Minot: 97
Morgan Cain & Associates: 45, 142, 145, 146, 169, 182, 184, 186, 202, 203
Ortelius Design Inc.: 57
Judith Pinkham: 90, 120, 128, 179, 186t
Matthew Pippin: 52, 116 (soil)
Pond and Giles: 77, 78, 93
Walter Stuart: 48
Alan Witschonke: 198–199
J/B Woolsey Associates: 22, 26, 33, 36, 47, 53, 54, 74, 101, 116 (spots), 206

Photography

Photo Research Sue McDermott
Cover image Robert Maier/Animals Animals

Nature of Science
Page 10,11t, Courtesy of Elroy Masters; **11b,** Pat O'Hara/DRK Photo; **12tl,** Vireo; **12bl,** Jeff Foott/Tom Stack & Assoc.; **12–13r,** M. Collier/DRK Photo; **13,** Gilbert Grant/Photo Researchers.

Chapter 1
Pages 14–15, Tony Craddock/TSI; **16,** Richard Haynes; **16–17,** Shin Yoshino/Minden Pictures; **17,** Carr Clifton/Minden Pictures; **17 inset top,** Corel Corp.; **17 inset,** S. Nielsen/DRK Photo; **18,** John Cancalosi/Tom Stack & Associates; **19,** Patti Murray/Animals Animals; **23t,** Richard Haynes; **23b,** Michlo Hoshino/Minden Pictures; **24,** C. Allan Morgan/DRK Photo; **25t,** Rob Simpson/Visuals Unlimited; **25b,** Bas van Beek/Leo de Wys; **27,** Mitsuaki Iwago/Minden Pictures; **28t,** Dan Budnick/Woodfin Camp & Associates; **28b,** Russ Lappa; **30,** Gary Griffen/Animals Animals; **31,** J. Alcock/Visuals Unlimited; **33l,** Patti Murray/Animals Animals; **33tr,** Wayne Lankinen/DRK Photo; **33br,** Ron Willocks/Animals Animals; **34l,** Michael Fogden/DRK Photo; **34r,** D. Holden Bailey/Tom Stack & Associates; **35l,** Stephen J. Krasemann/DRK Photo; **35r,** Donald Specker/Animals Animals; **35b,** Jeanne White/Photo Researchers, **37,** Daryl Balfour/TSI; **38,** John Gerlach/DRK Photo; **39,** Tony Craddock/TSI.

Chapter 2
Pages 42–43, Tom McHugh/Steinhart Aquarium/Photo Researchers; **44t,** Richard Haynes; **44b,** Byron Jorjorian/TSI; **45,** Breck P. Kent/Animals Animals/Earth Scenes; **46l,** Stephen J. Krasemann/DRK Photo; **46tr,** John Cancalosi/DRK Photo; **46br,** John Netherton/Animals Animals; **47,** S. Nielsen/DRK Photo; **49,** Stephen J. Krasemann/DRK Photo; **51t,** Richard Haynes; **51b,** R.J. Erwin/DRK Photo; **55,** Dr. Jeremy Burgess/Science Photo Library/Photo Researchers; **56t,** Richard Haynes; **56b,** J. Cancalosi/DRK Photo; **57,** D. Cavagnaro/DRK Photo; **58,** Stephen G. Maka/DRK Photo; **59t,** John Canalosi/DRK Photo; **59b,** Russ Lappa; **61,** Richard Haynes; **62,** Russ Lappa; **63t,** Renee Lynn/TSI; **63m,** Frans Lanting/Minden Pictures; **63b,** Mark Hones/Minden Pictures; **64l,** Joe McDonald/DRK Photo; **64 inset,** Michael Fogden/DRK Photo; **65,** Art Wolfe/TSI; **66l,** Carr Clifton/Minden Pictures; **66 inset,** **67r,** Stephen J. Krasemann/DRK Photo; **67 inset,** Michael Quinton/Minden Pictures; **68, 69,** Michio Hoshino/Minden Pictures; **70l,** David Boyle/Animals Animals; **70r,** Kim Heacox/DRK Photo; **71l,** Stephen G. Maka/DRK Photo; **71r,** Steven David Miller/Animals Animals; **72l,** Anne Wertheim/Animals Animals; **72r,** Gregory Ochocki/Photo Researchers; **73l,** Michael Nolan/Tom Stack & Associates; **73r,** Norbert Wu; **75l,r,** Russ Lappa; **76t,76b,** Tom & Pat Leeson/Photo Researchers; **79,** John Cancalosi/DRK Photo.

Chapter 3
Pages 82–83, Gay Bumgarner/TSI; **84,** Frans Lanting/Minden Pictures; **85l,** Inga Spence/Tom Stack & Associates; **85r,** Charles D. Winters/Photo Researchers; **85b,** Key Sanders/TSI; **86t,** UPI/corbis-Bettmann; **86b,** Corbis-Bettmann; **87t,** UPI/Corbis-Bettmann; **87bl,** Underwood & Underwood/Corbis-Bettmann; **87br,** William Campbell/Peter Arnold; **88,** Jeff Gnass/The Stock Market; **90,** Russ Lappa; **91,** Martin Rogers/Stock Boston; **92,** Gary Braasch/TSI; **94,** Tom Stewart/The Stock Market; **95,** Greg Vaughn/Tom Stack & Associates; **96,** Russ Lappa; **97,** Richard Haynes; **98tl,** Dave Watts/Tom Stack & Associates; **98tm,** Frans Lanting/Minden Pictures; **98tr,** George G. Dimijian/Photo Researchers; **98b,** Fred Bavendam/Minden Pictures; **99t,** Frans Lanting/Minden Pictures; **99b,** Jim Zipp/Photo Researchers; **100,** D. Cavagnaro/DRK Photo; **101,** Randy Wells/TSI; **102l,** John Shaw/Tom Stack & Associates; **102m,** Dan Suzio/Photo Researchers ; **102tr,** Stephen J. Krasemann/DRK Photo; **102–103,** Phil A. Dotson/Photo Researchers; **103tm,** Frans Lanting/Minden Pictures; **103m,** David Liebman, **103r,** Lynn M. Stone/DRK Photo; **104l,** Roy Toft/Tom Stack & Associates; **104r,** Frans Lanting/Minden Pictures; **105,** Tom McHugh/Photo Researchers; **106t,** Richard Haynes; **106b,** Greg Vaughn/Tom Stack & Associates; **107l,r,** G. Payne/Liaison International; **108,** D. Cavagnaro/DRK Photo; **109,** Gary Braasch/TSI.

Chapter 4
Pages 112–113, Nick Vedros, Vedros & Assoc./TSI; **114t,** Richard Haynes; **114bl,** Bertrand Rieger/TSI; **114br,** Chad Slattery/TSI; **115,** Jacques Jangoux/TSI; **117tl,** Kevin Horan/TSI; **117tr,** Tom Bean 1994/DRK Photo; **117bl,** Larry Lefever/Grant Heilman Photography; **117br,** Martin Benjamin/The Image Works; **118,** Chris Sattleberger/Panos Pictures; **119l,r,** Wally McNamee/Woodfin Camp & Associates; **120,** Richard Haynes; **121,** Russ Lappa; **123,** Hank Morgan/Science Source/Photo Researchers; **124l,** David Joel/TSI; **124r,** Hank Morgan/Science Source/Photo Researchers; **125,** Russ Lappa; **126,** David Lassman/The Image Works; **127,** Ray Pfortner/Peter Arnold; **128,** David Young Wolff/PhotoEdit; **129,** Richard Haynes; **130t,** Russ Lappa; **130b,** Galen Rowell/Peter Arnold; **131 all,** Russ Lappa; **132l,** Fred Hirschmann/TSI; **132r,** Stephen Agricola/The Image Works; **134,** Russ Lappa, **135,** Fred Hirschmann/TSI.

Chapter 5
Pages 138–139, G. Randall/FPG International; **140t,** Russ Lappa; **140b,** NASA/Liaison International; **141,** Conor Caffrey/SPL/Photo Researchers; **144,147,** Russ Lappa; **149t,** Richard Haynes; **149b,** NASA/The Stock Market; **150l,** Ed Wheeler/The Stock Market; **150r,** Robert Fried/Stock Boston; **151,** Bilderberg/The Stock Market; **152l,** Suzi Moore/Woodfin Camp & Associates; **152r,** Jeffrey Muir Hamilton/Stock Boston; **153,** Randy Duchaine/The Stock Market; **155t,** Richard Haynes; **155b,** Mike Booher/Transparencies, Inc.; **157t,** Courtesy of city of Arcata, CA; **157b,** Stephen Rose/Rainbow; **158,** Bob Daemmrich/Stock Boston; **159t,** Conor Caffrey/SPL/Photo Researchers; **159b,** Randy Duchaine/The Stock Market.

Chapter 6
Pages 162–163, Yamada Toshiro/TSI; **164,** M. L. Sinibaldi/The Stock Market; **167t,** Mike Abrahams/TSI; **167b,** Paul Harris/TSI; **168,** Jbboykin Oil Prod./The Stock Market; **170,** UPI/Corbis-Bettmann; **171,** Chad Ehlers/International Stock; **172,** Nadia MacKenzie/TSI; **174,** A & L Sinibaldi/TSI; **175,** Larry Ulrich/DRK Photo; **176,** Carlie Waite/TSI; **178,** NASA; **179,** Richard Haynes; **180,** Herb Swanson; **181t,** Russ Lappa; **181b,** Photograph by Johan Hagemeyer, courtesy AIP Emilio Segre Visual Archives; **184,** Y. Arthus-Bertrand/Peter Arnold; **185,** U.S. Dept. of Energy/Science Photo Library/Photo Researchers; **187,** Richard Haynes; **188l,** Mitch Kezar/TSI; **188r,** Leonard Lessin/Peter Arnold; **189,** Yves Marcoux/TSI; **190,** Wolf/Monkmeyer; **191l,** Nadia MacKenzie/TSI; **191r,** Yves Marcoux/TSI.

Interdisciplinary Exploration
Page 194tm, Frans Lanting/Minden Pictures; **194tr,** Alan Carey/Photo Researchers; **194bl,** Frans Lanting/Minden Pictures; **194br,** Roy Toft/Tom Stack & Associates; **195t,** Starin/Ardea London Ltd.; **195m,** Peter Steyn/Ardea London Ltd.; **195b,** Tom Brakefield/DRK Photo; **196t,** Dr. Migel Smith/ Earth Scenes; **196b,** Werner Forman Archive/Art Resource; **197l,** Christie's Images; **197r,** Jose Anzel/Aurora; **199,** Corbis-Bettmann

Skills Handbook
Page 200, Mike Moreland/Photo Network; **201t,** Foodpix; **201m,** Richard Haynes; **201b,** Russ Lappa; **204,** Richard Haynes; **206,** Ron Kimball; **207,** Renee Lynn/Photo Researchers.